# MAKING AND GROWING

# Anthropological Studies of Creativity and Perception

*Series Editor:* Tim Ingold, University of Aberdeen, UK

The books in this series explore the relations, in human social and cultural life, between perception, creativity and skill. Their common aim is to move beyond established approaches in anthropology and material culture studies that treat the inhabited world as a repository of complete objects, already present and available for analysis. Instead these works focus on the creative processes that continually bring these objects into being, along with the persons in whose lives they are entangled.

All creative activities entail movement or gesture, and the books in this series are particularly concerned to understand the relations between these creative movements and the inscriptions they yield. Likewise in considering the histories of artefacts, these studies foreground the skills of their makers-cum-users, and the transformations that ensue, rather than tracking their incorporation as finished objects within networks of interpersonal relations.

The books in this series will be interdisciplinary in orientation, their concern being always with the practice of interdisciplinarity: on ways of doing anthropology *with* other disciplines, rather than doing an anthropology *of* these subjects. Through this anthropology *with*, they aim to achieve an understanding that is at once holistic and processual, dedicated not so much to the achievement of a final synthesis as to opening up lines of inquiry.

*Other titles in the series:*

Design and Anthropology
*Edited by Wendy Gunn and Jared Donovan*

Imagining Landscapes
Past, Present and Future
*Edited by Monica Janowski and Tim Ingold*

Redrawing Anthropology
Materials, Movements, Lines
*Edited by Tim Ingold*

Conversations With Landscape
*Edited by Karl Benediktsson and Katrín Anna Lund*

# Making and Growing
Anthropological Studies of Organisms and Artefacts

*Edited by*

ELIZABETH HALLAM
*University of Aberdeen and University of Oxford, UK*

TIM INGOLD
*University of Aberdeen, UK*

**ASHGATE**

© Elizabeth Hallam and Tim Ingold and the contributors 2014

All rights reserved. No part of this publication may be reproduced, stored in a retrieval system or transmitted in any form or by any means, electronic, mechanical, photocopying, recording or otherwise without the prior permission of the publisher.

Elizabeth Hallam and Tim Ingold have asserted their rights under the Copyright, Designs and Patents Act, 1988, to be identified as the editors of this work.

Published by
Ashgate Publishing Limited
Wey Court East
Union Road
Farnham
Surrey, GU9 7PT
England

Ashgate Publishing Company
110 Cherry Street
Suite 3-1
Burlington, VT 05401-3818
USA

www.ashgate.com

**British Library Cataloguing in Publication Data**
A catalogue record for this book is available from the British Library

**The Library of Congress has cataloged the printed edition as follows:**
Hallam, Elizabeth, 1967–
    Making and growing : anthropological studies of organisms and artefacts / by Elizabeth Hallam and Tim Ingold.
        pages cm. – (Anthropological studies of creativity and perception)
    Includes bibliographical references and index.
    ISBN 978-1-4094-3642-3 (hardback : alk. paper) – ISBN 978-1-4094-3643-0 (ebook) – ISBN 978-1-4724-0260-8 (epub)
    1. Material culture. 2. Creation (Literary, artistic, etc.) – Social aspects. I. Ingold, Tim, 1948– II. Title.

GN429.H35 2014
306.4'6 – dc23

2013033632

ISBN 9781409436423 (hbk)
ISBN 9781409436430 (ebk –PDF)
ISBN 9781472402608 (ebk – ePUB)

Printed in the United Kingdom by Henry Ling Limited,
at the Dorset Press, Dorchester, DT1 1HD

# Contents

| | | |
|---|---|---|
| *List of Figures* | | *vii* |
| *Notes on Contributors* | | *ix* |
| *Preface and Acknowledgements* | | *xiii* |
| 1 | Making and Growing: An Introduction<br>*Tim Ingold and Elizabeth Hallam* | 1 |
| 2 | Silk Production: Moths, Mulberry and Metamorphosis<br>*Jacqueline Field* | 25 |
| 3 | Between Nature and Art: Casting from Life in Sixteenth-Century Europe<br>*Pamela H. Smith* | 45 |
| 4 | Anatomopoeia<br>*Elizabeth Hallam* | 65 |
| 5 | Artefacts and Bodies among Kuna People from Panamá<br>*Paolo Fortis* | 89 |
| 6 | Designing Body-Pots in the Formative La Candelaria Culture, Northwest Argentina<br>*Benjamin Alberti* | 107 |
| 7 | Stitching Lives: A Family History of Making Caribou Skin Clothing in the Canadian Arctic<br>*Nancy Wachowich* | 127 |
| 8 | Gardening and Wellbeing: A View from the Ground<br>*Anne Jepson* | 147 |
| 9 | Making Plants and Growing Baskets<br>*Stephanie Bunn* | 163 |
| 10 | Skill and Aging: Perspectives from Three Generations of English Woodworkers<br>*Trevor H.J. Marchand* | 183 |

| 11 | Movement in Making: An Apprenticeship with Glass and Fire<br>*Frances Liardet* | 203 |
| 12 | Growing Granite: The Recombinant Geologies of Sludge<br>*David A. Paton and Caitlin DeSilvey* | 221 |

*Index* 239

# List of Figures

| | | |
|---|---|---|
| 1.1 | A witch and a devil making a nail | 11 |
| 1.2 | Processing of pewter | 13 |
| 1.3 | Still life of leaves and flowers, Hong Kong | 14 |
| 1.4 | Two human bone-forming cells growing over crystals of the ceramic material, monetite | 16 |
| 2.1 | Silkworms. Fourth stage silkworms feeding on fresh mulberry leaves at a Japanese silk farm | 28 |
| 2.2 | Silkworm glands | 32 |
| 2.3 | Reeling silk | 35 |
| 2.4 | A Uyghur woman reeling silk. Kashgar, Western China | 36 |
| 3.1 | Wenzel Jamnitzer (attributed). Life-cast lizard. Lead | 46 |
| 3.2 | Wenzel Jamnitzer (attributed). Writing box | 50 |
| 3.3 | Bernard Palissy (follower of). Oval plate | 51 |
| 3.4 | Wenzel Jamnitzer, *Daphne* | 53 |
| 3.5 | Life-cast lizard. Silver | 58 |
| 4.1 | Photograph of David Tompsett with a corrosion cast | 67 |
| 4.2 | Corrosion cast of thoracic and abdominal viscera | 71 |
| 4.3 | Photograph of museum technician Sydney Bartlett | 75 |
| 4.4 | Tools used by David Tompsett | 82 |
| 4.5 | Corrosion cast of the arteries of a child at birth | 84 |
| 5.1 | Leopoldo Smith carving a female *nuchu* | 93 |
| 5.2 | *Nuchukana* | 95 |
| 5.3 | Nixia Pérez sewing a *mola* | 100 |
| 5.4 | Mikita Smith posing with her *nuchukana* and one of her nephews | 103 |
| 6.1 | La Candelaria body-pot | 108 |
| 6.2 | Detail of roughly incised lines | 112 |
| 6.3 | Faceless body-pot | 114 |
| 6.4 | Pierced nose of pot | 117 |
| 7.1 | Caribou skin mittens made by Damaris Ittukusuk Katdlutsiak | 132 |
| 7.2 | Photograph of Damaris Ittukusuk Katdlutsiak sewing a pair of mittens | 135 |
| 7.3 | Close-up of the back of a caribou skin parka | 136 |
| 7.4 | Qaumayuq and her family, Ellesmere Island | 139 |
| 8.1 | View of the garden project | 151 |
| 8.2 | Pumpkin in the garden | 155 |
| 8.3 | The youngest project participant watering his transplants | 158 |
| 8.4 | Working together, digging | 159 |

| 9.1 | Traveller's frame basket | 165 |
| 9.2 | *Na Hale 'Eo Waiawi*, by Patrick Dougherty | 170 |
| 9.3 | Willow in a variety of colours and tones | 172 |
| 9.4 | Shetland *kishie* made in a workshop led by Ewen Balfour | 175 |
| 9.5 | Spiral base of woven basket | 178 |
| 10.1 | Jack at the Building Crafts College | 187 |
| 10.2 | Jack machining a piece of timber | 189 |
| 10.3 | James Verner at his workshop in Devon | 191 |
| 10.4 | James mentoring a trainee | 193 |
| 10.5 | George Pysden, Master Craftsman | 196 |
| 11.1 | A core-formed alabastron | 204 |
| 11.2 | The order of procedures for the making of core-formed alabastra | 205 |
| 11.3 | Aspects of the experience of becoming dexterous with tools and materials | 210 |
| 11.4 | Top: core covering, knife technique. Bottom: core covering, trailing technique | 213 |
| 12.1 | '*The sludge stream negotiates and overflows a series of corroded steel drums ...* ' | 222 |
| 12.2 | '*Near the gathering piles of off-cuts ... I can still see the trace of suspended granite ...*' | 225 |
| 12.3 | '*I ... press my bare foot into the sludge ... and try to make my mark*' | 230 |
| 12.4 | '*The edges of the print gradually close in, erasing the surface trace ...*' | 231 |

# Notes on Contributors

**Benjamin Alberti** is Professor of Anthropology at Framingham State University and lectures at the Universidad Nacional de Córdoba, Argentina. He has published on sex/gender, masculinity and anthropomorphism in South American archaeology and Bronze Age Crete in a number of international journals and edited books. He is co-editor of the Special Section of the *Cambridge Archaeological Journal*, 'Animating Archaeology: of Subjects, Objects and Alternative Ontologies' (2009, with T. Bray), *Género y Etnicidad en la Arqueología Suramericána* (2006, with V. Williams), *Latin American Archaeology* (2000, with G. Politis) and *Archaeology After Interpretation* (2013, with A. Jones and J. Pollard).

**Stephanie Bunn** is Lecturer in Social Anthropology at the University of St Andrews. She has been conducting research among Kyrgyz pastoral nomads in Kyrgyzstan and Tajikistan for the past 15 years. Research themes include relationships with the environment, perception and creativity, home, space, and tent textiles. She also works as a practising textile artist and sculptor. Recent publications include *Nomadic Felts* (2010) and the website *Sound and Anthropology*.

**Caitlin DeSilvey** is a cultural geographer whose research investigates the aesthetics of obsolescence and the cultural significance of material change. Recent projects include a connective ethnography of copper-mining regions and a collaborative documentary project on mending and repair practices. She has also carried out research on themes of landscape and memory, adaptive heritage management, and the intersection between geography and contemporary arts practice. Recent publications include *Anticipatory History* (2011, with Simon Naylor and Colin Sackett) and the website *A Celebration of Repair* (with Steven Bond and James Ryan). She is based in the Environment and Sustainability Institute at the University of Exeter's Cornwall Campus.

**Jacqueline Field** is a textiles and dress historian. She was formerly Costume Curator at Westbrook College, Portland, Maine, where she taught textile and dress history. She researches silk production and consumption with a focus on the relationship between nineteenth- and early twentieth-century Asian sericulture and the United States silk industry. Currently she is investigating the manufacture and export of turn of the twentieth-century Canton (now Guangzhou) gambiered mud silk textiles and clothing. Her interests include developments in non-textile uses for silk. She is lead author of the co-authored *American Silk 1830–1930: Entrepreneurs and Artifacts* (2007). Recent articles include 'The North

American Silk Industry and Dress' (*Berg Fashion Library* electronic reference resource 2012), and 'Agriculture to Industry: Silk Production and Manufacture in Maine 1800–1930' (*Maine History* 2008).

**Paolo Fortis** is Lecturer in Social Anthropology at Durham University. He has been conducting fieldwork among Kuna people in the San Blas Archipelago of Panamá since 1998 and his main research concerns are art, aesthetics, ontology, personhood, and notions of power and violence. His main areas of ethnographic interest are the Lowlands of Central and South America. He has published articles on Kuna notions of design, sculptural forms, body and social praxis (in *Journal of the Royal Anthropological Institute*, *Tellus* and *Journal de la Société de Américanistes*), and his monograph building on his doctoral dissertation is entitled *Kuna Art and Shamanism: an Ethnographic Approach* (2013).

**Elizabeth Hallam** is Senior Research Fellow at the Department of Anthropology, University of Aberdeen, and a Research Associate in the School of Anthropology and Museum Ethnography, University of Oxford. She has conducted fieldwork, museum and archival research in Scotland and England. Her interests and publications focus on the historical anthropology of the body; death and dying; material and visual cultures; histories of collecting and museums; the anthropology of anatomy; three-dimensional modelling, especially in medical education; and mixed-media sculpture. Her books include the co-authored *Death, Memory and Material Culture* (2001, with Jenny Hockey) and the co-edited *Creativity and Cultural Improvisation* (2007, with Tim Ingold). She has recently co-edited *Medical Museums: Past, Present, Future* (2013, with Samuel J.M.M. Alberti), and her forthcoming book is *Anatomy Museum: Death and the Body Displayed*.

**Tim Ingold** is Professor of Social Anthropology at the University of Aberdeen. He has carried out ethnographic fieldwork in Lapland, and has written on environment, technology and social organization in the circumpolar North, on evolutionary theory in anthropology, biology and history, on the role of animals in human society, on language and tool use, and on environmental perception and skilled practice. He is currently exploring issues on the interface between anthropology, archaeology, art and architecture. His latest book, *Making*, was published in 2013.

**Anne Jepson** studied social anthropology 10 years after qualifying as a horticulturist. She has developed her research on gardens, plants and growing practices in Cyprus (for her PhD) and on the Isle of Skye. She is particularly interested in the power these have as vehicles for history, ideology, loss and relatedness. She has also set up and managed a therapeutic garden and allotment project for the National Health Service, UK. She continues to teach in the Department of Social Anthropology at the University of Edinburgh, as well supporting community gardening projects, in practical ways, across Scotland.

**Frances Liardet** was awarded her PhD from the School of History, Archaeology and Religion at Cardiff University, where she studied skilled crafting in ancient glass. Her research projects include the Core-Forming Project conducted with Mark Taylor and David Hill. Her research papers include presentations at the Theoretical Archaeology Group, and at Lancaster University's Institute of Advanced Studies workshop on experimentality in nature and in human culture. Her work has been funded by the Arts and Humanities Research Council and by the Rakow Foundation at the Corning Museum of Glass, USA. Her publications focus on glass vessel manufacture and boatbuilding. Further research interests include skill traditions in ancient boatbuilding and water flow technologies.

**Trevor H.J. Marchand** is Professor of Social Anthropology at SOAS and British Academy mid-Career Fellow. Marchand was trained as an architect (McGill) and received a PhD in anthropology (SOAS). He has conducted fieldwork with masons and craftspeople in Yemen, Mali and East London. He is the author of *Minaret Building and Apprenticeship in Yemen* (2001) and *The Masons of Djenné* (2009); editor of *Making Knowledge* (2010), and co-editor of *Knowledge in Practice* (2009, with K. Kresse) and *The Handbook of Social Anthropology* (2012, with R. Fardon et al.). In 2007 he co-produced the documentary film *Future of Mud* with S. Vogel, and he is presently curating a new exhibition on the masons of Djenné with M.-J. Arnoldi for the Smithsonian NMNH. His next monograph, *The Pursuit of Pleasurable Work*, is based on long-term fieldwork with UK woodworkers and furniture makers.

**David A. Paton** is a sculptor and PhD candidate in the Department of Geography at the University of Exeter's Cornwall Campus. His thesis, entitled *The Quarry as Sculpture: The Place of Making*, focuses on an ethnographic project in Trenoweth Granite Quarry in Cornwall, where he works as a sawman and mason. Expanding on the deep knowledge of the quarry generated through day to day labour, he has developed a series of creative engagements with the granite that examine the relationship between place and material. His recent projects include *Tilted Matter* (June 2012) – a performance-lecture held in the quarry at night, and *Slumped* – where granite slabs are melted in a kiln. Major public commissions include the West Park Arts Project in Darlington and the Herrington Colliery Sculpture Residency, UK. Arts Council England awards for artist-led initiatives include TEND (2007), a year-long residency at Trewidden Garden in Cornwall. He has also published in the journal *Environment and Planning A* (2013).

**Pamela H. Smith** is Professor of History at Columbia University and the author of *The Business of Alchemy: Science and Culture in the Holy Roman Empire* (1994) and *The Body of the Artisan: Art and Experience in the Scientific Revolution* (2004). She co-edited *Merchants and Marvels: Commerce, Science, and Art in Early Modern Europe* (with Paula Findlen 2002) and *Making Knowledge in Early Modern Europe: Practices, Objects, and Texts, 1400–1800* (with Benjamin Schmidt 2008).

In her present research, she attempts to reconstruct the vernacular knowledge of early modern European metalworkers from a variety of disciplinary perspectives, including hands-on reconstruction of historical metalworking techniques.

**Nancy Wachowich** is Lecturer in Social Anthropology at the University of Aberdeen. Most of her ethnographic fieldwork has been with people in the Inuit communities of Pond Inlet and Igloolik in Canada's Eastern Arctic. She focuses primarily on colonial histories and social movements, drawing on fields of historical anthropology, oral traditions, visual anthropology, museum studies and the anthropology of media. Her 1999 book *Saqiyuq: Stories from the Lives of Three Inuit Women*, written in collaboration with Apphia Agalakti Awa, Rhoda Kaukjak Katsak and Sandra Pikujak Katsak, won the 1999 Canadian Historical Association's Clio Award for the North and the 2000 Oral History Association (USA) Award for Best Project.

# Preface and Acknowledgements

This book began when Neil Jordan at Ashgate suggested that we might edit a volume on material culture. Our initial reaction was that there are already many edited collections in this field, and that yet one more would scarcely register on the academic radar. But we also felt that many mainstream studies of material culture were limited by an overriding concern with apparently finished objects and what happens to them in their use and circulation, rather than with processes of formation and dissolution wherein objects alternately come into and pass out of existence. Why not put together a book that would focus not on the relations between persons and things but on the becoming of persons and the becoming of things – that is on the intertwined processes of growing and making? And perhaps by doing so, we thought, we could tackle another lacuna in the literature on material culture – that in recalling to our attention the masses of 'non-humans' with which we surround ourselves, and without which everyday life would be impossible, there has been an overwhelming bias towards artefacts over organisms, or towards things that have been made rather than things that grow. We need a book, we thought, that would bring things back to life. But to do so, we would have to focus less on the 'objectness' of things and more on the flows of materials by which they come into being and carry on.

The book builds on interests that both of us have been pursuing for a long time. Tim discusses the theme of making and growing in several of the essays collected in his book *The Perception of the Environment* (2000), and has returned to it on many occasions since then. Liz's interest in the theme stems from her work on the anthropology and history of anatomy, involving research with museum collections across medicine, zoology and botany. We set about inviting contributions not only from anthropologists but also from archaeologists, historians and geographers. Over the last two years we have been very fortunate to work with all of the authors in this volume who have so capably and patiently developed their chapters in relation to our theme. All of them have helped us enormously in exploring what we found to be a much more difficult and protean topic than we initially thought when we wrote the book proposal.

Many colleagues and friends have also helped us bring the book to fruition. At the University of Aberdeen we would like to thank everyone in the Department of Anthropology, most especially Alison Brown and Neil Curtis. At the University of Oxford colleagues in the School of Anthropology and Museum Ethnography have been very generous with their support, especially Marcus Banks, Clare Harris, Elisabeth Hsu and Laura Peers. We are also very grateful to Elizabeth Edwards for her invaluable advice and encouragement. Tim would like to acknowledge the support of the Leverhulme Trust in the award of a Major Research Fellowship (2011–13), which freed up the time he needed for the project.

Finally, Liz would like to give heartfelt thanks to her family, especially Ian Maclachlan, for their loving kindness which makes her work possible, and Tim would like to thank Liz for doing most of the work!

Liz Hallam and Tim Ingold, Oxford and Aberdeen

# Chapter 1
# Making and Growing: An Introduction

Tim Ingold and Elizabeth Hallam

*The action of Make*: production, creation, construction, preparation; conversion into or causing to become something.

*The action of Grow*: to arise or come into existence, to manifest vigorous life, to flourish, to increase gradually in size by natural development, to increase in quantity or degree, to advance towards maturity.

(*Oxford English Dictionary*)

You come across a craftsperson, bent over his or her work. 'What are you making?' you ask. 'A pot', says the potter, as he gently presses hands against soft clay. 'A fine, inlaid table', says the carpenter, as he carves out a groove for a mortise joint with his chisel. 'Mittens for my daughter', says the seamstress, as she sews pre-cut pieces of prepared animal hide with fine, even stitches. 'A basket', says the basket maker, as she weaves lengths of willow in and out, in and out, in a mesmeric rhythm. Pot, table, mittens and basket are all examples of what people in contemporary western societies commonly regard as artefacts. In making an artefact, it is supposed, you start with some raw material such as clay, timber, hide or willow, and end at the point when this material has taken on the form intended for it. Indeed the question 'What are you making?' is one that invites an answer in terms of an end product, an objective, the completion or fulfilment of which will bring the project to a close. All the activity seems to be concentrated there, in the interval between start and finish, each of which presupposes the other: for how do you know when you have finished unless you have an idea, at the outset, of what is to be made; and how can you get started without some conception of an end?

Makers know better, however. They know that the simple answer, designed perhaps to fend off your unwanted attentions as a meddling onlooker, leaves almost everything about their craft unsaid, and implies a certainty about ends and means that, in practice, is largely an illusion. Making things, for them, often feels like telling stories, and as with all stories, though you may pick up the thread and eventually cast it off, the thread itself has no discernible beginning or end. The story of clay does not begin with the potter, since the material he throws on the wheel has already had to be dug out from the ground and kneaded so that it is sufficiently pure and of the right consistency. Before that, it was sedimented through the deposition of water-borne particles, over eons of geological time. And when does the story end? On leaving the pottery, the life of a pot has scarcely begun: think of all the hands or heads that will carry it and the substances it will hold until, cracked and discarded, it is returned to the earth. Even this does not rule out the possibility that it might, one day, be unearthed by an archaeologist and pieced together from the fragments, only for its life to continue as a museum exhibit. 'Finishing', in short, is but a moment in the life of the pot: a rite of passage, perhaps, where it crosses a threshold from preparation to employment.

So too with the carpenter, who works with timber that has first had to be harvested from living trees, prior to a lengthy process of seasoning, and whose handiwork never ceases to respond to heat and humidity, long after it is allegedly finished. As it takes in moisture from the atmosphere and, in turn, releases it, wood continues to 'breathe' (Marchand, Chapter 10). Is the table, then, a complete artefact or just a phase in the life-history of a piece of wood? And where wood comes from trees rooted in the earth, skins come from the animals that inhabit it. They require long and laborious preparation before the seamstress can even commence her sewing. Once the mittens or other garments are sewn, they will clothe a human life just as they had once clothed the living animals from which they were taken (Wachowich, Chapter 7). And lastly, the basket-maker's willow – which must be fresh, green and supple to be worked – will have first been cultivated and harvested, and will take root and sprout once again if reinserted in the earth (Bunn, Chapter 9). In effect, rather than standing over nature and effecting a change, from a seemingly raw to a completed or 'artefactual' state, makers of every profession appear to stand at the threshold, in amongst the stuff and tackle of their trade, easing the way for their ever-varying, protean material to pass from one form of life to another. Clay passes from earth-life to life as a pot, wood from arboreal life to living room, skin from animal shank to human hand and willow from bed to basket. As in rites of passage, one can discern in making the three phases of separation, in which the material is removed from its former life, of transition, in which it is treated in the seclusion of the workshop, and of reincorporation into the settings of its subsequent career.

It is customary, in many settings, to say that trees and shrubs, like garden plants, *grow* in the soil, and that skin and fur *grow* on the bodies of animals. Such growth amounts to a material accumulation, as the living plant or animal absorbs or ingests substances from earth, air and water, incorporating them into its own flesh through the expenditure of energy ultimately derived from sunlight. This accumulation can assume astonishing proportions, as in the caterpillar of the *Bombyx mori* moth which, in 38 days from hatching and through the energetic consumption of mulberry leaves, multiplies in size by a factor of 10,000 (Field, Chapter 2). What the caterpillar creates, in this manufacture of bodily tissue, is itself. Growth, in this sense, is a process of self-making or *autopoiesis*. The philosopher A.N. Whitehead coined the term 'concrescence' to describe the way in which, in life, beings continually surpass themselves (Whitehead 1929: 410). Concrescence is not necessarily confined, however, to the organic domain. Inorganic crystals, too, can grow, when immersed in supersaturated solution. Mineral deposits grow through the accumulation of sludge (Paton and DeSilvey, Chapter 12). And in the domain of the social – what in an earlier anthropology was known as the 'superorganic' – people grow too, not just in strength and stature but in skill and wisdom. Indeed, to take growth or concrescence as the fundamental condition of beings and things in a world that is always surpassing itself is effectively to dissolve the boundaries between the inorganic, the organic and the superorganic. People, animals, plants and pots are all immersed in the process, and all play their part in it.

But if things grow, they are also grown. The gardener grows plants and the forester trees; in Australia, sheep-farmers call themselves wool-growers. The *Bombyx mori* caterpillar, better known as the silkworm, is grown in the production of silk. In each case what the grower does is to contribute, in some way or other, to setting up the conditions under which the growth of the things in question proceeds. Growing plants, for example, is a matter of ensuring the adequate provision of nutrients and water, and eliminating competition from weeds, coupled perhaps with a degree of control over ambient temperature and exposure to light. To grow wool one must see to the needs of sheep, principally for pasture and for protection against predators and parasites. To grow silk entails unremitting labour in keeping the worms supplied with the only food they will eat, namely mulberry leaves, and removing excrement (Field, Chapter 2). We have a word, 'nurture', to refer more specifically to this sense of growing as care and nourishment. An ancient yet seemingly entrenched discourse on 'nature and nurture' seeks to partition responsibility for the manifest forms of things between intrinsic drivers and environing conditions, and it is one that we routinely extend to people as well. Parallels between raising plants and raising people are commonplace, and not only in the West. Japanese foresters say that the trees in their care require stern discipline if they are to grow strong and resilient, which is why those on the weather sides of mountains, exposed to the fierce storms of winter, are always superior to those on the lee sides (Knight 1998: 200).

**Making in Growing, Growing in Making**

Our concern in this book is to think again about *making* and *growing*. Both words are among the richest and most polysemic in the vocabulary of English, and the last thing we want is to be sidetracked into arid questions of definition. Making can be defined in any number of possible ways, all of which serve well enough in particular contexts, and the same goes for growing. To make a bed means something quite different in the home from what it does in the joinery; and neither has much to do with what it means, for example, to make hay, fire, peace, love or an observation. And growing a beard is not quite the same as growing potatoes, or growing weary. Our interest is not in the meaning of each word taken in isolation, but in the possibilities opened up by their juxtaposition. Why, to take one example, would a farmer choose to say that he is growing grass on his meadows, rather than making it, but that in harvesting the crop and stacking it to dry he is making hay and not growing it? What subtle inflection of meaning is encrypted in this distinction? Perhaps it has something to do with nouns and verbs. The predicate of making, let us say, is nominal in form. It is an entity or an event. But the predicate of growing is verbal; it is a 'going on'. Thus what the farmer brings about in the meadow, when he grows grass, is 'grassing' – the photosynthetic process which binds carbon dioxide in the air with moisture absorbed in the soil and taken up though the roots, in the presence of sunlight, to fuel the formation of plant tissues. And that is precisely what is brought to a halt when the crop is harvested to make hay. By analogy, the financier grows his investment, but makes a lot of money by cashing it in!

It would seem, in short, that making is to growing as being to becoming. So which comes first? Does growing span the intervals between fixed states of being, or does making punctuate the movements of a world in perpetual becoming? The first alternative is already presupposed in the conventional language of continuity and change, epitomized in what could be called the 'my, how you've grown' syndrome. As a child, you recall, a distant relative would make infrequent visits to your household, and every time, on first clapping eyes on you, she would exclaim 'my, how you've grown'. She remembers you only as she saw you last, and seeing you now she is struck by the change. Growth, for her, bridges the gap between then and now, and accounts for the difference between your previous and present appearance. But for you and for those around you, growth is going on all the time: you do not register it as change, or as a transition from A to B, but as life itself. Yet this life of yours was punctuated by significant events: looking back, you remember them as formative moments in your career that contributed to making you the person you are today. And this takes us back to the idea of making as akin to a rite of passage, and to our characterization of the maker as one who stands at the threshold, easing the persons and materials in his or her charge across from one phase of life and growth to the next. Writing of initiation rites in East Africa, Turner observes that 'to "grow" a girl into a woman is to effect an ontological transformation; it is not merely to convey an unchanging substance from one position to another by a quasi-mechanical force' (Turner 1967: 101–2). Likewise, according to this second alternative, the maker effects an ontological transformation in the material, not through the application of exterior force to inert substance, but through intervening in a play of forces and relations both internal and external to the things under production.

In rethinking making and growing, our aim is not to substitute for a view of the world in which everything is made – for example, nature by God, artefacts by man – one in which everything grows and is grown. The question is rather one of ontological priority. In a classic essay, Martin Heidegger (1971) asked this question of building and dwelling. Do we dwell in a world that is already built, with its structures in place for us to occupy, or can we build only because we already dwell, in body and mind, in the world in which we find ourselves? Heidegger's purpose was to reverse the prioritization of building over dwelling bequeathed by modern thought. We can do the same for making and growing. What would happen if we were to think of growing not as something that takes place in the space intermediate between God-given nature and man-made society – as the organic was once conceived to be sandwiched between the inorganic and the superorganic – but as the very ground of becoming from which the forms of the artificial take shape? What if we were to suggest, adapting Heidegger's turn of phrase (ibid.: 148, 160, with original emphasis) by substituting 'grow' for 'dwell' and 'growing' for 'dwelling', that 'we do not grow because we have made, but we make and have made because we grow, that is because we are growers ... *Only if we are capable of growing, only then can we make*'? This is to put culture, as it were, after nurture rather than before it: to think not of nurture as the projection of pre-existent cultural form upon natural material but of culture as the sum of emergent properties of a nurturing process. Is not culture, in one of its senses, something grown – that is, cultivated – rather than made?

Consider, for example, the difference between a pot and a baby. Is it enough to state the seemingly obvious: that the pot is made by the potter, whereas the baby grows and is grown within its mother's womb? That the former is an artefact, the latter an organism? This may seem obvious in western contexts, yet we know that in many societies, pots are compared to human bodies (Alberti, Chapter 6). Why are they attributed with such manifestly anthropomorphic features? Modern social theory, as exemplified in mainstream studies of material culture, answers that if pots are like bodies, it is not because pots are grown as bodies are, but because bodies – like pots – are actually made. They are socially constructed, say our theorists, through training and discipline into particular normative shapes and affects. They would not deny, of course, that babies grow, but this growth is put in parentheses, as a residually biological undercurrent that provides, as it were, the raw material for socialization. The organism grows, they say, but personhood is embodied. Amerindian potters, however – like carvers and seamstresses (Fortis, Chapter 5) – might put it precisely the other way around. Pots do indeed grow like babies, and are grown like them. As the potter's hands stroke the clay, so human hands caress and cradle babies. All this handling, this nurturance, gives rise to the form of the pot, just as it does to that of the growing baby. The form is not imposed onto the 'natural' material of the clay from a superior source in human society, as the notion of anthropomorphism implies. It rather emerges from the caressing and cradling hands of the potter, who is literally inaugurating a new life-cycle through his work.

We really need a new word, something like 'anthropo-ontogenetic', to describe how form, rather than being applied to the material, is emergent within the field of human relations. This is neither making nor growing, but a kind of making-in-growing, or growing-in-making. To knit an item of clothing could be regarded as anthropo-ontogenetic in this sense. The shape of the clothing might map onto the bodily form of the wearer, as mittens map onto hands, yet this shape arises from countless micro-gestures of threading and looping that turn a continuous strand of yarn into a surface. But is it any different with the body? 'For you created my inmost being', as it is written in the *Book of Psalms*; 'you knit me together in my mother's womb' (Psalms 139, verse 13). For the craftspeople of early modern Europe, this image of divine creation, as a knitting or weaving together of materials, provided the inspiration and the ideal for their own activity. Materials that were food for living, growing human bodies – such as bread, butter and honey – also fed their work, and vice versa, the materials of craft spilled into medicinal and other prescriptions for bodies. In bodies as in craftwork, materials would be mixed together, with a certain balance and proportion that corresponded to their temperament. This was art imitating nature not by the reproduction of its forms but in the exploration of its processes (Smith, Chapter 3): if there was a likeness between artefacts and organisms, it was not because the former had been modelled in the image of the latter but because similar processes would generate similar results.

**Organisms Against Artefacts**

> *Organism* (from the Greek *organon* – an instrument, tool, for making or doing; organ of sense or apprehension): a whole with interdependent parts, compared to a living being; an animal, plant or single-celled life form.
>
> *Artefact* (from classical Latin *arte* – skill – and *factum* – to make): an object made or modified by human workmanship, as opposed to one formed by natural processes.
>
> (*Oxford English Dictionary*)

How come, then, that in later modern sensibilities, growing and making, or generation and production, were so radically split apart? We reserve our answers for a later section; for now we wish only to highlight the separation. In 2010, when scientists announced the creation of the 'world's first synthetic life form', having assembled the genome of a bacterium, they were accused of 'playing God' (Sample 2010, see Calvert 2010, Shapin 2008). But their conceit was hardly an imitation of divine craftsmanship. It lay instead in their assumption of powers of prediction and command that, according to their critics, did not rightfully belong to them. To make in this way was no longer about following the ways of the world, and bending them to human purposes. It was rather a matter of compulsion, of forcing nature to do one's bidding even when it goes against the grain, if need be through the application of superior force. Make nature do what it will not of itself, and all will be revealed. Already in his *Novum Organum* of 1620, Francis Bacon had opined that 'the secrets of nature reveal themselves more readily under the vexations of art than when they go their own way' (Bacon 1858: 95). Art insists, while nature resists: thus making and growing were coming to pull in opposite directions. Four years later, in his *New Atlantis*, Bacon proposed a Utopian vision of a society in which every living thing had been 'made by art' to better serve human purposes, through the rigorous application of scientific principles. Crops would be 'made' to ripen earlier or later, fruits 'made' to be bigger and sweeter, animals 'made' to keep within their enclosures. In Bacon's New World, the maker no longer stood at the threshold of material transformation but had assumed sovereign power over the universe of things (Bacon 1965: 449–50).

Yet in the subsequent unfolding of European thought, the universe itself would come to be seen as an object of creation in the same deterministic sense. Machinic rather than organic, it was held to have been put together like clockwork and to testify to supreme powers of intelligent design, on the part of the Creator, and not to the skill of His handiwork. It was in this vein that the theologian William Paley, at the turn of the nineteenth century, famously compared the watch and the earwig, coming to the conclusion that since the watch is manifestly an artefact that has been made in accordance with a certain design, as a means to some end, and since the earwig has all the design features of the watch and more (since unlike the watch, it is capable of making copies of itself), the existence of the Deity is proved beyond doubt. 'The hinges in the wings of an earwig, and the joints of its antennae', Paley wrote, 'are as highly wrought, as if the Creator had nothing else to finish' (Paley 2006 [1802]: 280). Nor was this argument from design diminished in force by the substitution of natural selection for God as a design agent. Even today, evolutionary biologists write as if living organisms were assembled from component parts, much like a watch although of infinitely greater complexity (Dawkins 1986). Through the natural selection of the so-called 'building blocks' of life, otherwise known as genes, organisms are said to have been made even before they grow or are grown. For these biologists, growth is a secondary spin-off: it merely spans the interval between genotype and phenotype, revealing an architecture that is already prefigured at the outset. Once you have a design for an earwig, you have an earwig, period.

There is however one fundamental difference between the watch and the earwig, between object assemblies and living things or, more generally, between the respective orders of the machinic and the organic. Or so it would seem. Already adumbrated in the 1950s by anthropologist Claude Lévi-Strauss (1968: 283–6), in his comparison of mechanical and statistical models, it has to do with the nature of time. Mechanical time, as Lévi-Strauss pointed out, is reversible. Things put together can be taken apart; the assembly can be disassembled, and reassembled again. You can make and remake a jig-saw puzzle as often as you like. The same is true, at least in theory if not in practice, of the watch. Unmaking is possible. Ungrowing, however, is not. Organic growth exemplifies what Lévi-Strauss would call a statistical process, and its time is irreversible. That is why growing is also ageing. This distinction, however, is not quite as clear-cut as it appears at first glance. For it depends on our understanding of the relation between parts and wholes. Imagine a bird's nest, for example. The bird collects twigs and other materials from here and there. In no sense are these materials parts of the nest until they are assembled there. That is to say, they *become* parts in the course of the work, and only as they settle – as they adjust themselves and progressively hold each other in place (Ingold 2013: 69). Although the nest may subsequently be undone, that work of mutual adjustment can never be recovered. For the coherence of the nest – that wholeness which renders its constituents as parts – is no more prefigured in the constituents themselves than is the pattern of a knitted garment prefigured in a hank of wool.

Indeed the nest may be said to be 'ornitho-ontogenetic' in much the same way that pots, baskets and mittens, to return to our earlier examples, are 'anthropo-ontogenetic'. Through the bird's own activity, and not through the imposition of any plan or blueprint, the nest is shaped to the proportions of its body. But is it really any different with the watch? Are the tiny cogs and springs which the watchmaker assembles the 'parts' of a watch, any more than twigs on the forest floor are the parts of a nest (Spuybroek 2011: 67)? As many model-makers know, the first stages of an assembly tend always to be the most difficult, as it is so hard to hold things in place until other things are brought in to fix or balance them. So it is, too, with making a watch. That is why it is such a skilled activity. Once again we find that the distinction between making and growing, and correspondingly between the machinic and the organic, is not as hard and fast as we might have thought. Perfect coherence, of the kind that would allow us to speak of a totality and its parts, is an asymptote to which the work may approach ever closer as it proceeds, but which it can never finally reach. Finishing, as the designer and inventor Stewart Brand once wryly put it, is never finished (Brand 1994: 64). The maker, then, is no longer sovereign, a totalitarian ruler over a world of parts whose integration is already given, in the form of an intelligent design, before he even moves a finger by way of creation. Such was the great designer-God of Paley's imagination. The lowly craftsperson, by contrast, is a go-between, in amongst a world of non-parts that must be coaxed into getting along together.

A world of non-parts cannot be unmade. It cannot be taken apart and put together again without loss. What, then, can happen to it? What is the opposite of making if things cannot be unmade? What is the opposite of growing if things cannot ungrow? The immediate answer to the first question is breaking or dismantling, the answer to the second is decomposition or decay. And whereas the first may call for a remedial response in the form of repair, the second calls for healing. Yet just as it is hard to draw the line between making and growing, so the distinctions between breakage and decomposition, dismantling and decay, and repair and healing, are all problematic in their various ways. Moreover all making, in a sense, entails breaking, just as all growth entails decomposition. To grow, a living body must eat, and to be rendered digestible, foodstuffs have to be broken down by the myriad bacterial agents that inhabit the gut. So too the craftsperson must break down materials into manageable pieces to work on them. Consider the stonemason, who uses picks, hammers and chisels to break the stone into blocks, and to chip off pieces to obtain the required forms. Likewise the carpenter splits wood with the axe and cuts it with the saw, all of which does injury to the material in the interests of making. Both stonemasonry and carpentry generate quantities of waste – stone chippings and sawdust – yet in its very deposition, this so-called waste can accumulate into sediments that could even leave an archaeological or geological trace (Paton and DeSilvey,

Chapter 12). The most enduring legacy of human manufacturing industry often comprises growing mounds of slag, sludge or litter.

Thus growth goes on, as it were, in the shadows of making, and not just in the environment but in bodies as well, for which cumulative exposure to industrial waste leaves its malignant shadow in occupational disease. Sociologist Richard Sennett's (2008) somewhat rose-tinted portrayal of 'the craftsman' perhaps needs a dose of realism. For making is tough on bodies as well as materials. It can be mind-numbingly arduous and hazardous to health. Not only materials suffer the cuts and blows of the maker's practice. For every strike or punch recoils, on impact, in the body that delivered it. Months and years of repetitive effort leave their mark in bones, joints, muscles and calluses of the skin (Marchand, Chapter 10). Accidents happen, and materials can cause injury to their makers as well as makers to their materials. Most often, accidental damage can be repaired, and injuries heal, yet no repair is ever complete or perfect, and there is no healing that does not leave a scar. Over time, these mount up. Bodies age in performance. Though they may grow in skill and knowledge, and up to a point in strength and stamina, over time the stresses and strains of working with often recalcitrant materials take their toll. Yet lives of making and growing are never lived in isolation but always in the company of others (Liardet, Chapter 11). And since life is a process, as Schutz (1962: 16–17) puts it, of 'growing older together', one person's decline may be another's growth. Thus even as lives come and go, life itself is carried on.

## The Historical Division of Making and Growing

Above, we have highlighted the divisions between growing and making, and between the respective definitions of the organism and the artefact, that have become such an established part of modern thought. There is, as we have seen, nothing pre-ordained or absolute about these divisions. Wherever and whenever they have emerged – perhaps above all, in Europe – it has been in the course of a long and complex history, which we briefly trace here. Daston and Park (1998) have shown how in early modern Europe, the realms of art and nature were closely intertwined, and even merged, for example in the *Wunderkammern* (chambers of wonder) in which the wealthy housed their precious objects and materials. Here the rare, strange and intricate mingled with metamorphic entities such as coral, described by Ovid as 'a sea plant petrified by the blood dripping from Medusa's severed head' (Daston and Park 1998: 273). The ancient opposition of art and nature – which Aristotle had conceived in terms of the distinctive capacity of living things to move, grow and regenerate – was dissolved by material entities that breached or traversed these categories. These wonders included stones, metals, shells and plants that seemed artful, and paintings, casts and automata (in human and animal form) that counterfeited nature and appeared to be alive. Such wonders were testimony to the 'union of art and nature' (Daston and Park 1998: 291).

In this volume, Smith (Chapter 3) explores sixteenth-century casts which not only looked like products of nature but also arose from practices of making that imitated and provided knowledge of nature's processes. With casts as with many other inhabitants of *Wunderkammern*, what had been made and what was grown were in many ways pleasurably and inspirationally indistinct.

In popular belief during this period, too, making and growing were far from discrete processes. Magical practices in England, for example, presupposed connections between the bodies of human beings, animals and plants, as well as artefacts and substances. Witches were believed deliberately to cause sickness by occult means, and thereby to inhibit or distort growth, when they injured people and animals, and when they created problems with food production, especially the making of butter, cheese and beer (Thomas 1985 [1971]). Sharp instruments such as pins and nails were among the ritual artefacts used by witches; it was with such items that they were thought to pierce images or possessions of victims in order to cause physical harm (Darr 2011). In one woodcut a witch and a devil make a nail as an instrument for inflicting lameness on a boy (Figure 1.1). This form of making drew potency from a collaboration of human and supernatural agents to create an artefact for harmful intervention in another person's growth. It required the work of cunning (that is, knowledgeable) men and women to diagnose the cause, and ritually to counteract it in order to restore heath. Witchcraft as making was thus perceived as a kind of anti-nurturance, a corruption of growing achieved through the use of dangerous implements, the wastage of food, or disruption in the 'flow of nourishment', which caused affliction to human and animal bodies (Roper 1994: 207).

While the artificial and the natural were sometimes coincident, they could also be more clearly distinguished. That inanimate objects existed in a domain apart from those of nature was an ancient view, and distinctions between nature and art emphasized the power of living things to reproduce, in contrast to those that did not (Sawday 2007). Closely related to this notion of reproduction, however, was that of imitation or mimesis. The relations between nature's reproductions and art's imitations, which 'translate[d] objects or stories from one medium to another', were significant interests among early modern artists, craft workers, engineers, philosophers and poets: 'the makers of tools, machines, statues, images or literary texts were all … involved in that debate which pitted the Aristotelian world of *Techne* or the process of "bringing something into being" against nature and natural forms' (Sawday 2007: 174, 207). By the late seventeenth century one aspect of this relation, as we noted above with the work of Bacon, was the idea that a subordinate nature was available for harnessing by mechanical means for human use. From this perspective, nature was like a soft metal – matter to be 'pressured and moulded' (quoted in Sawday 2007: 212).

In the partition of the artificial and the natural, enlightenment collectors excelled with their programmes for systematic categorization and ordering. Scholarly collections of innumerable material entities, which were increasingly listed and catalogued, tended to reject ambiguity and resist heterogeneity.

**Figure 1.1**  A witch and a devil making a nail with which to make a boy lame. Woodcut in *The History of Witches and Wizards*, London 1720. Wellcome Library, London

Instead systematic classifications and arrangements were sought for domains (and sub-divisions) of art and of nature including animals, insects, plants, minerals and shells, many obtained through the expansion of trade and colonial territories (see MacGregor 2007, Sloan and Burnett 2003). Further characteristics of eighteenth-century methods and concepts developed in the pursuit of systematized knowledge were dissection and abstraction, which informed perceptions of entities that were grown, on the one hand, and made on the other (Stafford 1993). With regard to artefacts, these can be seen, for instance, in printed images of a huge range of practices – such as weaving, carpentry, pottery and bookbinding; wig-, bead-, cardboard-, lace-, parchment-, mirror- and coin-making; diamond working and the processing of metals – published in the *Encyclopédie* under the direction of Denis Diderot and Jean le Rond d'Alembert from 1751 to 1772. These images were enlisted in the work's aim to provide an analytical dictionary of human knowledge, including that involved in the labour of many trades.

Illustrations of pewterware making, for example, showed the workshop, the tools and moulds used, and the final product, in this case a wine jug (Figure 1.2). In the scene or context of making, at the top of the image, the pewter casting is broken down into several main operations performed by workers (seemingly ordered in reverse from lathe work, the fitting of lid and hinge, the soldering of the jug's parts, and finally the casting of molten metal in moulds). Below this the pewter artefact is shown removed or abstracted from the setting of the workshop. The artefact is further taken apart to reveal its several components (belly, neck, foot, lid, hinge, handle), and the moulds used to form it are dismantled and shown in cross-section to expose their internal composition. In this visual analysis, which was linked via a key to textual description, material things were extracted from the processes of their production, isolated, internally divided and named (or labelled) so that they could be better understood and known. So abstraction and dissection not only contributed to the differentiation of making and growing, they also helped to define the very nature of these processes. Here, making took place on a simplified trajectory 'from substance to object', where what grew, or was offered by nature, was worked from raw material to completed item, the latter understood as an amalgam of parts (Barthes 1980 [1964]: 26).

A century later, back in the world of museums (these institutions by this time massively expanding, with the growth of empire, and opening to the public), the separation of natural from artefactual was deemed necessary to the organization and advancement of knowledge. Such a separation made sense because it had become possible to conceive of phenomena in the universe that were 'independent of the agency of man' (Flower 1898 [1889]: 7). The study of these phenomena – natural history – was sub-dividing into such subjects as astronomy, botany, chemistry, geology, mineralogy and zoology, as William Henry Flower explained in 1889 when Director of the Natural History Museum in London (see Jardine, Secord and Spary 1996). Nevertheless, the term 'natural history' was still pertinent, Flower argued, for museums whose contents *contrasted* with those in museums concerned with the 'history of man and of his works'. Thus at the British Museum a significant division was made: 'the line of severance was effected at the junction of what was natural and what was artificial; the former, including the products of what are commonly called "natural" forces, unaffected by man's handiwork, or the impress of his mind' (Flower 1898 [1889]: 8). The Natural History Museum, therefore, gathered and exhibited 'natural objects' which were treated differently from 'works art'. In the case of the latter, Flower advised, items such as a picture or vase could come into the curator's hands in a completed state, requiring only cleaning and repair. By contrast, natural 'specimens' required special methods of preservation, skilled labour that, when conducted successfully, rendered the specimen 'itself a work of art, based upon a natural substratum' (Flower 1898 [1893]: 32).

In this conception of growing, nature was assumed to produce entities without human involvement, and the corresponding conception of making was that human skill was applied to natural substances without influencing their underlying essence. Once growing had ceased, then, human skill was required to maintain natural specimens, to protect them from decay and disintegration.

Making and Growing: An Introduction 13

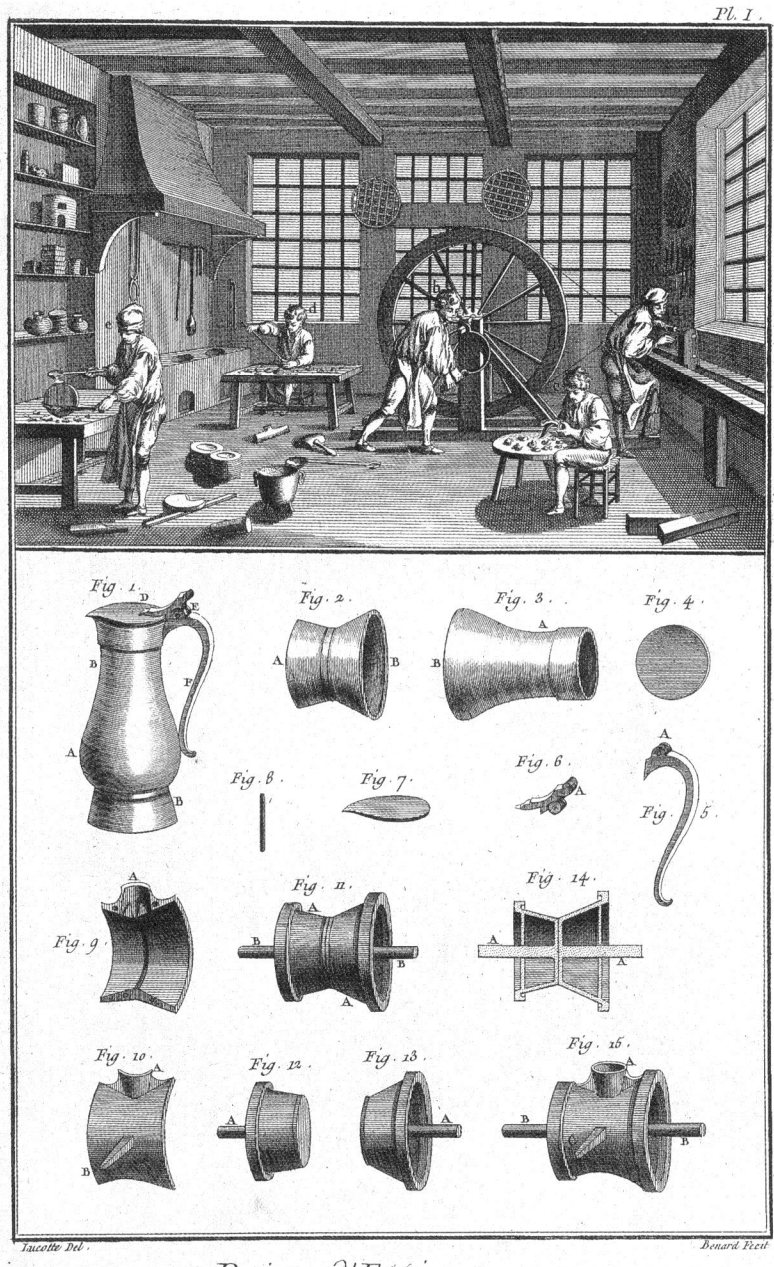

Figure 1.2   Processing of pewter, moulds used and final product. Etching with engraving, Paris 1768. Wellcome Library, London

**Figure 1.3** Still life of leaves and flowers, Hong Kong. Photograph by John Thomson, 1868/1871. Wellcome Library, London

As living organisms became specimens for science, 'biological' life also became still life as, for example, in John Thomson's photographs taken when travelling from Scotland to Singapore and China during the second half of the nineteenth century (Figure 1.3) (Flower 1898 [1893]: 32).

Photography was among the favoured techniques for collecting and preserving 'nature'; it was seen to capture organisms by way of imaging processes regarded, ideally, as independent of human interpretation. Yet Thomson's carefully composed photographs of plants, people and places crossed the expected (but difficult to maintain) boundary between the genres of scientific and aesthetic photography (including portraiture) (see Daston and Galison 2007). So too, the museum division of the grown and the made was far from straightforward. In particular, Flower pointed out, it was not helpful in all areas of investigation for 'it cuts man himself in two', artificially separating the study of his 'physical structure' from that of 'his mental development, his manners, customs, traditions and languages' as well as his 'art'. Dividing in this way certainly presented 'inconveniences' for the 'new science of anthropology', which was properly concerned with 'all that man is or ever has been, [and] all that he has ever done' (Flower 1898 [1889]: 8, 9). For these museum-based knowledge practices to physically and conceptually separate supposedly natural objects from what were designated as artefacts was to encourage analysis of growing and making as distinct processes. Notions of a partible nature and culture continued to play out in museum collecting and display into the twentieth century, in association with their respective university disciplines, fuelling divisions of academic labour between disciplines concerned, respectively, with the domains or orders of artefacts and organisms (see Alberti 2009).

**Beyond the Division: Contemporary Challenges**

Today, these divisions between artefacts and organisms, or between what is made and what is grown, are being increasingly challenged, in fields ranging from contemporary art to biomedicine. Artists Gerda Steiner and Jörg Lenzlinger, for instance, have set up installations in museums, art galleries, libraries, offices, gardens and other settings in Australia, Japan, Israel, Brazil and Europe, that confound attempts to distinguish growing from manufactured elements. Thus *Brainforest* (2004), displayed at Kanazawa's 21st Century Museum of Contemporary Art, was a sprawling amalgam of roots, vines, branches, discarded telephone and computer cables, paper and plastic flowers, and leaves covered in gold leaf. Steiner and Lenzlinger's projects fuse myriad discarded materials with living plants, animal bones, water, and minerals such as salt, as well as 'artificial' fertilizer, so that coral-like crystals grow for the duration of the exhibition. This fertilizer contains urea which the human body produces and excretes in urine but which is also industrially manufactured on a large scale. In Steiner and Lenzlinger's collaborations, assumed boundaries of human bodies, plants, insects, and all manner of material objects seem to have given way to fluid profusions that provoke reflection on processes of life and death, nature and artifice (Steiner and Lenzlinger 2010).

If these artists' experimental installations are ways of 'investigating the world' (Grimshaw, Owen and Ravetz 2010: 160), they also draw attention to – and participate in – the seemingly increasing permeability between domains once distinguished as nature and culture, thereby highlighting the inseparability of the organic and the artefactual. In the last two decades anthropologists, too, have documented and analyzed this permeability in industrialized contexts. Franklin and Lock (2003: 3) approach the 'remaking of life and death' by focusing on developments in biomedicine, science and technology, such as cloning, genetic modification and organ transplants. These practices call into question the notion that fabrication is distinct from growth, and that there are clear points at which life begins and ends (see Franklin 2007, Sharp 2006, Kaufman and Morgan 2005). Human reproductive technologies as well as animal and plant breeding are as thoroughly social as they are physical (see Cassidy 2007, Edwards and Salazar 2009). Bioengineering of human tissue cuts across the categories of organism and artefact when, for instance, blood vessels are produced for surgical procedures (see Graber 2011). A crucial issue in these and other medical practices, such as the use of prosthetic implants, is the capacity of human cells within the body to thrive in relation to – and not to reject – fabricated or grown replacements, which can comprise materials such as metals and ceramics (Figure 1.4). While according to Haraway (1991), hybrid human/machine and human/animal bodies took form in late twentieth-century medicine, current fibre and textile engineers are reconfiguring human/plant relations by, for example, combining 'natural' and 'synthetic' fibres to create 'technonaturals'. Some of these contain plant extracts for making garments that encourage health-giving 'active exchange' between fibre and skin (O'Mahony 2001: 34). Smart materials such as Bioglass, 'seeded' with stem cells from a patient and then implanted to encourage bone growth, are said to 'stand on the frontier between the animate and the inanimate', as does 'self-healing concrete' which is impregnated with bacteria whose excretions seal up emerging fine cracks (Harrod 2013, see Küchler 2010).

Despite these developments in art, biomedicine and materials science, which have confounded the division between making and growing, recent anthropological studies of material culture have continued to privilege the artefactual, somewhat at the expense of the organic. And while it has become fashionable to speak of humans and non-humans rather than of persons and things, or of subjects and objects, the non-humans almost invariably turn out to be artefacts rather than life-forms, leaving a gaping void so far as non-human life is concerned. The issues have tended to be framed around questions of agency, or the capacity to cause effects. Is this capacity confined to humans alone, or does it come into operation by way of their association with non-humans? On the one hand, Karp and Lavine

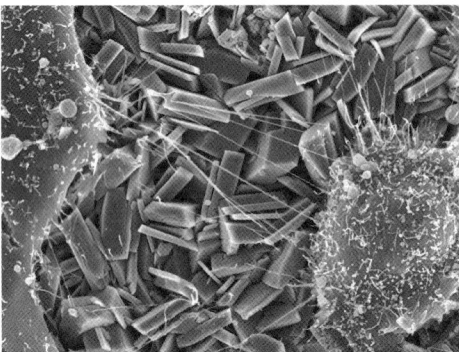

Figure 1.4    Two human bone-forming cells growing over crystals of the ceramic material, monetite. This ceramic coating on titanium hip joints and tooth-root posts encourages cell growth, making the metal more compatible with the body and therefore more effective in prosthetic implants. Scanning electron micrograph, c.2000. Karin Hing, Wellcome Images

(1991: 23) note that artefacts are produced 'by human agents who have goals and intentions', thus excluding 'natural' objects deemed to exist beyond the reach of such intentions (see Alberti 2008). The implication is that making is an intentional human act – an aspect of culture – whereas growing just happens. On the other hand, in their *Handbook of Material Culture* (2006), Tilley and his colleagues set out a broader approach, embracing both 'things as materially existing and having a significance in the world independent of any human action or intervention (e.g. a stone, a mountain, an animal or a tree)', and 'things as created by persons: artefacts'. However this framework still prioritizes relationships between persons and things that are characterized by reciprocal making ('persons make and use things … and things make persons'), leaving growing once again relatively neglected (Tilley et al. 2006: 4).

Expositions of 'materiality', which similarly tend to focus on artefacts, are likewise concerned with both human and non-human agency, either within hybrid networks comprising such entities as computers, bacteria and plants (following Latour 1993), or, following Gell (1998), with reference to relations between persons and material objects (see Miller 2005, Hicks 2010). Again there seems little room, either theoretical or ethnographic, for processes of growth. Even when attention shifts from artefacts to organisms, such as trees, it is their 'purposive' agency that is stressed. In this view, growth is the 'action' through which trees produce flowers, leaves and fruit, while contributing to the composition of landscapes, during their seasonal cycles and over long-term 'organic time' (Jones and Cloke 2002: 60, 69). Indeed it seems that the theoretical resort to the concept of agency is a by-product of the subsumption of growth under making, and with it, the suppression of animate life. What if we were to reverse our priorities, and subsume making under growth? Would not the concept of agency then take second place to that of animacy, as embodiment would take second place to ontogenesis, and being to becoming (Ingold 2013: 95–7)? Some aspects of what this might involve are suggested by studies in geography that explore, for example, 'entanglements' of nature through innovative discussions of such seemingly disparate entities as lichen, viruses, railways, bees, cities, ice and the moon (Harrison, Pile, Thrift 2004). That growth also entails rotting and disintegration – brought about by thriving algae, micro-organisms, insects, mosses, and small animals – is vividly documented in studies of buildings and ruins enmeshed in diverse ecologies (see Edensor 2011, DeSilvey and Edensor 2012).

The anthropological work on growth that is perhaps most relevant for material culture studies is to be found in explorations of gardens – yet these too have their limitations. Two examples are relevant here. The first takes its starting point from Malinowski's (1935) classic account of gardening in the Trobriand Islands, *Coral Gardens and their Magic*. Moving from the inorganic (the growth of stones) to the organic, Tilley develops an account of gardens in England which likens them to artefacts, especially as they have associated stories, memories and biographical meanings such that persons and the plants they cultivate grow together (2004, 2009: 176). Growing here becomes tantamount to making, even though plants are taken to have their own lives. The second example, Coupaye's (2009: 435) discussion of yam gardening in Papua New Guinea, works in the same interpretative direction by describing gardening as making, understood as the 'actions of humans on materials', intended to take them from a raw to a manufactured state. Although Coupaye acknowledges the 'agency' of such non-human entities as spirits, butterflies and worms in gardening, growing is again subordinated to making, just as yams are defined by the anthropologist primarily as artefacts – despite their recognition as deeply ambiguous botanical-cum-artefactual entities. Once more, the rendering of living things as artefacts, and the consequent appeal to agency, puts growth in the shade. Ethnography in Melanesia, such as Battaglia's (1990) classic study of Sabarl Island, indicates that growing is a far richer terrain, as does ethnobotanical research in England that focuses on people-plant interactions in ways that grant 'intellectual space' to forms of growth (Ellen and Platten 2011: 580).

So while anthropological analysis of growing has yet to fully develop in studies of material culture, making, by contrast, has flourished as an area of considerable contemporary interest. For example, Naji and Douny's agenda for understanding socially-situated making and doing emphasizes the 'embodied and cognitive engagement of human beings in their lived material world' (2009: 411). To approach making in this way is to acknowledge its emotional, sensual, material and technological dimensions. In 2010, The Museum Ethnographers Group (MEG), the UK-based international collective, organized their annual conference around the theme of 'making things', which provided a platform for discussions of artists' interventions, film, the sacred and community-making in relation to museum work and research (Douglas 2011). Further studies interrogate the issue of making as a means of generating and communicating knowledge in contemporary and historical practices (see Marchand 2010, Smith and Schmidt 2007, Klein and Spary 2010). Making blurs into re-making, and repair into everyday, mundane maintenance, so that practices of making and use become inseparable (see Colloredo-Mansfeld 2003, DeSilvey et al. 2012, Naji and Douny 2009). Making shapes perceptions of the past just as it forges into the future. At the newly founded Institute of Making, based at University College London, with its Materials Library full of the 'most unusual materials in the world' – such as the self-healing concrete mentioned above – multidisciplinary research and practice is facilitated, including collaborations across design, engineering, science and art (UCL 2013, see Howes and Laughlin 2012). Making applies not just to manipulations conducted with materials, but also to the very constitution of those materials (see Küchler 2008).

**The Book**

To sum up, while anthropological studies of material culture have devoted much attention to questions of making (involving artefacts), questions of growing (involving organisms) have so far been examined in much less depth. As historians have noted, understandings of what constitutes an 'organism' are diverse and shift over time (Cheung 2006). And if, as current debates in the philosophy of science suggest, the definition of the human organism may have to be radically re-examined – given the high proportion of bacterial and fungal cells in the human body, revealing the 'deep interconnection, or symbiosis, between living things' (Parry and Dupré 2010: 10, Dupré 2010) – then how might an anthropology of organisms inflect the analysis of material culture? This book extends the analysis of the relations between making and growing beyond the domains of science and technology, by turning not only to the work of biomedical engineers and medical educators but also to everyday working practices such as sewing, carving, gardening and glass-forming. Contributors explore these varied and changing relations from perspectives in anthropology, archaeology, cultural geography and history. In so doing, they reveal a whole spectrum of responses to the question of how, if at all, things created by people may be distinguished from what apparently comes into being 'naturally'.

Running through the book are three significant threads: bodies, materials and temporality. Here attention to bodies in processes of making and growing ranges from the bodies of human beings to those of insects, reptiles, mammals and plants, emphasizing the relational nature of these bodies, whether living or dead. These bodies are social, material and processual (see Lock and Farquhar 2007, Lambert and McDonald 2009) and, as authors in this volume show, they undergo development by way of diverse practices enacted in sites from the domestic to the industrial. Key to these practices and developmental pathways are materials, and the following chapters explore many, including silk, metals, plastics, wood, willow, clay, caribou skin, glass and granite. Such materials have implications for technique, form and use, just as bodily engagements with these materials draw out their particular qualities – qualities which in turn continue to have effects. Thus this book is concerned with the dynamics of substance and sensation, as well as with skill and sentiment. To address processes of making and growing, the contributors situate their analyses in particular material contexts and in terms of different time scales, be they in the immediate term or commensurate with the human lifespan, across several generations or centuries, or in deep geological time (see Gosden 2006). Depending on the time-scale or scales adopted, they conduct their research through apprenticeship and skilled practice, oral history, archival and museum-based research, ethnography, experimental investigation and documentation.

In the following chapters, then, the processes and relations of making and growing are explored through analysis that is sensitive to the social, epistemological and affective dimensions of the subject matter to hand. Each foregrounds a particular thematic through which to consider how making and growing are interrelated. In her discussion of *metamorphosis*, Jacqueline Field (Chapter 2) traces silk production in China, North America and Japan especially from the nineteenth century onwards. Pamela H. Smith (Chapter 3) is concerned with *transformation* in her examination of casting from life in early modern Europe. Elizabeth Hallam (Chapter 4) also explores casting – as a ritualized means to generate and disseminate anatomical knowledge, in mid-twentieth-century England, through a *material poiesis* entailing composition and decay. Paolo Fortis

(Chapter 5) focuses on *design* in carving, garment-making and the formation of human beings in contemporary Panama, as does Benjamin Alberti (Chapter 6) in his discussion of bodies and ceramic vessels from Argentina in the first millennium AD. Nancy Wachowich (Chapter 7) examines the sewing of animal-skin gloves as a form of *nurturance* in the Canadian Arctic over the last century.

The next five chapters are by scholars who are also active practitioners, in Britain, of the making-growing that they seek to interpret. *Cultivation* is integral to Anne Jepson's (Chapter 8) description of gardening in terms of a grounded therapeutics. Stephanie Bunn (Chapter 9) analyzes basket weaving as a form of *generation* – of knowledge as well as pleasure. Trevor Marchand (Chapter 10) takes up the theme of *learning*, in his case among woodworkers developing and relinquishing a range of embodied skills as they age. Frances Liardet (Chapter 11) approaches glass-forming as dextrous *movement* with tools and materials in workshop settings. David Paton and Caitlin DeSilvey (Chapter 12) develop an experimental narrative based at a granite quarry where they follow *flows* of 'waste' sludge as a way of thinking about production. Together these explorations seek to bring together making and growing so as to offer fresh insights into the myriad and ever-changing relations between organisms and artefacts.

## References

Alberti, S.J.M.M. 2008. Constructing nature behind glass. *Museum and Society*, 6(2), 73–97.

Alberti, S.J.M.M. 2009. *Nature and Culture: Objects, Disciplines and the Manchester Museum.* Manchester: Manchester University Press.

Bacon, F. 1858. *Works of Francis Bacon, Baron of Verulam, Viscount St. Alban and Lord High Chancellor of England, Vol. IV*, translated by J. Spedding, R.L. Ellis and D.D. Heath. London: Spottiswoode.

Bacon, F. 1965. *Francis Bacon: A Selection of His Works*, edited by S. Wahrhaft. Toronto: Macmillan.

Barthes, R. 1980 [1964]. The plates of the encyclopedia, in *Roland Barthes: New Critical Essays*, translated by R. Howard. New York: Hill and Wang, 23–39.

Battaglia, D. 1990. *On the Bones of the Serpent: Person, Memory and Mortality in Sabarl Island Society.* Chicago, IL: University of Chicago Press.

Brand, S. 1994. *How Buildings Learn: What Happens to Them after They're Built.* New York: Penguin.

Calvert, J. 2010. Synthetic biology: constructing nature? *The Sociological Review*, 58, 95–112.

Cassidy, R.L. 2007. *Horse People: Thoroughbred Culture in Lexington and Newmarket.* Baltimore, MD: Johns Hopkins University Press.

Cheung, T. 2006. From the organism of a body to the body of an organism: occurrence and meaning of the word 'organism' from the seventeenth to the nineteenth centuries. *British Journal for the History of Science*, 39(3), 319–39.

Colloredo-Mansfeld, R. 2003. Introduction: matter unbound. *Journal of Material Culture*, 8(3), 245–54.

Darr, O.A. 2011. *Marks of an Absolute Witch: Evidentiary Dilemmas in Early Modern England.* Farnham: Ashgate.

Daston, L. and P. Galison 2007. *Objectivity.* New York: Zone Books.

Daston, L. and K. Park 2001. *Wonders and the Order of Nature, 1150–1750.* New York: Zone Books.

Dawkins, R. 1986. *The Blind Watchmaker*. Harlow, Essex: Longman Scientific and Technical.

DeSilvey, C. and T. Edensor 2012. Reckoning with ruins. *Progress in Human Geography,* published online 27 November 2012, DOI: 10.1177/0309132512462271, 1–21.

Desilvey, C. et al. 2012. A celebration of repair (collaborative website), http://projects.exeter.ac.uk/celebrationofrepair/. Accessed June 2012.

Douglas, O. 2011. Making things: an introduction. *Journal of Museum Ethnography*, 24, 11–22.

Dupré, J. 2010. The polygenomic organism. *The Sociological Review*, 58(s1), 19–31.

Edensor, T. 2011. Entangled agencies, material networks and repair in a building assemblage: the mutable stone of St Ann's Church, Manchester. *Transactions of the Institute of British Geographers*, 36(2), 238–52.

Edwards, J. and C. Salazar (eds) 2009. *European Kinship in the Age of Biotechnology.* Oxford: Berghahn.

Ellen, R. and S. Platten 2011. The social life of seeds: the role of networks of relationships in the dispersal and cultural selection of plant germplasm. *Journal of the Royal Anthropological Institute*, 17(3), 563–84.

Flower, W.H. 1898 [1889]. Museum organization, in *Essays on Museums and Other Subjects Connected with Natural History*, by W.H. Flower. London: Macmillan, 1–29.

Flower, W.H. 1898 [1893]. Modern museums, in *Essays on Museums and Other Subjects Connected with Natural History*, by W.H. Flower. London: Macmillan, 30–53.

Franklin, S. 2007. *Dolly Mixtures: The Remaking of Genealogy.* Durham, N.C.: Duke University Press.

Franklin, S. and M. Lock (eds) 2003. *Remaking Life and Death: Toward an Anthropology of the Biosciences.* Sante Fe: School of American Research Press.

Gell, A. 1998. *Art and Agency: An Anthropological Theory.* Oxford: Oxford University Press.

Gosden, C. 2006. Material culture and long-term change, in *Handbook of Material Culture*, edited by C. Tilley, et al. London: Sage, 425–42.

Graber, C. 2011. Bioengineered blood vessels are state-of-the-artery. *Scientific American*, 7 February 2011. http://www.scientificamerican.com. Accessed May 2013.

Grimshaw, A., E. Owen and A. Ravetz 2010. Making do: the materials of art and anthropology, in *Between Art and Anthropology: Contemporary Art and Anthropology*, edited by A. Schneider and D. Wright. Oxford: Berg, 147–62.

Haraway, D. 1991. *Simians, Cyborgs, and Women: The Reinvention of Nature*. New York: Routledge.

Harrison, S., Pile, S. and N. Thrift (eds) 2004. *Patterned Ground: Entanglements of Nature and Culture*. London: Reaktion Books.

Harrod, H. 2013. Inside the materials library. *The Telegraph*, 22 April 2013. http://www.telegraph.co.uk. Accessed May 2013.

Heidegger, M. 1971. Building dwelling thinking, in *Poetry, Language, Thought*, by M. Heidegger, translated by A. Hofstadter. New York: Harper and Row, 143–161.

Hicks, D. 2010. The material-cultural turn: event and affect, in *The Oxford Handbook of Material Culture Studies*, edited by D. Hicks and M.D. Beaudry. Oxford: Oxford University Press, 25–98.

Howes, P. and Z. Laughlin. 2012. *Material Matters: New Materials in Design*. London: Black Dog Publishing.

Ingold, T. 2013. *Making: Anthropology, Archaeology, Art and Architecture*. Abingdon: Routledge.

Jardine, N., J.A. Secord, and E.C. Spary (eds) 1996. *Cultures of Natural History*. Cambridge: Cambridge University Press.

Jones, O. and Cloke, P. 2002. *Tree Cultures: The Place of Trees and Trees in their Place*. Oxford: Berg.

Karp, I. and S.D. Lavine (eds) 1991. *Exhibiting Cultures: The Poetics and Politics of Museum Display*. Washington, DC: Smithsonian Institution Press.

Kaufman, S. and Morgan, L.M. 2005. The anthropology of the beginnings and ends of life. *Annual Review of Anthropology*, 34, 317–41.

Klein, U. and E.C. Spary (eds) 2010. *Materials and Expertise in Early Modern Europe: Between Market and Laboratory*. Chicago, IL: University of Chicago Press.

Knight, J. 1998. The second life of trees: family forestry in upland Japan, in *The Social Life of Trees: Anthropological Perspectives on Tree Symbolism*, edited by L. Rival. Oxford: Berg, 197–218.

Küchler, S. 2008. Technological materiality: beyond the dualist paradigm. *Theory, Culture and Society*, 25(1), 101–20.

Küchler, S. 2010. Materials and design, in *Design Anthropology: Object Culture in the 21st Century*, edited by A. Clarke. Vienna: Springer.

Lambert, H. and M. McDonald 2009. *Social Bodies*. Oxford: Berghahn.

Latour, B. 1993. *We Have Never Been Modern*. Cambridge, MA: Harvard University Press.

Lévi-Strauss, C. 1968. *Structural Anthropology*. Harmondsworth: Penguin.

Lock, M. and J. Farquhar (eds) 2007. *Beyond the Body Proper: Reading the Anthropology of Material Life*. Durham, NC: Duke University Press.

MacGregor, A. 2007. *Curiosity and Enlightenment: Collectors and Collections from the Sixteenth to the Nineteenth Century*. New Haven: Yale University Press.

Malinowski, B. 1935. *Coral Gardens and their Magic*. London: Allen & Unwin.

Marchand, T.H.J. (ed.) 2010. *Making Knowledge: Explorations of the Indissoluble Relation Between Mind, Body and Environment.* Oxford: Wiley-Blackwell.

Miller, D. 2005. Materiality: an introduction, in *Materiality*, edited by D. Miller. Durham, NC: Duke University Press, 1–50.

Naji, M. and L. Douny 2009. Editorial. *Journal of Material Culture*, 14(4), 411–32.

O'Mahony, M. 2011. *Advanced Textiles for Health and Wellbeing.* London: Thames and Hudson.

Paley, W. 2006 [1802]. *Natural Theology: or, Evidences of the Existence and Attributes of the Deity, Collected from the Appearances of Nature*, edited by M. Eddy and D. Knight. Oxford: Oxford University Press.

Parry, S. and Dupré, J. 2010. Introducing nature after the genome. *The Sociological Review*, 58(s1), 3–16.

Roper, L. 1994. *Oedipus and the Devil: Witchcraft, Sexuality and Religion in Early Modern Europe.* London: Routledge.

Sample, I. 2010. Craig Venter creates synthetic life form. *The Guardian*, 20 May 2010. http://www.guardian.co.uk/science/2010/may/20/craig-venter-synthetic-life-form. Accessed May 2013.

Sawday, J. 2007. *Engines of the Imagination: Renaissance Culture and the Rise of the Machine.* London: Routledge.

Schutz, A. 1962. *The Problem of Social Reality*, collected papers volume I, edited by M. Nathanson. The Hague: Nijhoff.

Sennett, R. 2008. *The Craftsman*. London: Penguin (Allen Lane).

Shapin, S. 2008. *The Scientific Life: A Moral History of a Late Modern Vocation.* Chicago, IL: University of Chicago Press.

Sharp, L. 2006. *Strange Harvest: Organ Transplants, Denatured Bodies, and the Transformed Self.* Berkeley, CA: University of California Press.

Sloan, K. and A. Burnett (eds) 2003. *Enlightenment: Discovering the World in the Eighteenth Century.* London: The British Museum Press.

Smith, P.H. and B. Schmidt (eds) 2007. *Making Knowledge in Early Modern Europe: Practices, Objects, and Texts, 1400–1800.* Chicago, IL: University of Chicago Press.

Spuybroek, L. 2011. *The Sympathy of Things: Ruskin and the Ecology of Design.* Rotterdam: V_2 Publishing.

Stafford, B.M. 1993. *Body Criticism: Imaging the Unseen in Enlightenment Art and Medicine.* Cambridge, MA: MIT Press.

Stafford, B.M. 1994. *Artful Science: Enlightenment Entertainment and the Eclipse of Visual Education.* Cambridge, MA: MIT Press.

Steiner, G. and Lenzlinger, J. 2010. *The Mystery of Fertility.* Basel: Christoph Merian Verlag.

Thomas, K. 1985 [1971]. *Religion and the Decline of Magic.* Harmondsworth: Peregrine Books.

Tilley, C. 2004. *The Materiality of Stone: Explorations in Landscape Phenomenology*, Oxford: Berg.

Tilley, C. et al. 2006. Introduction, in *Handbook of Material Culture*, edited by C. Tilley et al. London: Sage, 1–6.
Tilley, C. 2009. What gardens mean, in *Material Culture and Technology in Everyday Life: Ethnographic Approaches*, edited by P. Vannini. New York: Peter Lang, 171–92.
Turner, V.W. 1967. *The Forest of Symbols: Aspects of Ndembu Ritual*. Ithaca, NY: Cornell University Press.
UCL 2013. Most extraordinary materials on earth housed in new Institute of Making, http://www.ucl.ac.uk/news/news-articles, 12 March 2013. Accessed June 2013.
Whitehead, A.N. 1929. *Process and Reality: An Essay in Cosmology*. Cambridge: Cambridge University Press.

# Chapter 2
# Silk Production: Moths, Mulberry and Metamorphosis

Jacqueline Field

'The structure of fabric or its weave – that is, the fastening of threads to each other – is as much a determining factor in its function as is the choice of raw material' (Albers 1966: 38). In the case of silk fabric the apparently raw material – the silk filaments – imparts the lustrous and tactile qualities that distinguish this textile from all others. At the same time silk materials are highly valued as the products of machine technology and deliberate design. While distinctions between 'raw' material and processed fabric might be readily made in some cultural contexts, this chapter explores the technology and design embedded in the very yarn itself and in its component silk filaments. In so doing it shows how the 'raw', or grown, and the processed, or made, are interrelated in the case of sericulture. What is termed raw silk is, therefore, far from raw in the sense of not having been treated or remaining free from human intervention. Sericulture – the plant and insect cultivation system that provides the material for silk textiles – is the foundation upon which the silk industry has developed. In what follows I explore these issues with reference mainly to parts of Asia and North America. I begin by discussing the agricultural activity of rearing silkworms and by providing a comparative overview of some of the ways market forces stimulated nineteenth-century silk production. From an examination of mulberry and worm relationships, and worm-to-moth metamorphosis, I go on to show the effects of cultivation and, more recently, science, on silkworms and their food source. Finally I focus on new uses for silk and bioengineering efforts to grow silk protein in forms other than filament. Attention to these processes highlights the plant–human–insect relationships that yield silk through growing and making.

## Sericulture: People, Plant and Insect Interactions

Sericulture is an agricultural activity involving mulberry tree cultivation, the rearing of delicate temperamental insects, and the reeling of filament from their cocoons. Silk has been known in China for more than five millennia. It is uncertain exactly when wild silkworm domestication – the subtly complex and labour-intensive silk rearing activity – originated, but it is likely that silk farming developed more than 4,000 years ago. Carved representations of worms and cocoons have been found dating from c.5,000–3,000 BCE, but it is the earliest surviving silk fabric fragments, datable to the middle of the fourth millennium, that provide evidence that silk farming had become well established by that time (Vainker 2004). Over the long term, as the system evolved, it had the effect of altering both the insect and its food source, the mulberry. Wherever sericulture has been practised, and regardless of whether it supplied major state workshops or smaller independent or domestic textile manufacturers, mulberry and silkworm growing has tended to remain a predominantly cottage industry, and a seasonal means of earning supplemental income. Although practised in many parts of the world and perceived in different ways, there are nevertheless some common patterns in this process of entwined making and growing.

The silkworms used for most textile production cannot be reared to successfully produce quality silk on food other than mulberry leaves (Feltwell 1990). They thrive best on white mulberry (*Morus alba*), which is cultivated as a crop and harvested to feed silkworms reared indoors (Duran 1921). To avoid having to discard worms, or to waste weeks of labour and therefore lose anticipated silk income, silk growers determine the number of mulberry trees or shrubs required to provide sufficient feed for the quantity of worms to be raised (Min-hsiung 1976). Leaf food must be fresh every day, and the leaf harvesting required to sustain a going operation hatching tens of thousands of silkworms per season is considerable. During the week preceding cocoon building, when maturing silkworms are at their most ravenous, the feeding task becomes extremely arduous. For example a stock of 36,000 worms will require an average of 80 kg of leaves per day (Handschin 1946a, 1946b). In temperate regions deciduous trees support a major spring and a brief autumn sericulture season. In areas where tropical mulberry shrubs (*Morus multicaulis*) leaf all year round sericulture can be continuous.

The purpose of sericulture is the production of silkworm cocoons that will yield silk filament to be made into thread. The most dominant and productive silkworm is the caterpillar of the *Bombyx mori* Linné moth, a member of the Asian *Bombycinae* family of about 80 species whose larvae have the ability to make a silk cocoon (Handschin 1946 a, 1946b, Tweedie 1977). *Bombyx mori* stands out for its capacity to produce the most useful silk filament cocoon and because, in contrast to others, it is not difficult to contrive conditions in which the organism will thrive. For these reasons *Bombyx mori* has been singled out for domestication, an accomplishment made possible by its docile temperament, a trait enhanced over time by human intervention. In terms of length, silk filament is unique among natural fibres used for textiles: while other fibres such as cotton and wool are measured in fractions of inches, continuous silk filaments average from 500 to 1,500 yards (455 to 1370 m).

*Bombyx mori* varieties include monovoltines that breed once a year, bi-voltines which breed twice, and polyvoltines that annually produce many generations. Between seasons dormant monovoltine eggs require an interval in cold storage. Polyvoltine eggs do not. The organism has a four-stage life cycle: egg, larva, pupa and moth. During 33 to 38 days from hatching (less for polyvoltines) larvae pass through four phases (instars), shedding skin four times until the fifth instar when they become greyish white, very fat and thumb sized, reaching a weight of five grams and a length of nine centimetres: from hatching, this is a proportional growth rate of one to 10,000 (Duran 1921). At this point the caterpillar stops eating, finds a nook among specially provided mounts, spins out silk, and encases itself in an egg-shaped cocoon where metamorphosis takes place. Within ten days or so the moth breaks out and lives for three to four days. In the domesticated situation only a small number of selected cocoons are set aside for the moths to emerge and be placed on prepared papers where mating occurs and each female subsequently deposits 300–500 eggs. In a necessary intervention, however, most cocoons are smothered by heat or other means to kill the pupae because moths destroy the filament's valuable continuity when they break out. The pupae must die so that their intact cocoons can be successfully harvested.

Through domestication these organisms have lost the urge to forage; they scarcely move and have become totally dependent on human care, attention and feeding. Relationships between people, plants and insects that emerge through these practices have often been ones where people become cultivators, caretakers, and conservators, who safeguard and maintain the valuable plants and insects so crucial to silk production. These relationships develop in specific cultural contexts. The archaeological evidence referred to earlier indicates that as far back as the third and fourth millennia BCE silk crops and textile production had become an established part of the Chinese agricultural cycle. It is likely that then, as later, the business of rearing the silkworms was organized within the domestic sphere. Bray (1997) shows how this rearing was very much part of women's work. They supervised worm care, nurturing, cleaning, and feeding – a demanding and time-consuming task akin to, and carried out in addition to, childrearing. Like childrearing, silkworm rearing, reeling, and weaving were practices that women were highly invested and competent in. Until about 1,000 CE it was the female peasants and women of manorial households who produced most of China's textiles, including important quantities of silk. The majority of these silks were made on domestic looms. They were highly valued for tax payment purposes and as commercial commodities.

When changing conditions stimulated the market during the tenth to eleventh centuries, textile manufacture moved out of household production to more sophisticated workshops. Carried out in the home, sericulture became the only domestic textile-related female activity, a situation that emphasized the importance of women's work in rearing silkworms – the fabric maker's source of raw material (Bray 1997). While men undertook the labour of mulberry plant maintenance and leaf gathering, the indoor worm rearing and eventual reeled silk production thus primarily occupied women. Silkworm eggs were referred to as seeds and women nurtured them, tucking small packets of pin-head sized eggs in their clothing, or around their bodies, for several weeks until their physical warmth quickened the dormant eggs and induced hatching (Bray 1997). In the meantime ancillary preparatory tasks included preparing silkworm tray racks, and weaving mats to line the trays to allow frass (faecal matter) and leaf detritus to sieve through for removal. Hatching heralded the beginning of almost 40 days of ceaseless work.

**Figure 2.1** Silkworms. Fourth stage silkworms feeding on fresh mulberry leaves at a Japanese silk farm, 2011. Photograph copyright Jacqueline Field

Miniscule, hairy, black and ant-like at first, the baby silkworms are a mere three millimetres long and a half a milligram in weight (Duran 1921). Spread out on trays the tiny worms were fed with finely chopped newly budded mulberry leaves. Growing rapidly and always hungry, the insects required continual feeding and cleaning, and as their size increased, frequent redistribution by hand to new trays to alleviate crowding that could cause disease (Figure 2.1). Such human interaction with these insects has had significant effects on silk, as have further social, economic and political factors, which are briefly discussed next.

**Producing Silk: Comparative Historical Perspectives**

The silk industry consists of two distinct divisions. One is the agricultural activity of growing mulberry, raising silkworms and reeling silk filament that is marketed as raw silk. The other involves the use of raw silk and the activity of making useable threads and weaving textiles. Increases in demand for raw silk have stimulated concerted efforts to produce more of it, as in nineteenth-century

Asia when shortages caused by devastating silkworm disease in Europe were compounded by rapidly escalating silk fabric manufacture and silk consumption (Min-hsiung 1976). A brief overview of nineteenth-century agro-sericulture, as it was practised in China, North America and Japan, indicates how market forces have influenced raw silk production, altering established sericulture and reeling practices, as well as social relationships, and ultimately precipitating research and development by scientists seeking to improve production levels – an issue discussed later in this chapter. In the nineteenth century China had the longest established and most widespread raw silk production, while that in the United States has been the most recent, limited and shortest-lived.

The Lower Yangzi Valley and Lake T'ai area in the north, and the Canton (now Guangzhou)/Pearl River Delta region of Guangdong province in the south, dominated mid-nineteenth- and early twentieth-century Chinese silk production. In the Yangzi/Lake T'ai area deciduous mulberry trees provided leaves sufficient for a major spring and a small autumn crop of large white cocoons that yielded the best, most lustrous silk. However, because cocoons in this area were reeled without smothering the pupae, labour shortages often made it necessary for both husbands and wives to reel, working day and night to complete the job before the moths broke out. Due to hasty reeling the quality of this *tsatlee* silk was often less than good, as North American importers often complained (Kuhn 1988, Min-hsiung 1976). Rural devastation, and the cutting down of mulberry trees during the Taiping Rebellion (1850–64), as well as the later establishment of filatures (reeling factories) with year round reeling, affected the region's productive capacity.

Developed in the mid-nineteenth century, Guangdong's Pearl River Delta system of canals, excavated ponds and dykes supported the most intensive sericulture in China. The landscape was patterned with 'fields of closely set dark green mulberry shrubs with ponds of water scattered irregularly between them' (Howard and Buswell 1925). In this seamless ecological system mulberry leaves fed silkworms, worm litter fed fish, and fishpond waste and sludge became fertilizer for tropical *Morus multicaulis* mulberry shrubs that leafed continuously and fed seven or more generations of polyvoltine worms each year. Raising, feeding and reeling crop after crop permanently engaged entire families (Howard and Buswell 1925, Stockard 1989). The polyvoltine *Bombyx* silkworms they reared produced small soft cocoons that yielded less lustrous, thinner, lesser quality filament in amounts half that of monovoltines (Gaddum 1979).

In south China reeling was specifically women's work. When late nineteenth century demand kept raw silk prices high in some areas to the south of Canton city daughters became so valued for their skills that it became customary for young married women to continue to work at home with their natal families, where they reeled unhampered by children or household responsibilities, and to indefinitely delay joining their husbands. Work opportunities in filatures encouraged other marriage resistance practices. Wage earning women could afford to opt to live independently of their families and to remain single. For this group of female workers dependence on family transitioned to dependence on factory employers (Stockard 1989, Bray 1997).

The introduction of European-style filature or factory reeling increased raw silk output. In the process it turned reeling into a year-round business and separated it from household mulberry and cocoon production, thereby undermining Yangzi and Canton family-based sericulture. Farmers instead began to concentrate on growing cocoons to sell to filatures. Overseen by a foreman, as many as 50 to 500 women worked in filatures where individual reeling basins were arranged side by side in long rows. Hours were long and working conditions in crowded, hot and steamy filatures were harsh. Until the 1920s the quantity of Guangdong province filature reeled silk far exceeded that of the Yangzi / Shanghai region.

Sericulture in North America, apart from small colonial and localized sericulture episodes, began more or less from scratch in the early nineteenth century. With a view to eventually establishing a silk industry, the Secretary of the Treasury circulated a sericulture handbook known as *The Rush Letter* (1828) (Field 2007). At first sericulture seemed to be easily accommodated within the spaces of established agricultural and domestic work. Trays of silkworms crowded barns, attics and kitchens. As in Maine (Field 2008), large and small tracts of newly introduced rapid-growing *Morus multicaulis* mulberry cuttings proliferated throughout the eastern seaboard and elsewhere (Brockett 1876). The initial enthusiasm for sericulture stemmed from expectations that raw silk production would quickly generate good financial returns. However, although excellent silk could be cultivated, inadequate worm care often resulted in small cocoons of low quality and yield. Despite the availability of published literature and oral advice on basic reeling, sufficient expertise did not develop, and with the existence of more remunerative employment in other areas of work, the successful reeling of raw silk remained problematic (Brocket 1876).

Other entrepreneurs concentrated on manufacturing processes and applied themselves to the development of efficient machinery to turn raw silk into useable threads and to the mechanization of silk looms. Local hand-reeled silk was never produced in either the quality or quantity required for the new thread-making machines, developed by American manufacturers, and was never available in amounts adequate for textile production (Field 2008). Filatures were not introduced. Sericulture faded away, and by the middle of the century most of the mulberry orchards had been pulled up. Furthermore, there was no pressure to pursue sericulture in this context because the burgeoning North American domestic silk fabric making industry – the first mechanized silk textile industry in the world – obtained plentiful supplies of reeled raw silk for textile manufacturing from Chinese and, later, Japanese imports.

Silk production in Japan expanded beyond the country's domestic needs after commercial treaties, in 1858 and 1866, opened Japan to unrestricted international trade. Raw silk was one of the few commodities Japan could market to generate hard currency that would build a new economy and fuel modernization. Under government direction, mulberry planting and cocoon production expanded and the Tomioka Silk Mill was founded in 1872 to introduce French reeling machinery and reeling expertise (Kiyokawa 1987). Recruited from all parts of Japan, young and older women learned the new reeling process at Tomioka and then returned home and trained other women to work in smaller local family-owned filatures that opened across the country.

With sericulture a national priority, silk production increased rapidly. State operated research institutes improved mulberry varieties, and began to use the Mendelian theory of how inherited traits are passed from generation to generation to hybridize silkworms. Egg production was centralized, and the Government oversaw the wide take-up of new sericulture agro-technology by silk farmers (Honda 1909, Kiyokawa 1987). Vastly expanded cocoon production and filature reeling took Japan's raw silk exports from negligible in 1870, to 20 per cent of the world's supply by 1897. Quantities surpassed Chinese silk exports by 1905 and made up 80 per cent of the world market by 1930. The greatest percentage of it was shipped to North America for silk textile manufacturing.

As these examples indicate, myriad factors have come into play in increasing the rate and scale of the production of raw silk, from international markets to technologies, and from government policies to transport systems. We may point in this sense to a growth in production. But processes of physical growth – of leaves, larvae and cocoons, all inextricably enmeshed in their wider environments – are just as crucial. These processes, and their interrelation with those of making, are examined in the rest of this chapter, with regard to metamorphosis in silkworms as well as other modifications in these creatures, their food (mulberry trees) and their silk.

**Cocoon: Organism or Artefact?**

Consider how a cocoon grows, and what it is made of. This subject has been intensively investigated by the disciplines of entomology, agronomy, and engineering studies and in the biomedical, tissue and materials sciences (Omenetto and Kaplan 2010a, 2010b, Hussain et al. 2011). As indicated above, the larvae of *Bombyx mori*, after its fourth skin shedding, enters the fifth instar during which period its appetite is at its most voracious. Replete, with gorged glands, the plump and mature worm stops feeding as it is instinctively driven to cocoon-build in preparation for metamorphosis. Lodged in its chosen spot, spinnerets on each side of the worm's head begin to cast out fine streams (brins) of liquid protein. A gum (sericin) coating helps the two streams stick together and solidify as one filament (bave) upon exposure to the air. At this point the long glands stretching down both sides of the larva's body are full of liquid protein composed of haphazardly floating long chain molecules, and as the liquid silk is channelled and extruded through the worm's spinnerets the long chain molecules line up in the direction of the flow (Figure 2.2) (French, 1988: 68–9).

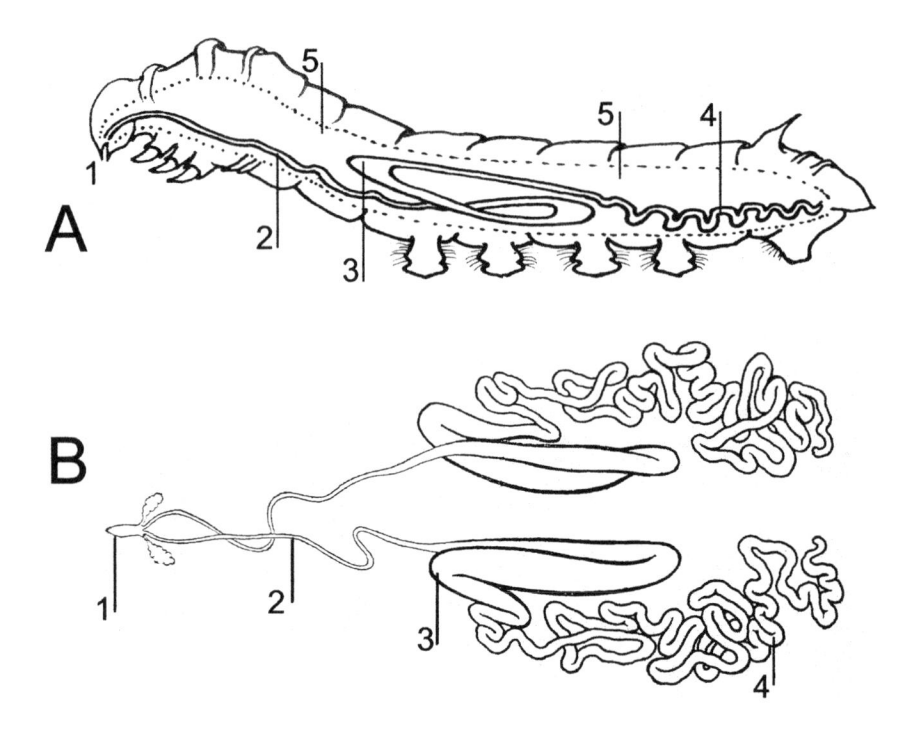

**Figure 2.2    Silkworm glands**

**Diagram A: Mature silkworm, longitudinal cross section: 1. Spinneret at the tip of the head; 2. Fore silk gland; 3. Middle silk gland; 4. Hind silk gland; 5. Intestinal gland containing ingested food. Diagram copyright Jacqueline Field**

**Diagram B: Function and view of glands from both sides of the silkworm: 1. Spinneret. This gland makes the liquefied silk extruded from the spinneret orifice; 2. Fore silk gland is the liquefied silk conduit; 3. Middle silk gland secretes sericin (gum) to coat the surface of the fibroin that comes from the hind silk gland and progresses to the fore silk gland; 4. Hind silk gland produces the fibroin (the main part of the silk filament) that transfers from here to the middle silk gland. Anatomical drawing and information by Katsuo Koizumi. Courtesy Mr Katsuo Koizumi former Director of the Yokohama Silk Center Silk Museum, Yokohama, Japan**

This phenomenon contributes to the silk filament's unusual strength. As the worm sets to work shaping the cocoon the continuous action of bobbing its head from side to side makes the extruded filament swish into figure of eight loops. Irregular rows of loops curve round and overlap to create a net wall that, within the first day, takes on the ovoid shape concealing the worm while it continues working on the inside for another two days, making additional net layers until the silk glands are emptied.

The filament's gummy sericin coating firmly cements the layers into a dense hard shell, housing the drained, slack and shrunken larva that now, at the end of its fifth instar, sheds its last skin ready to transform into a pupa. In his discussion of museum artefacts Beckow (1986: 122) notes that function may be inferred from such aspects as shape, size, and colour, or form. A cocoon's egg-like form indicates its function as a container, a structure enclosing the worm. The cocoon is an elegant solution to the problem of providing a secure shelter for the pupa's metamorphosis into a moth. Developed around a living organism, the cocoon is composed of many layers of worm-grown filament, but the extruded hardened filament is itself inanimate. The mode of construction is the head-bobbing action, which shapes the flow of silk into loops. Following Ingold's (2000: 345, 372) argument that an object is formed by regular repetitive physical motion – in this case layers of net resulting from silk extrusion and loop making by head-bobbing – the cocoon can be recognized as a constructed artefact.

While an aspect of the worm's genetic code steers the process it does not guarantee a perfect cocoon. At all stages the silkworm is a creature sensitive and responsive to its environment. Quality of care and feeding influences the amount of protein developed in the glands and available for cocoon construction. During cocoon-making, noises, fumes, changes in humidity, temperature and other variables can shock the organism, causing it to hesitate and disrupt the filament flow, or to stop spinning entirely, or even to die. Cocoons may be so weak and puny that pupation fails. Worms working too close together accommodate each other to make a double cocoon. Whatever the final size and quality, the cocoon is a three-dimensional construction, emanating from an organism in its material and social environment. Made of silkworm protein generated from plant cellulose, it is a structure with a function within the living egg-to-larva-to-moth continuum of growth. But once the moth has broken out of it, or once the larva has been killed, it is, for the insect, a purposeless shell – becoming, then, a source of raw material for people to re-make into silk thread.

**From Metamorphosis to Reconstitution**

Alive inside the completed cocoon the drained larva reaches the end of the fifth instar. It moults its skin and the penultimate instar begins. The interior of the cocoon becomes a ferment of activity as histolysis, or the breakdown of tissue, sets in and pupa formation commences with cells (called phagocytes) digesting and liquefying dead or dying caterpillar muscles, and any internal organs not useful for the imago. The resultant fluid mass and groups of cells that remain alive provide the energy and material to build the imago's new organs, body parts and limbs. Reconstitution progresses inside the quickly formed and hardened pupa shell upon which the imago features are clearly outlined (Tweedie 1977, Handschin 1946a, 1946b).

Dissolution of the larva provides the substance that grows into the moth, which emerges from the cocoon complete with nervous system, legs, wings, antennae, sexual organs, the ability to emit pheromones to attract a mate, and if a female, to deposit eggs within its brief few days of existence.

Mining silk, the process of reeling or unwinding cocoons, deconstructs the insect-made container and recovers the building material: silk filament. Cocoons are placed in hot water to soften the binding sericin gum. The coarse outer silk is brushed away, and the clean filament ends are released. When a cocoon's filament has all been unwound the hard dead pupa sinks to the bottom of the basin for later retrieval for use as fish food or fertilizer. Barely visible, a single filament is too fine to use alone (Gaddum 1979). So filament ends from three, six, ten, or many more cocoons are caught up together as a group (Figures 2.3, 2.4). Due to the gum they stick together and form what appears to be a single hair-like strand winding onto the reel. Each time a cocoon runs out of filament either the skilled deft-fingered hand reeler or a mechanized factory device maintains the strand's uniform size by quickly attaching a new end. Reeling is a means of controlling a set number of individual filaments and ensuring that they adhere together in a single cohesive strand of a predetermined size (Huber 1929). The strand of conjoined filaments grows, and keeps on growing, into what theoretically could be an endless yarn, while at the same time the regular motion of reeling, joining filaments on – by hand or machine – and maintaining consistent thickness or diameter make it into a consciously constructed artefact. Given these processes, the yarn's growing length is inseparable from its making.

Filaments from damaged and broken cocoons are not continuous. They may be teased out or cut into short lengths and spun like cotton, or wool to be made into different kinds of threads, or the cocoons may be stretched into a mesh useful for making wadding. By one means or another cocoon filaments are made available for purposes other than that for which they were originally grown by insects – they are manipulated into artefacts with entirely different forms and functions. Thus it is that the hard inanimate cocoon and its soft living contents are respectively subject to reconstitution and recycling: the latter by the process of metamorphosis from larva to insect and the former by manufacture from cocoon into strands of raw silk ready for further processing to make textile threads.

**Making Organisms Grow**

Not only silkworms and their cocoons undergo change; mulberry trees also transform through their utilization in sericulture. The silkworm-mulberry leaf relationship developed prior to domestication and is described as an example of insect-plant co-evolution (Feltwell 1990). As the silk-producing organism's only food, mulberry has long been subject to cultivation. Indeed, given China's long history of expansive silk manufacture, vast areas of land in different regions at different times were devoted to mulberry plantations. From the days of early

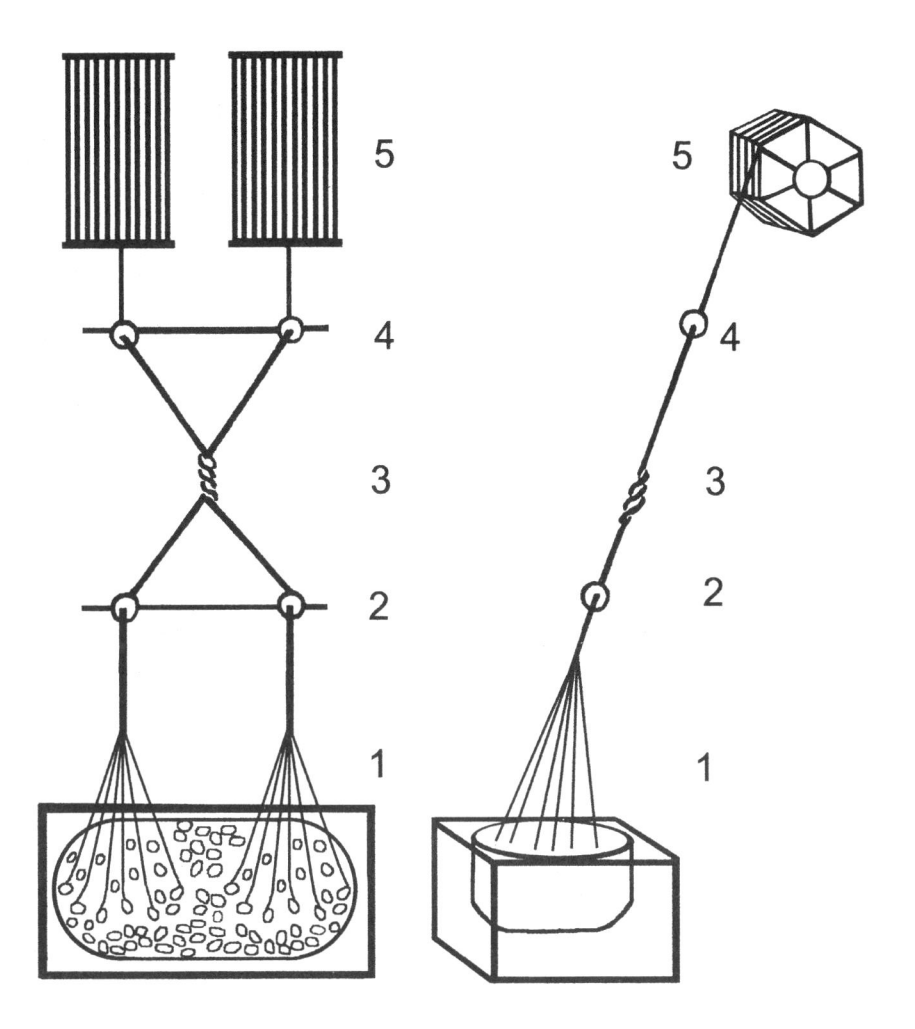

Figure 2.3  Reeling silk. 1. Cocoons in a basin of hot water; 2. Groups of filaments form a strand and pass through a guide; 3. The *croisieur* twists the two strands together, squeezes out water, and aids filament cohesion; 4. The strands pass through a second guide; 5. Each strand winds onto a revolving reel that may be powered by hand, treadle, or steam (the entire process tends now to be mechanized). Removed from the reel the silk is wound into hanks and further processed into finished textile threads. Diagram copyright Jacqueline Field

Figure 2.4  A Uyghur woman reeling with the large reel commonly used throughout central Asia. A single strand consisting of many filaments passes through guides on the reeling frame (here supported by a gourd) and winds onto the reel turned by a second person. Kashgar, Western China, 2004. Photograph copyright Jacqueline Field

silkworm domestication until as late as the fourteenth century CE, plantation trees were large, descendants of the huge, often multi-trunked, indigenous white mulberry trees that grew in mountainous areas. Reaping leaves from tall trees was difficult, variously involving slashing branches, pulling branches down with hooked poles or climbing on cumbersome platforms and ladders (Kuhn 1988). Steps towards alleviating the arduous leaf-harvesting task came with the introduction and gradual dissemination of tree-shaping practices in the fourteenth century CE (Kuhn 1988). Grafting the low-growing domestic white mulberry variety *Morus multicaulis* onto the sturdy wild mulberry (*Morus bombycis*) produced a short-trunked tree that grew large dark green leaves, was restrained to an overall height of around six feet, and was easier to prune and harvest.

In South China sericulture relied on the tropical white mulberry, *Morus multicaulis*, a low growing bushy shrub. Pruned to the ground each winter, it grew new shoots rapidly and leafed profusely all year. The market created by nineteenth-century maritime traders stimulated increased mulberry growing to support expanded sericulture (Howard and Buswell 1925). Most silk farmers cultivated mulberry for their own worm stock. Others grew and sold leaves to those in need. However, the plants had a limited life span, which led to the development of nurseries that concentrated on growing replacement seedlings. To breed continuously high leaf-yielding plants that could annually feed multiple worm generations, nursery growers carefully selected seeds and paid close attention to soil preparation, seedlings, fertilization, transplantation, and spacing between plants (Howard and Buswell 1925, Huber 1929). Late nineteenth- and early twentieth-century Japanese agronomists took these practices to new levels and developed very precise methods of grafting, cutting, pruning, planting, training and feeding (Honda 1909). Breeding programs produced numerous varieties from high and low bush to types specially suited to various terrains and climates. Analysis of the correlation between leaf nutrients, larvae growth and the amount of silk in cocoons encouraged chemical analysis of regional soils to identify deficiencies and provide appropriate fertilizer formulae to help produce heavy, highly nutritious leaf crops (Honda 1909). By way of these practices, mulberry trees have come to be made as much as grown.

The process continues with present day researchers utilizing resources such as Japan's National Institute of Sericulture and Entomological Science germplasm data (genetic material) from 1,300 mulberry varieties to help identify desirable morphological and agronomic traits. One project, for example, uses the database for complex polyploidy breeding trials, which entail identifying and using organisms with more than the two basic paired sets of chromosomes typical of most species. The significance of this, as Machii explains, is that crossing between plants with two paired sets of chromosomes and those with a greater number of sets may make it possible to grow high yielding mulberry hybrids with much larger, good quality leaves (Machii and Koyama 2002). Another mulberry specialist, Kasushige Touhara of Tokyo University, recently found that the hitherto unexplained connection between silkworm and mulberry may be attributable to the organism's attraction to a mulberry leaf oderant: cis-jasmone (Tanaka et al. 2009). This significant discovery might be the key to making an artificial food that does not even require the proportion of powdered mulberry leaf necessary in the artificial food compounds that breeding laboratories use. Cis-jasmone may be a step towards entirely dispensing with mulberry leaves as silkworm food.

If agriculture, genetics and research have moved mulberry leaves towards possible obsolescence, how have mulberry leaf-eating silkworms fared under cultivation? *Bombyx mori* has been classified into numerous breeds and sub-species since people first took an interest in the wild silkworm's cocoons, poking out the protein-laden pupae to eat. At that early time it would have been possible to make tangled cocoon fibres into felt-like materials or coarse thread. The process of unwinding very long thin wispy filaments onto a rotating reel evolved later, after the wheel came into use. The development of continuous filament for use in textiles was conducted in concert with the emergence of spinning and weaving technologies (Kuhn 1988). With this there was probably also an incentive to domesticate wild silkworms.

With selective breeding the domesticated silk moths and their caterpillars changed: the caterpillars became docile and almost immobile and the moth's flying ability became limited in the male moth and lost in the female. Mouthparts atrophied and digestive systems were dispensed with, so moths mate but do not eat during their brief few days of existence (Handschin 1946a, 1946b). From about 1000 CE to the present time hybridization steadily increased the number of silkworm varieties, and present day cocoons come in different sizes (1–3 cm), shapes (from egg-like to pointed ovoid) and colours (white, lemon or pale green) (Kuhn 1988, Duran 1921). During the early twentieth century in Japan, Mendel's laws were drawn upon to realize preferred qualities in moths, and a standardized cocoon, which was particularly convenient for filature reeling, was distributed nationally (Kiyokawa 1987). With publication, in 2005, of the first silkworm genetic map and with the advent of transgenic breeding (transference of a gene or part of a gene sequence from one organism into another), silkworm and cocoon engineering have moved on to produce further vigorous hybrids with special traits such as superior disease resistance, increased fecundity, reduced larval duration, greater cocoon size, and enhanced silk yield. In the interests of standardization, large hard white or yellow cocoons dominate commercial production today. Now that the chromosomes carrying cocoon traits have been identified, it has become possible to try to produce cocoons with still further desirable characteristics (Dingle at al. 2005). With these practices organisms have been made to grow in particular ways that are conducive to the industrial manufacture of silk threads and fabrics.

**Bioengineering Silk**

Since the second half of the nineteenth century scientists have been moving silkworms and silk into medical and technological domains, and with these developments processes of growing and making become ever more integrated.

In the 1860s, Louis Pasteur's work in finding a cure for pebrine and flasherie, the silkworm diseases then devastating European sericulture, helped confirm germ theory and establish the field of microbiology. Count Hilaire Chardonnet conducted some of the earliest experiments, in the 1880s, designed to replicate the silkworm's ability to digest cellulose, polymerize it and extrude a silk-like filament, but the resultant fibre, called artificial silk, did not exactly resemble the silkworm product. Nor, indeed, have any of the many chemically made and mechanically extruded filaments, such as nylon and polyester, manufactured since then. Silk replication still eludes scientists and the insect remains the only maker of silk fibroin protein. Burgeoning twenty-first century green chemistry, devised to minimize or eliminate the generation of hazardous materials, and nanotechnologies capable of making atomic and molecular scale structures and systems, have made the fibroin protein substance so desirable for uses other than in textiles that significant research is directed towards the complex task of replicating silk fibroin protein and achieving a means of its large-scale production. Environmentally friendly and with properties including tensile strength exceeding that of steel of a similar dimension, the insect-made fibroin protein substance, silk, is being developed and utilized for previously unimagined purposes.

Biomedical engineers Fiorenzo Omenetto and David Kaplan, of Tufts University's (Massachusetts) Department of Chemical and Biological Engineering, are currently modifying fibroin protein from silk filaments to fashion a new generation of novel materials for diverse medical and other applications. Compatible with human tissue, silk sutures have been in use for millennia, but now with new silks with controllable degradation rates the Tufts team envisages exploiting fibroin protein from *Bombyx mori* silk cocoons or replicated fibroin protein, for applications such as cell scaffolding in human tissue engineering, for tubes to replace clogged arteries and perhaps even for bone and other repairs (Omenetto and Kaplan 2010a, 2010b). At the National University of Singapore James Goh and his team have implanted stem cells in silk scaffolding used to recreate ligament in a live pig's knee, a process with potential human applications (Omenetto and Kaplan 2010a, 2010b).

The only way to obtain the substance, silk fibroin protein, is to unwind the insect-made cocoon to extract the silk filament. Scientists are endeavouring to take this reverse engineering process a step further back: they want to move from the filament in the cocoon to the starting material synthesized in the silkworm glands, and thereby to discover how to mimic the process in order to grow fibroin protein in the laboratory. In the meantime Omenetto and Kaplan are engaging in a form of metamorphosis – their work involves reprocessing silkworm filament to convert *Bombyx* fibroin protein into a silk solution, which can be used to form a gel, sponges, fibres, or sheets of transparent film. This non-toxic material has many anticipated applications, for example in the making of degradable implants carrying drug delivery systems within human bodies; in making optical fibres and mechanical objects; and in making items such as biodegradable cups to replace those made of polystyrene (Omenetto and Kaplan 2010a, 2010b, Omenetto 2011).

Jeney Zhang and colleagues (2012) report on a Tufts team's finding that vaccines and other medications retain their potency without refrigeration when stored in packets made of silk fibroin film. Materials made from fibroin protein can be fashioned as either highly stable or rapidly biodegradable, extending their functional reach. Furthermore, this protein can be used to manufacture transistors used in e-paper, and it is expected that this will speed the page-turning capabilities of next generation e-books with flexible displays (Wang, Hsieh and Hwang 2011).

Omenetto (2011) explains that biocompatibility and biodegradability mean fibroin implants simply dissolve in the human body, eliminating the need for invasive or painful retrieval procedures. Differences in light absorbency make it possible to see the interface between implant or scaffold and human cell material, so that degradation levels may be monitored. Another line of research involves transgenic and other methods of producing coloured silk. Although *Bombyx* cocoons may have a green or yellow appearance, the colour is only in the gummy sericin coating that is always removed, leaving the commercially valuable white fibroin underneath. At the Institute of Materials Research and Engineering, Singapore, Natalia Tansil and her colleagues (2011) found that feeding silkworms a mulberry leaf compound diet containing a particular type of dye made it possible to produce coloured silkworms that grow coloured fibroin in their glands and spin coloured cocoons made of intrinsically coloured and luminescent fibroin filament. If the standard white silk scaffolds used in engineering cell growth in human tissue were made of coloured luminescent silk, then it could further help scientists to see the cells and better understand the scaffold's performance (Tansil et al. 2011). As an environmentally friendly alternative to established highly polluting chemical silk dyeing, this method of biologically colouring silk may turn out to be valuable for the textile industry. Now that the process of integrating molecules into silk filament's core is understood, chemicals other than dye may be similarly integrated. Tansil and her co-workers (2011) foresee production of novel biomaterials with added functionalities, such as silk containing drugs that can be applied as wound dressings, and as tissue engineering scaffolds with anticoagulant or anti-inflammatory features.

Bioengineers have harboured hopes that silkworms could be co-opted to circumvent the problem of obtaining silk from spiders that are impossible to domesticate. Spider silk is similar in structure but much stronger than worm silk and is perceived to have even greater development potential, such as in making new fibres that are even tougher and more elastic than the chemically manufactured filament, marketed as Kevlar, which is currently used to make textiles for protective clothing such as loggers' aprons and bulletproof vests. In September 2010 Kraig Biocraft Laboratories in Lansing, Michigan, announced that they had genetically altered silkworms to produce spider silk (Omenetto and Kaplan 2010a, 2010b). Transgenic breeding and other manipulations have made new kinds of silkworms. Through bioengineering practices, making becomes an integral aspect of growing.

## Conclusion: Growing, Making, and Replicating

As the historical comparisons discussed earlier in this chapter suggest, a variety of factors have influenced silk production, from climate to practices of nurturing. In each cultural context silk production depends on how successfully people have manipulated and maintained an environment conducive to mulberry and silkworm growth. People, plants and insects are intimately interconnected in the labour-intensive silk production process. More skilful and diligent husbandry has meant more nutritious mulberry leaves, and thus a healthier and more productive worm. The nature of the insect–cultivator relationship has influenced the quantity and quality of the filament that forms the cocoon. This filament is far from raw material; rather it is fashioned and nurtured through the interactions of cultivator and silkworm. It is both grown and made, such that design and technology are integral to it.

Filaments are the necessary material for all silk textile products. Originally unravelled by hand, and now by machine, continuous filaments progress from reeling to be wound into hanks. From hanks the strands are wound onto bobbins, and from there are combined and twisted in a variety of ways, sometimes minimally and sometimes very tightly, depending on the size, strength and characteristics of the thread that is required. Threads are designed for specific end uses, some for strength, and some for appearance. Densely clustered together, multitudes of microscopic filament surfaces reflect light, giving the thread, and fabric made from it, a lustrous appearance that many regard as beautiful. In this way the spinning procedure transforms the silkworms' filament into thread, which can then be further worked into textiles.

Efforts to increase silk production for textile manufacture have led to the use of biology and genetics to create new strains of silkworms with the ability to grow more filament and filament with specific characteristics. This research has exploited the potential of silk fibroin protein as a basis from which new biotechnical industries can make medical and other products. Such developments hinge upon the availability of fibroin in amounts beyond what it is possible to produce from silkworms. For the insect the fibroin protein making process is integral to its life cycle. In an interlinked sequence its digestive process transforms mulberry leaves into liquid protein filament suitable for cocoon making and metamorphosis transforms the worm into a moth, the reproductive agent that guarantees continuity and future protein filament production. Bioengineers now aim to develop their knowledge of the silkworm gland's ability to produce protein, so that silk can be made in the laboratory. If this is achieved, then reliance on *Bombyx mori* silkworm fibroin would cease and substantial supplies would become assured. Although the capacity to replicate silk would make the mulberry–silkworm cycle virtually obsolete, the close connection between people and fibroin protein would continue. In the replicated fibroin growing process human activity would be, as in sericulture, integral to production just as replicated silk protein, and the products made of it, would be as interrelated as silkworm-grown filaments and the processed threads they are used to make.

## References

Albers, A. 1966. *On Weaving*. London: Studio Vista.

Beckow, S.M. 1986. Culture, history and artifact, in *Material Culture Studies in America,* comp. T. J. Schlereth. Nashville, Tennessee: The American Association for State and Local History.

Bray, F. 1997. *Technology and Gender: Fabric of Power in Late Imperial China*. Berkeley, CA: University of California Press.

Brocket, L.P. 1876. *Silk Industry in America*. New York: The Silk Association of America.

Dingle, D.J. et al. 2005. *Silk Production in Australia: A Report for the Rural Industries Research And Development Corporation*. RIRDC Publication No 05/145. RIRDC Project No UQ-96A.

Duran, L. 1921. *Raw Silk: A Practical Handbook for the Buyer*. 2nd Revised Edition. New York: The Silk Publishing Company.

Feltwell, J. 1990. *The Story of Silk*. New York: St. Martin's Press.

Field, J. et al. 2007. *American Silk 1830–1930: Entrepreneurs and Artifacts*. Lubbock, TX: Texas Tech University Press.

Field, J. 2008. From agriculture to industry: silk production and manufacture in Maine. *Maine History Journal*, 44(1), 19–49.

French, M.J. 1988. *Invention and Evolution: Design in Nature and Engineering*. Cambridge: Cambridge University Press.

Gaddum, H.T. 1979. *Silk*. Macclesfield, England: H.T. Gaddum Company Ltd.

Handschin, E. 1946a. The silkworm or *Bombyx mori Linné*. *Ciba Review*, (53), 1902–7.

Handschin, E. 1946b. The breeding of silkworms and their diseases. *Ciba Review*, (53) 1910–13.

Honda, I. 1909. *The Silk Industry of Japan*. Tokyo: The Imperial Tokyo Sericulture Institute. General Books.

Howard C.W. and K.P. Buswell 1925. *A Survey of the Silk Industry of Southern China*. Hong Kong: Commercial Press Printer.

Huber, C.J. 1929. *The Raw Silk Industry of Japan*. New York: The Silk Association of America.

Hussain, M. et al. 2011. Evaluation of silkworm lines against variations in temperatures and RH for various parameters of commercial cocoon production. *Psyche: A Journal of Entomology*, Volume 2011, Article ID 145640.

Ingold, T. 2000. *The Perception of the Environment: Essays on Livelihood, Dwelling and Skill*. London and New York: Routledge.

Kiyokawa, Y. 1987. Transplantation of the European factory system and adaptations in Japan: the experience of the Tomioka model filature. *Hitotsubashi Journal of Economics*, 28(1), 27–39.

Kuhn, D. 1988. *Science and Civilization in China. Textile Technology: Spinning and Reeling*. Vol. 5, part 9. Cambridge: Cambridge University Press.

Machii, H. and A. Koyama 2002. Mulberry breeding, cultivation and utilization in Japan, in *Mulberry for Animal Production. Proceedings of an Electronic Conference Carried Out Between May and August 2002*, edited by M.D. Sanchez. New York: Food and Agriculture Organization of the United Nations. Available at: http://www.fao.org/DOCREP/005/X9895E/X9895E00.HTM, 63–9. Accessed January 2011.

Min-hsiung Shih. 1976. *The Silk Industry in Ch'ing China*, translated by E-tu Zen Sun. Ann Arbor Center for Chinese Studies, University of Michigan.

Omenetto, F. 2011. Silk, the Ancient Material of the Future. TED2011 Video. [Posted May 2011] Available at: http://www.ted.com/talks/fiorenzo_omenetto_silk_the_ancient_material_of_the_future.html. Accessed June 2011.

Omenetto, F. and D. Kaplan 2010a. From silk cocoon to medical miracle. *Scientific American*, 303(5), 76–7.

Omenetto, F. and D. Kaplan 2010b. New opportunities for an ancient material. *Science Magazine*, 329, 528–31.

Stockard, J.E. 1989. *Daughters of the Canton Delta: Marriage Patterns and Economic Strategies in South China, 1860–1930*. Stanford, CA: Stanford University Press.

Tanaka, K. et al. 2009. Highly selective tuning of a silkworm olfactory receptor to a key mulberry leaf volatile. *Current Biology*, 19(11), 881–90.

Tansil, N.C. et al. 2011. Intrinsically colored and luminescent silk. *Advanced Materials,* 23(12), 1463–6.

Tweedie, M. 1977. *Insect Life*. Newton Abbot, England: Collins Countryside Series, Readers Union.

Vainker, S. 2004. *Chinese Silk: A Cultural History*. London and New Brunswick, NJ: British Museum Press and Rutgers University Press.

Wang, C-H., C-Y. Hsieh and J-C. Hwang 2011. Flexible organic thin-film transistors with silk fibroin as the gate dielectric. *Advanced Materials*, 23(14), 1630–34.

Zhang, J. et al. 2012. Stabilization of vaccines and antibiotics in silk and eliminating the cold chain. *Proceedings of the National Academy of Sciences*, 109 (30), 11981–6.

Chapter 3

# Between Nature and Art: Casting from Life in Sixteenth-Century Europe

Pamela H. Smith

Early modern European humanist *studioli* and princely *Kunst- und Wunderkammern* (chambers of art and wonder) almost invariably contained small, perfectly formed plants and animals moulded in metal by the technique of 'casting from life' (Figure 3.1). Casting from life was accomplished by moulding plants or recently killed animals in plaster, burning out or removing the plant or animal (the pattern), then pouring molten metal into the hollow left by the animal or plant. This technique resulted in precise replicas of the cast creature, creating stunningly lifelike objects. Life casting was especially favoured for animals that inhabited more than one elemental zone within the early modern view of the cosmos, such as lizards, snakes, toads, and crabs, which lived both on land and in water, as well as insects and birds, which inhabited both air and land. In addition, many of the animals preferred for life casting were regarded as spontaneously generated from putrefying matter. Despite this seemingly unsavoury connection, noble inventories of collections throughout Europe in the sixteenth and seventeenth centuries record hundreds of life-cast animals and plants in silver, tin, lead, plaster, and other media, and life casting was so popular that even German princes of the sixteenth century practised it (Smith and Beentjes 2010).

In this chapter I argue that these objects were not regarded as mere curiosities in early modern Europe; rather, they functioned as true epistemic objects that embodied concepts and even entire knowledge systems. They thus have the potential to reveal to the modern scholar much about how the craftspeople making them and the audience viewing and handling them understood a range of phenomena, including natural materials and processes, the transformation of materials by the human hand, the generation of living creatures, and the power of the human hand not only to make objects, but also to generate new materials and transform matter. Additionally, the techniques of life casting, recorded in traces in extant museum objects and written down in a remarkably detailed sixteenth-century manuscript, tell us much about the lifeworld of the craft workshop and the entanglement within it of the human body and natural materials. In the early modern workshop, making and growing were very much enmeshed. The transformation of materials in processes of making presupposed organic models of growth and change, especially those of the human body, and it involved processes based on bodily fluids, as well as processes of fermentation and growth. The 'made' world and the 'grown' world were not sharply differentiated in the artisan's workshop.

**Figure 3.1** **Wenzel Jamnitzer (attributed). Life-cast lizard. Lead. Staatliche Museen zu Berlin-Preußischer Kulturbesitz (Kunstgewerbemuseum, inv. no. K5912). Photo: Pamela H. Smith and Tonny Beentjes**

**The Lifeworld of the Workshop**

The human body was an integral component of the early modern European workshop, functioning as a tool in myriad ways – for warming, blowing, handling, manipulating, sensing, tasting, and providing force and dexterity, to name just a few; as a source of substances used in manufacture – including urine, excrement, blood, ear wax, and saliva; and as a model for natural processes, since the fermentation, digestion, purging, and excretion performed by the human body provided a conceptual framework for the transformation of materials in nature. Moreover, the quotidian stuff that sustained growth in the human body – including bread, butter, eggs, milk, honey, and garlic – was also employed on a daily basis in workshop practices (Smith 2004: Chapter 3). It was also by means of the body and its learned gestures and techniques that the embodied knowledge of craft was produced and reproduced, passed on from one generation to the next.

Craft recipes might express volume measures in terms of 'four drops of spittle', or size measurements as 'two-fingers wide' (Anon. 1966: 67). Time in recipe books was measured by reciting pater nosters, which doubtlessly were also regarded as having prophylactic effects. A lock of woman's hair was used to measure the temperature of material being heated (Anon. 1531: ix verso), and human touch could measure whether an object was 'cool enough to be held for a short time in your hand' (Theophilus 1979: 181), before being subjected to the next process. All five bodily senses were fully employed in the workshop: vitriol could be identified by its biting, sharp-to-the-taste, pungent-to-the-tongue, astringent nature, while rock alum had 'a bitter taste with a certain unctuous saltiness' (Biringuccio 1943: 95–8). Other measurements relied upon hearing: 'Put your cuttlefish bone very close to the fire, if you hear little cries it means that your bone is dry enough' (Anon. probably late sixteenth century: 145v). In a process for hardening mercury, the material in the crucible was supposed to sound a loud bang to signal that it had had enough of the fire (Anon. 1531: iv). And, in another, 'If the tin cries very much it means you added enough lead and not too much, if the tin cries softly it means you added too much lead' (Anon. probably late sixteenth century: 131v). The purity of tin was tested by biting to see whether it made cracking sounds, 'like that which water makes when it is frozen by cold'. Good iron ore could be indicated by the presence of a red, soft, fat earth that made no crackling noise when squeezed between the teeth (Biringuccio 1943: 60–67). In a dramatic account of casting bells, a medieval metalworking text advises the caster to 'lie down close to the mouth of the mould', as the metal is poured into the bell mould, 'and listen carefully to find out how things are progressing inside. If you hear a light thunderlike rumbling, tell them to stop for a moment and then pour again; and have it done like this, now stopping, now pouring, so that the bell metal settles evenly, until that pot is empty' (Theophilus 1979: 173). An anonymous goldsmith's treatise advises the assayer to make certain that an acid bath has dissolved all available silver in an alloy by listening carefully to see if the glass vessel makes a 'bott, bott, bott' sound when tapped (Anon. c.1604: 22v–24r).

Even such a cursory glance at early modern craft recipes reveals the role the artisanal body played within the processes of production and the ways in which the workshop functioned as an extension of the capacities and products of the human body. But the body was more than a tool in production. Within the early modern Christian framework, the body was seen simultaneously as the source of sin and an instrument of redemption, a view expressed repeatedly by artisans in their artworks and writings. By expulsion from the garden of Eden, humans had been destined to labour for the things they might have enjoyed freely in Paradise, but this was the means of both their eternal and temporal salvation, for in the temporal world, the labour of the craftsperson extracted the divine virtues implanted by God in created nature for human sustenance and healing (Smith 2004: Chapter 3). A sixteenth-century metalworker, Vannoccio Biringuccio, expressed this as 'those things that have such inner powers [implanted by God], like herbs, fruits, roots, animals, precious stones, metals, or other stones, can be understood only through oft-repeated experience' (1943: 114). Moreover, Christ's incarnation as a humble craftsman and His bodily sacrifice provided an explicit model and valorization of manual labour in early monastic formation and particularly in the fifteenth and early sixteenth centuries, leading up to and during the early Protestant Reformation (Lavin 1977–8, Smith 2004).

Working with natural materials could entail a struggle with the unpredictable forces and qualities of matter, for matter was a constantly transforming and surprising thing, like a living being one only came to know through intimate and bodily acquaintance. Matter behaved in idiosyncratic ways, which artisans had to learn – and to master – through experience. The painter Cennino Cennini wrote in the late fourteenth century about white lead and verdigris as each other's 'mortal enemies in every respect' (1960: 33) and azurite as being 'very scornful of the [grinding] stone' (36). Varnish was

> a powerful liquid ... and it wants to be obeyed in everything .... And immediately, as you spread it out on your work, every colour immediately loses some of its resistance, and is obliged to yield to the varnish, and never again has the power to go on refreshing itself with its own tempera. (99)

Size (used to prepare wooden panels for paint) could be lean or fat (68), and size with a water base could give the wood panel a good appetite: 'Not being so strong, it is just as if you were fasting, and ate a handful of sweetmeats, and drank a glass of good wine, which is an inducement for you to eat your dinner. So it is with this size: it is a means of giving the wood a taste for receiving the coats of size and gesso' (70). In explaining why a stone figure must be varnished and coated with mordant and charcoal before gilding, he wrote: 'stone always holds moisture, and when gesso tempered with size becomes aware of it, it promptly rots and comes away and is spoiled: and so the oil and varnish are the instruments and means of uniting the gesso with the stone, and I explain it to you on that account. The charcoal always keeps dry of the moisture of the stone' (119).

Magnets in particular exhibited active behaviour: 'the lodestone loves iron, and iron loves the lodestone so passionately that the lodestone hungers for the iron and seeks to attract it with all its strength, while the iron, in turn, acts toward it as if it were alive, leaps up to meet it and clings to it' (Ercker 1951 [1574]: 289). Biringuccio said of the lodestone: 'it appears that Nature has put into this stone a certain spirit of vivacity, so that it seems to have – I would like to say – hands, although they are not seen' (Biringuccio 1943: 114). Gold could be 'fastidious' about the stone with which it was burnished (Cennini 1960: 83). The struggle with refractory matter engaged the whole body of the artisan, for materials had to be sounded out, tasted, smelled, and touched through the bodily senses, a process that was often conceptualized as gaining knowledge through bodily union, sometimes on the model of mystical religious knowledge that could be recognized only through signs marked on the body (Smith 2004: Chapter 3, 2011). St Francis was marked with the stigmata, for instance, and Mother Julian of Norwich prayed that Jesus might cause her pain and disease as a mark of her religious experience.

The human body and natural materials shared many properties. To take just one example from metalworking: the idea of *temper* was crucial in the mental world of early modern Europeans. The term 'temper' meant to balance by mixing, and a person's temperament was determined by a balance of the four humours: black bile, phlegm, blood, and yellow bile. Each individual's unique combination of the four humours could be tempered by diet, exercise, purging, and so on, and this process of tempering was crucial to human health. Metals too partook in this system and their balance of qualities could be rectified by tempering, as steel was tempered (sometimes using the urine of young boys). Paints were also tempered to achieve the right balance of pigment and media. Minerals and humans alike received their temper from the movements of the heavens, for the sun was a source of growth for all living things – gold grew better along riverbanks warmed by the sun and in south-facing veins – and, in the common understanding of health and individual identity in early modern Europe, the celestial spheres and bodies determined the temperament of human beings at their conception and birth, just as they did for metals (Pieper 1955: 71–3, Anon. 1575, Sisco and Smith 1949: 39–40).

Artisans daily employed processes in the production of goods that are now often conceptualized as typical of organic growth, as in a pigment recipe for a gold colour that calls for mixing mercury with a fresh hen's egg and then putting it back under the hen for three weeks (Anon. 1538: 19v), or the frequent use of constant slow heat produced by thermophilic bacteria in putrefying horse manure for metalworking procedures (Anon. probably late sixteenth century: passim.). Artisanal manuals and recipe collections mix procedures for grafting and growing plants, fermenting liquids, and healing humans and animals indiscriminately with instructions for producing objects from ingredients now regarded as inorganic. For example, the first book of Hugh Plat's 1594 *Jewell-House of Art and Nature Conteining Divers Rare and Profitable Inventions, Together with Sundry New Experimentes in the Art of Husbandry, Distillation, and Molding* offers all manner of household tips and recipes including scouring pewter and killing rats, keeping prawns fresh, and knowing 'when the moone is at the full by a glasse of water', while the second book details instructions for new fertilizers and soils for husbandry. The third book contains distilling and fermenting instructions, and the fourth book processes of casting and working metals (including casting from life) and other materials.

Even from this very brief overview, it is evident that productive practices in the early modern European workshop involved more than just the handling and transformation of inert and inorganic materials; they allowed the artisan to investigate and to engage in bodily ways with life forces, to explore the relationship of matter to spirit, and to imitate processes of generation and transformation. In that exploration of the transformation of matter, the craftsperson might even imitate profound mysteries such as incarnation, in, for example, the making of the flesh tone pigment '*incarnatio*' (Kruse 2000, Lehmann 2008). On the one hand, craft practices were mundane and oriented to the production of goods, but, on the other, artisanal techniques gave access to the greater powers and mysteries of the universe.

## Making Life Casts

Casting from life was probably practised by the Romans, and extant life-cast crabs in bronze putatively go back to Roman antiquity. The earliest reference to life casting in the Renaissance appears in the fourteenth-century painter Cennino Cennini's *Libro dell' Arte*, which includes entries on casting faces, whole bodies, 'a bird, a beast, and any sort of animal, fish, and other such things' (Cennini 1960: 129, see also Kris 1928, Gramaccini 1985, Klier 2004, Didi-Huberman 1997, Stöckler 1990, Lein 2004, 2006, 2007). Lorenzo Ghiberti (1378–1455) cast plants from life on the doors of the Florence Baptistery, and Donatello (1386/7–1466) used wax-impregnated fabrics to model the draperies on some of his sculpture (Gramaccini 1985: 207–10, Stone 2001: 55–67). Life casts were produced in great numbers in northern Italy in the sixteenth century, and life-casting was carried out on an even grander scale in northern Europe, particularly in Nuremberg (Stone 1981). There, nature casts of textiles – in which the mould was formed directly by draped textiles – were made in the Vischer workshop, where life casting was a well-known technique by the first half of the sixteenth century, and it reached a high point in the work of the master goldsmith Wenzel Jamnitzer (1508–85) (Diemer 1996) (Figure 3.2). During the same period in France, Bernard Palissy (c.1510–90) experimented extensively with moulding flora and fauna from life for his ceramic works, which he regarded as an imitation of natural processes (Figure 3.3).

Figure 3.2  Wenzel Jamnitzer (attributed). Writing box, 1560–70, with plants, insects and reptiles cast from life. Cast silver, 6.0 × 22.7 × 10.2 cm. 1155/64. Kunsthistorisches Museum, Vienna. Photo: Tonny Beentjes and Pamela H. Smith

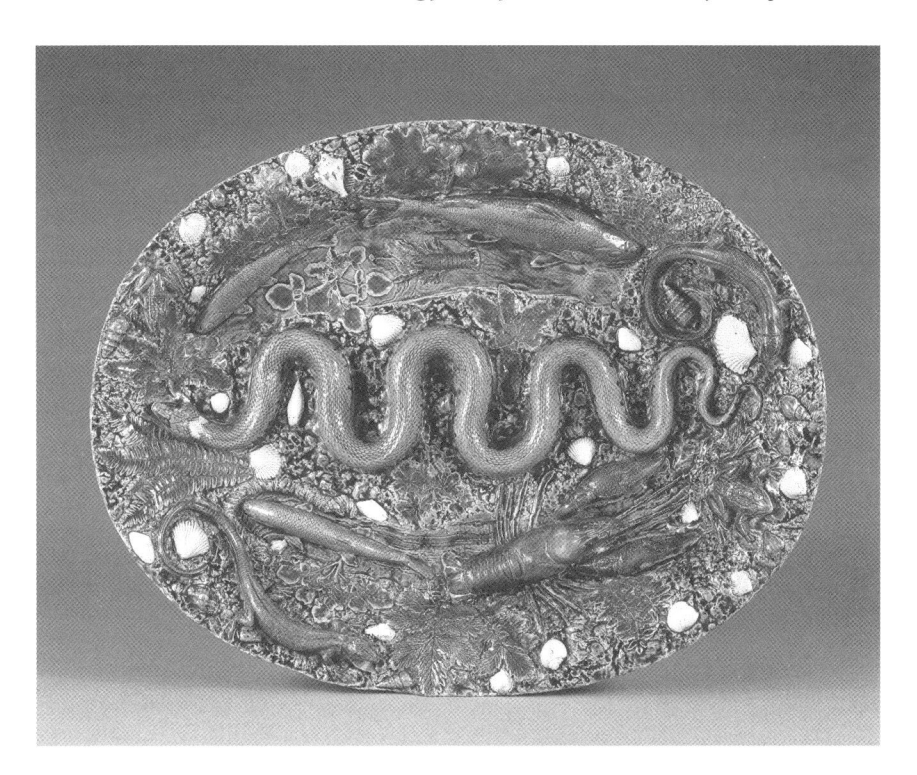

Figure 3.3  Bernard Palissy (follower of). Oval plate, decorated with serpents, crawfish and fish. Faience, l. 52.5 cm. MR2293. Louvre, Paris © RMN-Grand Palais / Art Resource, NY. Photo: Daniel Arnaudet

It is worth dwelling on the work of these two sixteenth-century artisans, for they exemplify several important dimensions of casting from life. Wenzel Jamnitzer's portrait, painted in 1562–3 by Nicholas Neufchatel, shows him to be a particularly ambitious and successful master goldsmith, as well as an esteemed citizen of Nuremberg. He is surrounded by objects of his own making that embodied his designs, ideas, skills, and knowledge. In his right hand, he grasps a pair of compasses, perhaps those he describes in his instrument book for scaling up a statue. In his other hand he holds another of his inventions, an instrument for comparing specific weights of metals in order to use them in sculpture. In a niche in the upper left corner stands a vase (similar to ewers made by Jamnitzer) full of delicate plants and flowers cast from life, a technique for which Jamnitzer attained particular fame. Two further examples of Jamnitzer's objects sit before him on the table: a statuette representing Neptune and the statuette's preparatory drawing. This too refers the viewer to Jamnitzer's methods for producing sculptures of the same weight in different metals, while indicating his ability to realize in metal a paper design (Pechstein 1970). The book before him may refer to his ambitions for publication that resulted after many years of work on the *Perspectiva corporum regularium* (1568). Represented here was the full range of Jamnitzer's artisanal production, both of objects and of knowledge.

The objects that survive from Jamnitzer's busy workshop almost all make reference to the relationship of nature and art, and, more particularly, to the relationship of the artifice of nature and that of art. Jamnitzer was especially known and admired for his 'casting from life'. This technique gave artisans the opportunity to display their art – their ability to imitate nature – not only because the finished product was a perfect imitation of nature, but also because they imitated nature in the very processes of working and casting metals. This imitation of nature comprised a form of natural knowledge, both in the techniques used to produce it as well as in the epistemological claims made by the artisans (Smith 2004: Chapter 2).

Jamnitzer's claims to expert knowledge of the behaviour of matter and the natural processes that produced valuable goods can be seen encapsulated in his extraordinary sculpture depicting the moment at which Daphne was turned into a laurel tree in order to escape the unwanted attentions of Apollo (Bimbenet-Privat 2007) (Figure 3.4). The theme of Apollo and Daphne alerts us to the fact that this is a meditation on metamorphosis and transformation, and we can see Jamnitzer's control and understanding of the processes of nature, as he noted the flow of silver and gold from the ores and minerals at the base of the statue, through the blood-red coral arms, from which tiny naturalistic green leaves begin to sprout. The sculpture embodies multiple levels of meaning: the tiny fragments of ore at the base of the sculpture allude to the transformation of raw ores by human art into precious metals, many of the mineral specimens in the base also refer to metamorphosis, the coral of the arms is seen as a 'juice of the earth' that causes stones and metals to grow in the earth, and coral is the result of metamorphosis likened in the sixteenth century to blood flowing in the veins. The sprouting leaves, cast from life, represent the new life in which all these processes of transformation culminate. Moreover, Apollo's hand transformed Daphne just as the goldsmith's hand produced this marvel of artisanal theorizing about metamorphosis (Cole 2002: 155).

But Jamnitzer's works did not simply proclaim his knowledge; they also embodied a long apprenticeship in metalworking. An anonymous metalsmith's workshop account, probably written in the Toulouse area in the late sixteenth century, makes this dimension of casting from life particularly clear (Anon. probably late sixteenth century). This manuscript appears to be a record of practice and contains a fascinating array of information and asides on all kinds of subjects, such as pigment production, drawing and painting, making mortars, casting, planting trees, an early form of taxidermy for manufacturing curiosities in the form of composite animals (kittens and bats), attracting pigeons, making papier mâché masks, concocting medicines, tips for using clysters on people suffering with haemorrhoids, and a great number of other activities. But by far the bulk of the

Figure 3.4  Wenzel Jamnitzer, *Daphne* (around 1570–75). Gilded silver, coral and semi-precious stones. H .665 m. E. CL 207750. Musée national de la Renaissance, Château d'Ecouen, France. Photo: Pamela H. Smith

manuscript is given over to metalworking techniques. It is one of the few sources that provides insight into the techniques of casting from life during this period, and the entire manuscript testifies to the constant experimentation undertaken in the workshop in order to produce mould material that would be fine enough to take the imprint of the animal's or plant's delicate surface texture; light enough not to flatten the animal; durable enough to withstand the burnout, the heating of the mould before casting, and the pouring of the red-hot metal; and friable enough to crumble easily when breaking the mould to reveal the finished cast object. Such qualities could be discovered only by repeated experiment with natural materials (Smith 2012). The author of this manuscript experiments constantly, noting, for example that he 'tried four kinds of sands for use with [casting] lead and tin: chalk, crushed glass, tripoly, and burned cloth' (Anon. probably late sixteenth century: 68r). And on another day he 'tried ox foot bone well-burned, pulverized and ground well on the porphyry until it becomes very small, as fine as possible' (84v). Under the heading 'Excellent Sand for Use with Lead, Tin and Copper' he records, 'I moulded with burned bone, clinker, and burned felt, all of them carefully ground on the marble slab and well mixed together. I moistened them with beaten egg white' (86v).

But the process of life casting also meant that animals had to be caught, kept alive, fed, killed gently in order not to mar their surface, and finally moulded. This too forms a constant theme in the manuscript, and it is filled with observations and experiments on the behaviour of animals. The techniques by which casting from life was achieved involved significant investigation into the behaviour of animals and materials, an investigation akin to natural history. For example, in making a snake mould:

> Before moulding your snake, if possible never remove [?] their teeth … because when their teeth are removed [?] they suffer in the gums and the mouth and can no longer eat. Keep your snake in a barrel full of bran, or, better, in a barrel full of earth in a cool place, or in a glass bottle. Give your snake some live frogs or other live animals, for snakes do not eat dead animals. Also, I have noticed that when snakes want to bite or eat something, they do not strike straight on. On the contrary, they attack sinuously and obliquely as do Satan and his henchmen. Snakes have small heads, but very large bodies ... they can abstain from eating for seven or eight days, but they can swallow three or four frogs, one after the other. Snakes do not digest food in the stomach all at once. Some parts are digested little by little and other parts remain fresh. For, if you bother and shake your snake, it will bring up partly digested food as well as food that is as fresh as if it were still alive. Sometimes two or three hours after swallowing a frog, it can bring it up still living.
> 
> If your snake is long, mould it hollow, and, if you want to mould it with its mouth open, put some cotton into the mouth and add some melted wax on the cotton. (109r–v)

In this passage, explicit natural historical observations stand alongside numerous experiments on the behaviour of sands, clays, and firing techniques, as well as directives for the best methods of casting reptiles. It can be seen, then, how this metalsmith sought out the behaviour of animals and natural materials in a systematic and empirical way. This is echoed in other artisans' manuals, which advise constant trial. 'It is necessary to find the true method by doing it again and again' (Biringuccio 1943: xvi), 'to have a superabundance of tests ... not only by using ordinary things but also by varying the quantities, adding now half the quantity of the ore and now an equal portion, now twice and now three times ... ' (143–4). This anonymous manuscript demonstrates that casting from life (and craft knowledge more generally) was not just productive but also investigative. This investigation extended seamlessly from natural historical observation and experiment to exploration of the properties of stones, woods, metals, and all manner of other materials, as well as inquiring into the transformation of matter by means of fire, acid, grinding, crushing, and other forms of brute disaggregation.

Bernard Palissy, a Huguenot potter, also experimented with materials and processes to produce extraordinary glazed ceramics: large platters, crawling with moulded-from-life ceramic reptiles, amphibians, and plants, and glazed in deep greens, blues, browns, and pure white – all produced for the tables and curiosity cabinets of the highest nobility in France. Most of these pieces, which he began producing in about 1555, imitate a shoreline or a marshland. Some have a deep blue centre with fish thrusting out of the plate, swimming down the length of the platter. On others, snakes coil on small islands protruding from the surface of the dish, every scale of the wet reptiles perfectly moulded from nature (Lestringant 1992, Amico 1996, Musée National de la Reniassance 1997). Around the rims of the platters creep snails, salamanders, and crabs – all amphibious creatures inhabiting the edges of the water – surrounded by deep green vegetation (Kris 1928, Amico 1996: 86–96). Palissy's larger works, the grottos and pleasure gardens he designed and built for his noble patrons, no longer exist, but he described one such garden of delight in his 1563 *True Recipe by Which All the Men of France Would be Able to Multiply and Augment Their Treasures*, and they too included creatures and plants moulded from life and glazed to produce a lifelike imitation of natural springs and caves (Morley 1855: 317–18, Amico 1996: Chapter 2). For Palissy, his grottos were not solely places of pleasure; rather, his ability to recreate a grotto and the freshwater spring it contained demonstrated his understanding of the most fundamental processes of nature. Grottos and their springs were considered primary sites of nature's generative and transformative powers (Bredekamp 1981, Morel 1990), and their imitation was an attempt to mimic the generative forces of nature. They were regarded as holding the key to knowledge about the processes by which rocks, minerals, and fossils were formed.

In his 1580 *Admirable Discourses on the Nature of Waters and Fountains, Either Natural or Artificial, on Metals, Salts and Salines, on Rocks, Earths, Fire and Enamels*, Palissy was particularly concerned with processes of generation, growth, and change, and the book as a whole explored springs and waters, ice, salts and their central place in the generation of terrestrial bodies, as well as stones, clays, and marl earths and their generative potential for agriculture. Palissy theorized that salt formed the generative principle of all things (130), and spring waters imbued with salts and running through the earth were the cause of generation (104–6). The *Admirable Discourses* contains a chapter in which Palissy makes clear that he discovered and developed his theories about subterranean generation through his experimentation with clays and glazes in producing his life castings, in what he called 'the art of the earth'. By his art, Palissy was able to imitate processes of nature in order to produce an exact imitation of nature, and even to gain insight into the processes by which stones, earths, and all subterranean formations (including what we call fossils) were generated in the earth (188–203).

## Nature and Art

The stunningly lifelike objects created by life casting encouraged conversations in Renaissance *Kunstkammern* about the interplay of human art and created nature. In playing on the relationship between nature and art, life casts in Renaissance collections served several purposes: they could provide proof of rare and odd natural phenomena, such as the crippled and seven-fingered hands of peasants and the misshapen lemons cast in plaster in the Bavarian Wittelsbach *Kunstkammer* (Fickler 2004: 130); they could stand in for the real objects that soon withered and died, like the bouquets of flowers cast in silver by Wenzel Jamnitzer; and, as we have seen above, they could display the talent of the artist in producing fine moulds and in understanding the casting properties of metals. But life casting also possessed a more profound significance, namely, that of demonstrating the human ability to imitate the transformative powers of nature, for humans might imitate nature not just by producing exact replicas of these natural creatures, but also in mastering the flow and structure of materials to produce lifelike forms.

Many of the animals cast from life, such as lizards, snakes, and toads, were associated with spontaneous generation and material transformation, while the plants and insects called up ideas about metamorphosis and the ephemeral nature of life on earth. These creatures, which appeared seemingly spontaneously from putrefying matter, lent support to the common sense principle that generation involved a process of decay (a process also evident in the germination of seeds). But lizards also regenerate their tails if detached, snakes shed their skins, adult frogs and turtles emerge from the ground after freezing winters, and living crustaceans were reported to be found alive in solid stone (Beringer 1963 [1726]: 196 n.8). Such creatures were approached ambivalently, on the one hand as impure and associated with putrefaction, yet on the other, as crucial in processes of transformation and generation. This ambivalence appears to reach at least as far back as the Hebrew bible (Wilson 2000: 150, 417–20, Crowther-Heyck 2003: 253–73, Smith 2004: 117–23), and continued at least until the early twentieth century when Jewish silversmiths in Morocco adorned birth amulets with naturalistic lizards and salamanders (Behrouzi 2002: 25, 70–71). Lizards in particular appear to have had significance for metalworkers and were sometimes employed in metalworking recipes, ostensibly to produce gold and gold coloured pigments (Smith 2009b). Thus, the types of animals used most frequently for life casting were those that seemed to give the most insight into processes of putrefaction, generation, regeneration, and, perhaps ultimately, into the essence of what quickened living beings, or even into the place of spirit in life. Life casts thus declared both the powers of nature and the power of art to transform nature by the human hand.

We find evidence for all these meanings of life casts in the collection of the Basel jurist and city official Basilius Amerbach (1533–91) (Smith and Beentjes 2010). A quintessential humanist, Amerbach evinced a typical interest in Roman antiquity, taking part in the first excavations of the Roman settlement near Basel. Like other humanists, he collected large numbers of coins, seeing them as valuable historical sources for Roman life. Remarkably, from early in his life, he also had a profound interest in the working processes of goldsmiths. In 1560, when he was training at the Imperial Law Court in Speyer, his father (also a lawyer) desired that he lodge with a fellow jurist, but Basilius angered his father by choosing instead to lodge with a goldsmith, Jacob zur Glocke. In the 1570s and 1580s, he collected the entire contents of at least two goldsmiths' workshops, including preparatory drawings, moulds, patterns, and tools, all listed carefully in the inventory in his own hand (Landolt and Ackermann 1991: on goldsmith's lodging 142, for inventories 151). Amerbach's interest, however, was not just in the materials and tools, but rather in all the steps of the creative process, as can be seen in his collection – today in the Basel Historisches Museum – by which goldsmiths transformed lead plates into ornamental gilt foliage on sculpture. He collected the unworked templates and each of the progressively more finished metal pieces that documented every stage of the metalsmith's work of hammering these templates into ornamental foliage. Amerbach's fascination with the precise stages of the process by which artisans produced objects was unusual in Europe, even as his fellow humanists began to express greater interest in practical knowledge and workshop techniques.

Amerbach also treasured a silver life-cast lizard inherited from his father, singling it out in his inventory and his last will (Figure 3.5). Its location in his collection indicates the significance it had for him: it was kept with silver casts of flowers, a unicorn horn (about which he expressed scepticism in the inventory), and various metal ores of silver, gold, and lead (Landolt and Ackermann 1991: esp. 30–31, 102, 122).

A clue to why he kept the lizard with these particular objects can be found in the 1565 plan for a collection written by Samuel Quiccheberg (1529–67), librarian to Duke Albrecht V of Bavaria (1528–79). Trained as a physician, Quiccheberg placed the animals cast from life in the Duke's collection with several other categories of materials involved in processes of generation and transformation. These included 'juices of the earth', which could bring about generation and healing;

**Figure 3.5** Life-cast lizard. Silver, 5.5 cm long. Listed in the inventory of Basilius Amerbach. Historisches Museum Basel (inv. no. 1882.117.64). Photo: Tonny Beentjes and Pamela H. Smith

natural growths, such as horns and bladderstones; and striated rocks that Quiccheberg believed grew in the earth (Quiccheberg 2000: 54–61). It is thus no wonder that Quiccheberg placed life casts with 'juices of the earth' and stones that grew in the earth. Like these substances, the animals employed for life casting – lizards, snakes, frogs, toads, turtles, and all kinds of insects – also alluded to generation. It seems safe to conclude that Amerbach kept his lizard with the metal ores because, to him, lizards suggested transformation. But life casts were made by the human hand, so they also demonstrated that human art could imitate natural processes of transformation and perhaps even of generation. The stunningly precise imitation of nature exhibited by the life-cast animals was a visual proof of knowledge about the processes of transformation, including the properties of sand, plaster, salts, metals, and fire employed in their making. Life casts thus demonstrated the powers of nature and their employment by the human hand to transform and generate. Moreover, life casting suggested that imitation through the work of the human hand was the means to know nature.

**Conclusion**

The artisan's workshop was a site for the transformation of the raw materials of nature into objects made by the human hand. The processes undertaken in the workshop often involved bodily fluids, natural processes of fermentation, as well as the generative power of 'juices of the earth'. Such transformation produced not just objects, but also knowledge about the nature and behaviour of materials, and about growth and life. Growing and making, and generation and production, were not sharply differentiated for the early modern craftsperson. The practice of using reptiles associated with generation and metamorphosis in order to capture the appearance of life, or life casting, highlighted how inseparable were the processes of nature and the practices of human art.

About a century after Quiccheberg and Amberbach included life casts in their collections, Gottfried Wilhelm Leibniz (1646–1716) noted that the process of fossilization could be explained by observing the technique of casting from life:

> We find something similar in the art of the goldsmith, for I gladly compare the secrets of nature with the visible works of men. They cover a spider or some other animal with suitable material, though leaving a small opening, they drive the animal's ashes out through the hole, and, finally, they pour silver in the same way. When the shell is removed, they uncover a silver animal, with its entire complement of feet, hairs, and fibres, which are wonderfully imitated. (Leibniz 2008: 49)

For Leibniz, as for many other seventeenth-century natural philosophers, knowing nature would become synonymous with knowing how to imitate the processes of nature. In the seventeenth century, many self-described 'new experimental philosophers' began to revise Aristotle's definition of *knowing* as the knowledge of causes and to declare instead that *making* was knowing; that is, a made thing was a known thing. By extension, to harness natural processes to produce objects and effects was to know those processes, objects, and effects, and thereby to co-opt the artisanal bodily engagement with nature in the development of an epistemology which held that making an imitation of nature was itself a form of knowing.

## References

Amico, L.M. 1996. *Bernard Palissy: In Search of Earthly Paradise*. Paris: Flammarion.

Anon. 1531. *Rechter Gebrauch der Alchimei/Mitt vil bisher verborgenen uund lustigen Künstien/Nit allein den fürwitzigen Alchmisten/sonder allen kunstbaren Werckleutten/in und ausserhalb feurs. Auch sunst aller menglichen inn vil wege zugebrauchen*. [No publisher noted].

Anon. 1538. *Kunstbüchlein, Auff mancherley weyß Dinten und allerhandt farben zu bereiten. Auch Gold unnd Silver/sampt allen Metallen auß der Federn zu schreiben/Mit viel anderen nützlichen künstlin. Schreybfedern unnd Pergamen mit allerley Farben zu ferben. Auch wie man Schrifft und gemälde auff stähelene/Eysene Waffen/und dergleichen etzen soll*. Augsburg: Michael Manger.

Anon. 1575. *Speculum metallorum*. Stadtarchiv Calw .

Anon. c.1604. *The Goldsmith's Storehouse*. V.a. 179. Folger Library.

Anon. probably late sixteenth century. Ms. Fr 640. Bibliothèque Nationale, Paris.

Anon. 1966. *The Strassburg Manuscript. A Medieval Painters' Handbook*, translated by Viola and Rosamund Borradaile. London: Alec Tiranti.

Behrouzi, N. 2002. *The Hand of Fortune: Khamsas from the Gross Family Collection and the Eretz Israel Museum Collection*, an exhibition at the Eretz Israel Museum, Tel Aviv, 2002. Tel Aviv: Eretz Israel Museum.

Beringer, J.B.A. 1963 [1726]. *The Lying Stones of Dr Johann Bartholomew. Adam Beringer being his Lithographiae Wirceburgensis*, translated and annotated by M.E. Jahn and D.J. Woolf. Berkeley: University of California Press.

Bimbenet-Privat, M. 2007. La Daphné d'argent et de corail par Wenzel Jamnitzer au musée national de la Renaissance. *Revue du Louvre et des musées de France*, 4, 62–74.

Biringuccio, V. 1943 [1540]. *Pirotechnia*, translated by C.S. Smith and M.T. Gnudi. New York: Basic Books.

Bredekamp, H. 1995. *The Lure of Antiquity and the Cult of the Machine*. Princeton: M. Wiener.

Cellini, B. 2005 [1568]. *Traktate über die Goldschmiedekunst und die Bildhauerei (I Trattati dell' Oreficeria e della scultura di Benvenuto Cellini)*, edited by E. Brepohl, translated by R. Fröhlich and M. Fröhlich. Cologne: Böhlau.

Cennini, C.D'A. 1960. *Il libro dell'Arte (The Craftsman's Handbook)*, translated by D.V. Thompson, Jr. New York: Dover.

Cole, M.W. 1999. Cellini's blood. *The Art Bulletin*, 81(2), 215–35.

Cole, M.W. 2002. *Cellini and the Principles of Sculpture*. Cambridge: Cambridge University Press.

Cole, M.W. 2003. The Medici *Mercury* and the Breath of Bronze, in *Large Bronzes in the Renaissance*, edited by P. Motture. New Haven: Yale University Press, 129–53.

Crowther-Heyck, K. 2003. Wonderful secrets of nature: natural knowledge and religious piety in reformation Germany. *Isis*, 94(2), 253–73.

Didi-Huberman, G. 1997. *L'Empreinte*. Paris: Editions du Centre Georges Pompidou.

Diemer, D. 1996. Handwerksgeheimnisse der Vischer-Werkstatt. Eine neue Quelle zur Entstehung des Sebaldusgrabes in Nürnberg. *Münchner Jahrbuch der bildenden Kunst*, 3rd series, 47, 24–54.

Eamon, W. 1994. *Science and the Secrets of Nature: Books of Secrets in Medieval and Early Modern Culture*. Princeton: Princeton University Press.

Ercker, L. 1951 [1580 ed., first published 1574]. *Treatise on Ores and Assaying*, translated by A.G. Sisco and C.S. Smith. Chicago: University of Chicago Press.

Fickler, J.B. 2004. *Das Inventar der Münchner herzoglichen Kunstkammer von 1598*. n.s., 125, *Bayerischen Akademie der Wissenschaften, Abhandlungen der Philosophisch-Historische Klasse*, edited by P. Diemer. Munich: C.H. Beck.

Gramaccini, N. 1985. Das genaue abbild der natur – Riccios Tiere und die theorie des naturabgusses seit Cennini, in *Natur und Antike in der Renaissance*. Frankfurt: Liebighaus Museum Alter Plastik, 198–225.

Klier, A. 2004. *Fixierte Natur: Naturabguss und Effigies im 16. Jahrhundert*. Berlin: Reimer.

Kris, E. 1928. Der stil 'rustique': die verwendung des naturabgusses bei Wenzel Jamnitzer und Bernard Palissy. *Jahrbuch der Kunsthistorischen Sammlungen in Wien*, n.s., 1, 137–208.

Kruse, C. 2000. Fleisch werden – fleisch malen: malerei als 'incarnazione'. Mediale verfahren des bildwerdens in Libro dell'Arte von Cennino Cennini, *Zeitschrift für Kunstgeschichte*, 63, 305–25.

Landolt, E. and Ackermann, F. 1991. *Sammeln in der Renaissance: Das Amerbach-Kabinett. Die Objekte im Historischen Museum Basel*. Basel: Öffentliche Kunstsammlung Basel.

Lavin, I. 1977–8. The sculptor's 'Last Will and Testament'. *Allen Memorial Art Museum Bulletin*, 25, 4–39.

Lehmann, A.-S. 2008. Fleshing out the body: the 'colours of the naked' in workshop practice and art theory, 1400–1600, in *Body and Embodiment in Netherlandish Art*, edited by A.-S. Lehmann and H. Roodenburg. Zwolle: Waanders, (*Nederlands kunsthistorisch jaarboek; 58.2007/08*), 86–109.

Leibniz, G.W. 2008. *Protogaea*, edited and translated by C. Cohen and A. Wakefield. Chicago: Chicago University Press.

Lein, E. 2004. *Ars Aeraria: Die Kunst des Bronzegießens und die Bedeutung von Bronze in der florentinischen Renaissance*. Mainz: P. von Zabern.

Lein, E. 2006. 'Wie man allerhand Insecta, als Spinnen, Fliegen, Käfer, Eydexen, Frösche und auch ander zart Laubwerck scharff abgiessen solle, als wann sie natürlich also gewachsen wären' – Die Natur als Modell in J. Kunckels Beschreibungen des Naturabgusses von Tieren und Pflanzen, in *Das Modell in der bildenden Kunst des Mittelalters und der Neuzeit – Festschrift für Herbert Beck*, edited by P.C. Bol and H. Richter. Petersberg: M. Imhof, 103–19.

Lein, E. 2007. Über den Naturabguss von Pflanzen und Tieren, in *Goldglanz und Silberstrahl*, edited by K. Tebbe. Nuremberg: Verlag des Germanischen Nationalmuseums, 2, 205–15.

Lestringant, F. (ed.), 1992. *Bernard Palissy 1510–1590. L'Écrivain, Le Réformé, Le Céramiste*. Paris: Coédition Association Internationale des Amis d'Agrippa d'Aubigné.

Morel, P. 1990. La théâtralisation de l'alchimie de la nature. Les grottes artificielles et la culture scientifique à Florence à la fin du XVIe siècle. *Symboles de la Renaissance*, 30, 155–81.

Morley, H. 1855. *Palissy the Potter*. 2nd edition. London: Chapman and Hall.

Musée National de la Reniassance. 1997. *Une Orfèverie de Terre: Bernard Palissy et la Céramique de Saint-Porchaire: Musée National de la Reniassance, Chateau D'Écouen.* Paris: Seuil.

Palissy, B. 1580. *Admirable Discourses on the Nature of Waters and Fountains, Either Natural or Artificial, on Metals, Salts and Salines, on Rocks, Earths, Fire and Enamels*, translated by A. la Rocque (1957). Urbana: University of Illinois Press.

Pechstein, K. 1970. Zeichnungen von Wenzel Jamnitzer. *Anzeiger des Germanischen Nationalmuseums*, 81–95.

Pieper, W. 1955 [1505]. *Ulrich Rülein von Calw und sein Bergbüchlein, Freiberger Forschungshefte.* Berlin-Ost: Akademie Verlag. Facsimile reprint of the first edition of the Bergbüchlein, Bibliothèque Nationale, Paris.

Plat, H. 1594. *The Jewell House of Art and Nature: Containing Divers Rare and Profitable Inventions, Together with Sundry New Experimentes in the Art of Husbandry, Distillation, and Molding.* London: Peter Short.

Quiccheberg, S. 2000. *Der Anfang der Museumslehre in Deutschland: Das Traktat 'Inscriptiones vel Tituli Theatri Amplissimi' von Samuel Quiccheberg*, edited by Harriet Roth. Berlin: Akademie Verlag.

Sisco, A.G. and C.S. Smith (eds) 1949. *Bergwerk- und Probierbüchlein; a Translation from the German of the Bergbüchlein, a Sixteenth-century Book on Mining Geology, by Anneliese Grünhaldt Sisco; and of the Probierbüchlein, a Sixteenth-century Work on Assaying.* New York: American Institute of Mining and Metallurgical Engineers.

Smith, P.H. 2004. *The Body of the Artisan: Art and Experience in the Scientific Revolution.* Chicago: Chicago University Press.

Smith, P.H. 2009a. Science on the move: recent trends in the history of early modern science. *Renaissance Quarterly*, 62(2), 345–75.

Smith, P.H. 2009b. Vermilion, mercury, blood, and lizards: matter and meaning in metalworking, in *Materials and Expertise in Early Modern Europe: Between Market and Laboratory*, edited by U. Klein and E. Spary. Chicago: Chicago University Press, 29–49.

Smith P.H. 2011. What is a secret? Secrets and craft knowledge in early modern Europe, in *Secrets and Knowledge in Medicine and Science, 1500–1800*, edited by E. Leong and A. Rankin. Burlington, VT: Ashgate, 47–66.

Smith, P.H. 2012. In the workshop of history: making, writing, and meaning. *West 86th: A Journal of Decorative Arts, Design History, and Material Culture*, 19, 4–31.

Smith, P.H. and T. Beentjes 2010. Nature and art, making and knowing: reconstructing sixteenth-century life casting techniques. *Renaissance Quarterly*, 63(1), 128–79.

Stöckler, I. 1990. *Die Entwicklung der Naturabgüsses von Padua bis Nürnberg: Eine nähere Betrachtung des silbernen Schreibzeugkästchen des Wenzel Jamnitzer.* Zürich: Lizentiatsarbeit Zürich University.

Stone, R. 1981. Antico and the development of bronze casting in Italy at the end of the Quattrocento. *Metropolitan Museum Journal*, 16, 87–116.

Stone, R. 2001. A new interpretation of the casting of Donatello's *Judith and Holofernes*, in *Small Bronzes in the Renaissance*, edited by Debra Pincus. *Studies in the History of Art*, 62. New Haven: Yale University Press, 55–67.

Theophilus. 1979. *On Divers Arts*, translated and with an introduction by J.G. Hawthorne and C.S. Smith. New York: Dover Publications.

Wilson, S. 2000. *The Magical Universe: Everyday Ritual and Magic in Pre-Modern Europe.* London: Hambledon and London.

Vasari, G. 1907. *Vasari on Technique*, edited by G. Baldwin Brown, translated by L.S. Maclehose. London: J.M. Dent.

# Chapter 4
# Anatomopoeia

Elizabeth Hallam

**Introduction: Making and Growing Anatomical Models**

For centuries anatomists, with their assistants and associates, have practised anatomopoeia to produce knowledge of bodies, human, animal and vegetable. Here I develop the concept of anatomopoeia to refer to the processes involved in making and growing anatomical knowledge, which cut across any clear distinctions between the mental and the material, the organic and the artefactual. To generate and communicate knowledge of anatomy for medical purposes, practitioners in Europe, especially from the sixteenth century onwards, have developed a wide range of techniques for preserving, modelling and displaying bodies and parts thereof. To arrest putrefaction after death, bodies have been dried or immersed in fluid, and to exhibit various aspects of these bodies practitioners have engaged in such work as sculpting, inflating, injecting, macerating, painting, sewing, drawing and writing. From robust bones to delicate membranes, and from voluminous organs to the tiniest intricate vessels, practitioners have rendered anatomy effectively, sometimes strikingly, visible and tangible.

The products of anatomopoeia, many of which are now maintained in medical schools and museums, are extensive and composed in diverse materials, often mixed: 'preparations' or 'specimens' preserved in the flesh; models in wax, wood, plaster, plastics and many other materials; printed books (for example anatomical atlases) and visual images (for instance, x-rays, photographs and MRI scans). Given the processes of their production and use, however, these entities are neither discrete (clearly bounded) nor completed; rather they are open, caught up in relations with further material entities and with people in ways that shape their matter and meanings over time (Hallam forthcoming). How making and growing are entangled and mutually implicated in the development of these open, relational entities is explored in this chapter with reference to one particular form of anatomopoeia: corrosion casting to produce three-dimensional anatomical models for medical education as practised in Britain from the 1940s to the 1970s. In this casting, parts of deceased bodies, such as blood vessels, were injected with fluids that solidified and then the surrounding flesh was corroded away to give the very interior of bodies visible and enduring form.

I develop the concept of anatomopoeia partly from the nineteenth-century use of the term 'skeletopoeia': 'that part of practical anatomy which treats of the preparation of bones, and the construction of skeletons' (Dunglison 1868: 888, Hallam 2010).

Rather than focusing specifically on the preparation and construction of skeletons, however, anatomopoeia refers to a broader domain of anatomical production, as suggested above. The concept also draws on current historians' concerns with the poetics of science, that is, with the ways in which science is constituted or made (see Golinski 2005 [1998]). James Bono (2010: 559, 555), for instance, argues that science should be analyzed as a 'form of *poiesis*, of making' involving 'material practices, and a panoply of meaningful artifacts – instruments of thought and action – that refuse any simple dichotomy between "text" and "action"'. Material practices, including writing, therefore crucially participate in this poiesis.

With reference to a very different context – that of mortuary ritual – Seremetakis analyzes interrelated spoken words and practices enacted when disposing of the dead (in Mani, southern Greece) in terms of poiesis or the processes by which 'things and persons are made and unmade'. This poiesis took place through women's labour with deceased kin during burial, the performance of laments and the later exhumation of skeletal remains for storage in ossuaries, as documented by Seremetakis in the 1980s (1991: 1). Significantly, poiesis in these ritualized mortuary practices was inseparably material and metaphorical. So, for example, women's mortuary labour in Mani drew upon and metaphorically alluded to their domestic and agricultural work thereby supplying ritual practice with additional 'material force' (1991: 230).

Similarly, processes of anatomopoeia entwine materials and metaphors as this chapter goes on to discuss by focusing not just on making but also on growing. For the making of anatomical models, in the context examined here, entailed an extension of the growth undergone by the deceased bodies from which the models were cast, and also growth on the part of those who produced and interacted with them, especially with regard to their embodied knowledge and skills. In this co-constitution of models and practitioners, the latter gained in expertise as they engaged intensively with the former. This relational growth was stimulated and sustained in a working environment where relationships among models and practitioners can be understood in terms of kinship, forged and expressed in interrelated material and textual forms.

To examine the dynamics of anatomopoeia as both making and growing I focus on one practitioner – David Hugh Tompsett (1910–91) – at the Royal College of Surgeons of England (RCS), in London. From 1945 for over 30 years, Tompsett was employed as a 'professional' prosector in the College's department of anatomy, preserving and dissecting bodies of the recently deceased, as well as non-human bodies, for use in anatomical teaching and learning (Tompsett 1956: vi, see Alberti forthcoming). Tompsett became expert in corrosion casting – experimenting, improvising and achieving recognition as an 'important pioneer', especially with the use of plastics (Lewis 1971: 586) (Figure 4.1). Producing over 150 models during his career, Tompsett worked with colleagues at the RCS to rebuild this institution's museum collections after the bombing during the Second World War. His area of particular expertise – explained in two editions of his manual *Anatomical Techniques* (1956, 1970) – was the corrosion casting of vessels and ventricles (i.e. tubes and cavities) through which fluids and air flow during life.

*Anatomopoeia* 67

**Figure 4.1** Photograph of David Tompsett with a corrosion cast of the human lungs and heart, 1950s. Hunterian Museum at the Royal College of Surgeons of England

Casts of these anatomical structures rendered their three-dimensional form visible as intricate and vibrantly coloured 'trees'. Although Tompsett was acknowledged as the maker of these material entities, in practice they were generated through collaborative anatomopoeia, as I argue here, so that his oeuvre developed through social and material interactions sustained over several decades.

By attending to growing as much as making, this analysis of anatomopoeia highlights the relational aspects of practitioner and model in anatomical practices, situating both within relations, including those of 'kin', generated at a medical institution for research and education. As Gell (1998) has suggested, material entities such as artworks can bear kinship to one another, finding positions within genealogies, as do people. What follows, then, provides an anthropological and historical account of bodies which differs from those that foreground the medically constituted body as a bounded 'biomechanical entity' (Farquhar and Lock 2007: 2). Rather than highlighting dominant conceptions of the body in western anatomical practices as a machine (see Prentice 2013), or as muscular form, this chapter explores the modelling of bodies as plants – an association usually deemed more significant in non-western medical traditions (Kuriyama 2002), though such western/non-western distinctions have been questioned in recent studies (Degnen 2009). Examining anatomopoeia in this way reveals the interrelation not only of the organic and the artefactual, but also of the living and the dead, and of disintegration and composition.

## Loss and Reconstruction

After a night of German air raids in May 1941, Arthur Keith, conservator of the Hunterian Museum of the RCS from 1908 to 1933, described the bombing of the Museum and the consequent loss of many 'rare and irreplaceable objects, the harvest of two centuries' which 'perished in the flames' (Keith 1950: 673–4). Over 38,000 specimens (mainly preserved and dissected body parts) were destroyed, but around 27,000 survived and museum staff salvaged what they could from the 'charred mass'. Many specimens were transported to safe storage outside London, which was increasingly 'battle-scarred' with buildings, hospitals and homes reduced to rubble (Anon. 1942b, Anon. 1940). The RCS reported on the event as a terrible blow to the 'development of British biological science', and just prior to the war's end professor of surgery George Grey Turner continued to stress the Museum's value, underlining the medical community's 'duty' to ensure its complete restoration (RCS Annual Report, quoted in Wakeley 1965: 339, Turner 1945: 249). In a prominent lecture he announced 'the Museum will be reborn', taking inspiration from the past – from John Hunter (1728–93), anatomist and surgeon whose esteemed collection had formed the basis of the Museum – whilst promoting 'present-day knowledge'. This rebirth was labour-intensive and had to be 'patiently done', he counselled: 'we must plod on and on till the task is well under way, knowing full well that it can never be completed' (Turner 1945: 249–50). An effective medical museum conceived in these terms required endless maintenance if it was to reach into the future rather than slipping, deteriorated, into the past.

The medical press joined Grey Turner, supporting medical museums whilst also airing critical views of their sometimes 'obsolete' holdings, such as ageing wax models and defunct specimens without a 'vestige of colour' (Anon. 1945: 376, Hallam and Alberti 2013). When the RCS's collections returned from remote storage, the aim was for the Museum to be 'restored and built up around the surviving collections to illustrate the development, structure and functions of man' as well as accidents and diseases (Turner 1945: 249). So animal skeletons and other comparative anatomy specimens were not to clutter the Museum if they had little capacity to enhance comprehension of human anatomy and pathology (though animal specimens were still studied as a route to understanding the human body). Furthermore, this museum planning emerged at a time when many medical school educators were shifting away from teaching methods that focused on the dead body *per se* towards a 'new anatomy', which directed students' attention to living bodies, to the relation of form and function and to processes of 'growth, repair and adaptation to functional demands' (Royal College of Physicians of London 1944: 13). With this focus on 'living anatomy', the dissection and study of deceased bodies were not, however, abandoned. Rather, the dead were dissected and preserved within pedagogical strategies that mobilized further teaching materials, depicting anatomy – and encouraging students to visualize it – as alive. Dedicated photographs of living bodies with muscles 'in action' and three-dimensional anatomical models, for example, had the perceived capacity to aid in the difficult 'task of raising anatomy from the dead' (Lockhart 1960 [1948]: n.p.).

The Hunterian Museum's reconstruction was initiated in the context of wider post-war rebuilding and recovery in Britain where, as the medical journal *The Lancet* reported, 'reconstruction is the watchword' (Anon. 1945: 377). Here medicine and science were seen to have key roles (de Chadarevian 2002). According to consulting physician and Oxford professor of medicine Edward Farquhar Buzzard, the reconstruction of medical practice in Britain was required amid changes in diagnosis and treatment with, for example, the use of x-rays, and the expansion of 'clinical, bacteriological and bio-chemical laboratories' – developments linked to the acceleration of biomedicine from the post-war period onwards (Buzzard 1942: 343, Quirke and Gaudillière 2008). While Buzzard described these 'advances' as examples of the 'scientific mechanization of medical practice', he also used organic metaphors to convey the need for changes in medical education. A key aspect of reconstruction was, thus, the 'cultivation of the tree of knowledge' that would guide the 'growth' of various 'branches' of medical knowledge (Buzzard 1942: 343). So in addition to the establishment of the National Health Service (introduced in 1948 to provide free health care for all), Buzzard recommended the 'designing' of medical education so that it would generate thorough understanding of 'man as a living animal' (1942: 345, see Stewart 2008). Properly utilized in the training of professional practitioners, therefore, medical museums, including the Hunterian, were seen by their supporters as important resources for medical education and research that would save the lives of many and promote widespread health (Anon. 1945).

Analysis of museum reconstruction at the RCS through the production of anatomical models indicates that organic metaphors in medical discourse – which could communicate, for instance, a sense of regeneration (museum rebirth) and growth (cultivating the tree of knowledge) – were not confined to words as they were intimately bound up with material practices: the interrelation of metaphorical and bodily processes was central to anatomopoeia at work. In the next sections of this chapter I analyze Tompsett's model-making at the RCS from 1945 onwards as a significant instance of anatomopoeia, focusing on the role of making and growing in his working techniques and relationships, his ritualized treatment of deceased persons, and his intensive engagement with materials including commercially manufactured plastics.

**Anatomical Techniques: The Casting Complex**

In 1956 Tompsett published his 'instructive and very practical book', *Anatomical Techniques*, based on his first decade of work as prosector at the RCS (Wakeley 1956). It was intended to guide and instruct 'workers' who produced specimens – of which there was a perceived 'pressing need' – for teaching purposes in anatomy museums. At medical schools and teaching hospitals, many lecturers and students had been preparing such specimens in their 'spare time', Tompsett noted. Given that he was able to devote all his energy to 'the perfection of the art of dissection and the development of various techniques', he aimed to share his know-how widely (1956: vi). Tompsett's book and his 1970 revised second edition, therefore, contributed to a body of publications by practitioners concerned to disseminate methods for maintaining medical museums and for keeping them 'up to date' with 'modern techniques' (Edwards and Edwards 1959: 158).

In deliberate contrast to a previous RCS prosector, who kept his special techniques a 'jealously guarded secret', Tompsett aimed in his book to 'reveal as completely as possible all the tricks of his trade' (1956: 3). Such revelation, with detailed description of complex action, is never complete, as much anthropological and historical analysis of making practices shows, especially with reference to embodied and tacit knowledge (see for example Lawrence and Shapin 1998, Marchand 2010, Smith 2012). Tompsett was aware of this difficulty, and sought various means to convey knowledge through visual as well as textual means, by working with drawings, diagrams and photographs. Indeed he emphasized the importance of pictures in that they 'give a clearer idea than any amount of printed description' (1956: 39). He also encouraged observation of his practice by holding demonstrations, by teaching, and through the display of his work at the RCS in the Hunterian Museum and the post-war Wellcome anatomy museum (Tompsett 1970: x). Tompsett instructed on a range of related techniques for which no formal training was available: preparing and mounting anatomical specimens, illustrating dissections, and casting to produce anatomical models. Of these practices he had gained 'intimate practical experience' at the RCS, building on his general science degree in chemistry, botany and zoology, his PhD in the latter subject and his training in engineering (1956: vi).

The majority of his *Anatomical Techniques* was devoted to corrosion casting (Figure 4.2). He detailed the materials, tools and equipment used, giving comprehensive guidance on how to prepare and inject vessels and ducts –

Figure 4.2  Corrosion cast of thoracic and abdominal viscera of a 14-year-old boy, 1965. Hunterian Museum at the Royal College of Surgeons of England

in limbs and in the lungs, liver, kidney, spleen, brain and heart – with 'cold-setting synthetic unsaturated polyester resins'. Once injected this resin solidified, and the surrounding 'organic' tissues were corroded or dissolved away when immersed in concentrated hydrochloric acid. Further procedures were needed to clean and improve the appearance of resin casts – especially 'pruning', as I describe later – which readied them for museum display and for teaching anatomy (1956: 95, 119).

Anticipating potential problems that practitioners might encounter, Tompsett underlined the need for thorough understanding gained through practice and considered reflection on that practice:

> To produce the best results this work has to be done intelligently; it is not enough to just follow blindly the instructions given. Therefore a special effort has been made to explain the reason for each detail of procedure, so that, if something goes wrong, the worker will be able to diagnose correctly the cause of the failure. Then it is not difficult to avoid making the same mistake again. (1956: 109)

Stressing that practitioners' abilities develop only with 'considerable experience', Tompsett directed attention towards dextrous action (for example, cutting, picking, gripping, stretching, pulling, tearing, scraping, trimming, sewing); processes such as solidification, decay and cleaning; working conditions (for example lighting and room temperature); and the variable and changing properties of materials such as weight, texture and colour (1956: 39). Tompsett's skill in describing perceptual, bodily and material processes was appreciated by readers of his book: one reviewer praised the lucid explanations of this 'craft' that put into print 'much information which was previously handed down by word of mouth from one generation of prosectors to the next' (Brown 1957: 689).

The same reader saw in Tompsett's work a 'charming combination of the ancient traditions of the Royal College of Surgeons and the newer cult of "Do it yourself"' (Brown 1957: 689). This was a sharp insight, as Tompsett linked his casting work with accomplished, prominent predecessors in his field whilst innovating with materials. In the RCS's museum collections he found a 'trace' of lost eighteenth-century wax corrosion casts in a 1760s portrait of anatomist William Hunter (1718–83), John's elder brother, with a cast human heart and lungs in a glass bell jar (Tompsett 1956: 178, see Chaplin 2009). While Tompsett studied and wrote about previous practitioners from whom he had learnt, thereby placing his casts within a prestigious genealogy, he also emphasized the importance of materials and methods more suited to the 'modern' anatomy museum (Tompsett 1956: 178). Here plastics were important, along with products originally designed for other purposes but nevertheless adaptable for producing corrosion casts.

Tompsett's do-it-yourself (DIY) approach to modelling was informed by an ethos of frugality in museums – cultivated during war time and persisting to a certain extent with rationing into the 1950s – which encouraged the careful and creative use of materials (Anon. 1942a). He was committed to experimentation in his casting, including improvisation with products many of which were perceived as mundane and associated with the household and domestic work. Tompsett's corrosion-casting equipment, for example, included silk thread, button thread and linen carpet thread used in his assemblies of rubber-tubing apparatus for injecting vessels; and an adapted whistling kettle (for giving jets of steam) was in his tool kit among medical instruments, such as enema syringes, aural (ear) syringes and dissecting forceps (Tompsett 1956). Improvisation in anatomical practices, involving the appropriation of materials, tools and techniques from other domains of work and activity, has a long history; it is apparent in descriptions by sixteenth-century anatomist Andreas Vesalius, for example (Hallam 2010). Tompsett's anatomical improvisation developed in particular ways in the post-war context where DIY was widely embraced as a productive approach among, for instance, scientists and artists: fields of research such as biophysics (later molecular biology) were investigated and communicated via DIY models (as in James Watson and Francis Crick's models of human DNA, developed in Cambridge during the early 1950s), and at the same time artists, internationally, experimented with notions of DIY, engaging in bricolage by drawing upon everyday things and materials (de Chadarevian 2002, Dezeuze 2010).

For Tompsett DIY anatomical models were crucial, especially as he deemed many commercially produced models 'inaccurate'. Although anatomical models imported from leading commercial firms (many based in continental Europe) were considered useful in teaching anatomy, the on-site production of DIY models – often with 'home made' equipment characterized by its 'simplicity' – in Britain's medical schools was also important (Tompsett 1956: 162, 95, 1970: 74, Tompsett and Bartlett 1961, Hamlyn and Thilesen 1953, Fitzgerald at al. 1979, see Hallam 2013). One of the main perceived advantages of Tompsett's models was that they were cast inside parts of bodies from which they acquired form and surface impressions, thereby giving vivid and compelling shape to vessels and ventricles that were very difficult to dissect and otherwise observe in medical education. Thus Tompsett's casts were highly valued for 'making it easy to visualize the form' of previously invisible anatomical parts (Tompsett 1956: 153). Indeed, body part and cast were so intimately related that the latter was not clearly distinguished from the former: a cast therefore oscillated between the status of model and of actual body, it was an ambiguous entity – both artefact and organism.[1]

This ambiguity was compounded by the interrelation of the human and the botanical, in the material form, treatment and metaphorical elaboration of casts. Bodily tubes, channels and cavities rendered as trees were described as such in anatomical terminology: lungs were cast to show the 'bronchial tree'; casts of the heart displayed the 'trunk' and 'branches' of arteries and veins, and limb casts revealed the 'arterial tree'; liver casts disclosed the vessels of the biliary tree,

---

1  Definitions of, and distinctions between, casts and models were contextual: while Tompsett (1956) distinguished casting from the preparation of models, other practitioners in Britain at the time referred to casts as a type of model (see for example Hamlyn and Thilesen 1953).

and brain casts exhibited the cerebral arterial tree as well as the ventricles in this organ which also comprises an anatomical part that, due to its branching shape, is known as the *arbor vitae* or tree of life (Tompsett 1956: 134, 157, 161, 1970: 170). If body part became tree, in visual appearance and in anatomical discourse, it did so through a casting process that was inseparably social and material, as well as ritualized.

## Relational, Ritualized Casting

Tompsett's models were DIY in that they were improvised in a hands-on experimental way with mundane materials, but he did not, however, do this work by himself. Its doing was highly dependent on collaboration with colleagues at the RCS and associates elsewhere. In addition to support from professors in the department of anatomy, Tompsett was especially appreciative of assistance from the technicians with whom he worked closely for many years. He publicly credited those who advised and helped him at a time when the labour of technicians and museum workers in the fields of science and medicine – often previously 'invisible' or unrecognized, as surgeon Cecil Wakely noted in the 1960s – was increasingly acknowledged (Wakely 1965: 337, see Tansey 2008). Sydney Bartlett, for instance, who became chief technician in the Wellcome anatomy museum, aided Tompsett with information on embalming and also on mounting techniques especially those for the construction of transparent Perspex cases in which to display specimens and casts (Figure 4.3). From the late 1950s Tompsett gave Bartlett tuition, so that he too learned corrosion casting. In this collaboration, the two were part of a community of practitioners engaged in anatomical work, a community in which long-term working relationships, although somewhat hierarchically organized, were characterized by mutual support and learning (see Wenger 1998). Facilitating the growth of knowledge relating to working practices and to anatomical knowledge of the body, these relationships aided Tompsett's development among practitioners who became his working 'kin', professionals who could still feel like 'family' (Keith 1950: 308).

If corrosion casts were relational – collaboratively produced within a specific working environment – they were also made possible by the deceased persons whose bodies they were cast within. Indeed this kind of anatomical modelling was impossible without access to human remains. In Britain human bodies were legally obtained, prior to burial (or, later, cremation), for purposes of medical education under the Anatomy Act of 1832. This legislation allowed anatomists to obtain the bodies of those who died in hospitals and other institutions when they were unclaimed by relatives, but by the mid-1940s the number of people donating their own bodies to medical schools was rising, especially in England, so that donors eventually replaced the unclaimed as the source of bodies for medical teaching and research (Goodman 1944, Hallam 2007, see Richardson 2001). It was through this system of supply that the RCS's department of anatomy received the bodies with

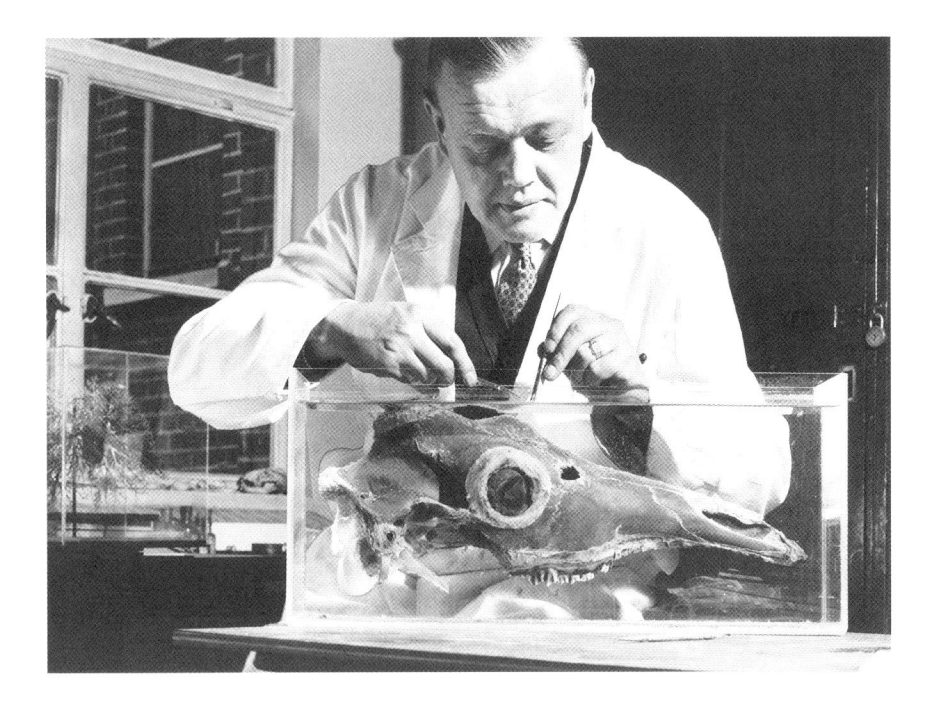

Figure 4.3  Photograph of museum technician Sydney Bartlett placing a giraffe specimen in a display case, 1961. A corrosion cast can be seen in the background (left). Hunterian Museum at the Royal College of Surgeons of England

which Tompsett worked. Additionally, the department appears to have obtained some amputated limbs from surgical operations as well as organs (for example hearts, brains, lungs and livers) removed from the dead, according to Tompsett, in 'the post-mortem room' (probably in one or more of the London hospitals) – and these body parts were also used to produce casts (Tompsett 1956: 4, 63).[2]

Once within the department, the deceased were referred to as anonymous bodies or parts thereof: a deceased person became a 'body' and a 'cadaver' as well as 'material', a term also used to refer to organs and tissues that had been separated from bodies (Tompsett 1956: 9, 31, 109). The use of such terms suggests an objectification of the deceased, which would be consistent with anthropological studies of western anatomical and medical practices in terms of their propensity to turn persons into passive objects (see Lock and Nguyen 2010). Yet during the casting process, although deceased bodies were anonymized and their personhood dissolved, they were not reduced to inert, disconnected objects.

---

2  The sources of human bodies and body parts with which Tompsett worked is the subject of further research by the author.

The anatomical technique of corrosion casting, as practised by Tompsett and his colleagues, was a form of mortuary ritual that eased the modification of body into model. Many of the deceased bodies with which Tompsett worked were women and men in their 70s and 80s, but he also cast from the bodies of children and stillborn babies (Tompsett 1956: 1970). Bodies and body parts were required as soon as possible after death, before decomposition could begin. Their preservation and treatment necessitated a particular kind of intensive 'labour' on the part of practitioners involving 'great care' and 'patience' that, over time, generated in-depth knowledge of the dead regarding their bodily interiors. Key procedures were to wash out blood and remove air from vessels so that molten resin could pass, unobstructed, into them: the flow of blood and air that once sustained life was replaced with the flow of resin. When solidified, the resin cast was exposed through corrosion so that soft tissue gave way to rigid, self-supporting, anatomical 'structures' (Tompsett 1956: 95, 10, 5, 32). In this shift from body or body part to cast the imprint of an individual's physical interior was retained while the personhood of the deceased was displaced by their status as an anonymized anatomical model labelled only with details of age, sex and sometimes medical condition.

Casting to produce models in this way was achieved, then, through ritualized procedures that disposed of unstable flesh in order to compose a durable form moulded by that flesh. Just as dissecting rooms in medical schools and operating theatres in hospitals have been interpreted as ritual spaces (see Good 1994, Prentice 2013), the prosector's laboratory can be seen as a site of ritual practice: particular activities were performed to reconstitute the dead as models and in the process practitioners gained knowledge such that they were themselves reshaped. Casting in this way gave the dead a version of what Seremetakis (1991) – drawing on Hertz in her discussion of the exhumation of bones in Maniat double burial – refers to as a second body. When the decayed body is unearthed from the grave the rotten flesh is separated from the bones and this durable, reconstructed second body is preserved in an ossuary, becoming a 'communication device' between the living and the dead (Seremetakis 1991: 178). The poiesis or making of the second body which Seremetakis discusses involves the labour of retrieving and cleaning the skeleton as well as the narration of this process, interrelated actions and words that create the second body or set of bones which are treated as the remains of a particular person, not as 'inert artefacts' (1991: 189). The anatomopoeia in which Tompsett engaged produced models that were similarly *not* inert (although they were not explicitly identified with particular persons). For these models were entities with which, during their production, practitioners became physically and subjectively engaged, and once cast these models were perceived to have particular capacities and effects in the generation and transmission of anatomical knowledge. They therefore strengthened the medical education of professionals who aimed to promote health and save lives. Casting thus deployed the dead as a resource for the living, and this ritualized undertaking translated death into life.

Tompsett referred to his work as *making* – in that he said casts were 'made from' bodies or body parts (1956: 109) – yet this relational and ritualized making also entailed *growing*, as evidenced by Tompsett's own descriptions of working practices. Next I focus on two aspects of growth in the process of anatomopoeia: firstly in the behaviour and manipulation of modelling materials, and secondly in the emergent relations between practitioner and anatomical model which shaped the latter whilst cultivating the embodied self of the former. Here distinctions between the living and the dead, between subject and object, what was made and what grown, were far from stable (see Hallam and Hockey 2001).

**Plastic Processes: Working with Resins**

Just as Tompsett looked to previous practitioners with whom he connected his work, thereby situating himself within a genealogy or family tree, so he discerned connections between his working materials and those previously used in corrosion casting. Through his exploration of the properties of materials he traced generations of materials from wax and metal to his preferred plastics. Molten wax, as he explained, used in anatomical casting and injecting since the early sixteenth century, was very fragile when solidified. Low-melting-point metals, employed from the seventeenth century onwards, were stronger than wax but the weighty metal distorted the delicate vessels that it was meant to cast. While Tompsett noted techniques for casting with plastics from the 1880s, it was the availability of polyester resins in 1948 in England (earlier in the USA) which, he enthused, 'opened up completely new possibilities in the sphere of anatomical casting'; it facilitated the production of models without the need for costly and elaborate equipment (Tompsett 1956: 95).

Recognized as one of the first practitioners to 'appreciate the possibilities' of synthetic resins for modelling, Tompsett exploited what were seen as advances in manufactured materials that had properties such as malleability, setting capacity, strength and lightness (Anon. 1957b: 209). Although referred to as 'raw materials' these plastics were 'designed', engineered (Brown 1971: 467, Hamlyn and Thilesen 1953: 474, see Küchler 2010). And when put to use, these materials were perceived to have vital qualities, as is evident in Tompsett's experimental casting with polyester resins. While what were defined as 'natural' resins were derived from plants, especially coniferous trees, 'synthetic' resins were industrially produced from chemicals (Mossman 2008). Tompsett understood that success in casting with this material required not only 'manual skill' but also 'thorough knowledge' of its 'properties and behaviour' (1956: 96). The resins Tompsett selected were marketed by a London firm as Marco Resin 26C and, later, Crystic Resin 700. Beginning by casting the bronchial tree in the lungs of deceased dogs and sheep, and then moving on to humans, Tompsett developed in depth his knowledge of the combined effects and reactions of his working materials – principally human bodies, plastics, and corrosive agents such as acids.[3] The orchestration of interactions between these materials was compelling in both process and results.

Tompsett's account of the properties of resin during the casting process highlights the perceived vitality of this material. To resin – described as a pale yellow transparent fluid – was added a liquid (monomer) in which a catalyst had been dissolved. Immediately prior to use, an accelerator (a 'mobile violet liquid') was stirred into the mixture, causing the resin to darken slightly. At this point, the viscosity of the resin would increase until it gelled. The period of time between the addition of accelerator and the gelling was referred to as the 'working life' of the mixture – a life that could be adjusted, from minutes to days, by altering the proportions of the blend. Tompsett recommended an ideal working life of 15 minutes, giving sufficient time to inject the mixture into the vessels of a body or body part via polythene, rubber or glass tubing attached to those vessels. After injection the resin would harden for about a week until fully 'matured', a stable state when no further changes were expected (1956: 97, 101). Resin, once activated, therefore had a life during which its behaviour had to be understood and managed; resin had its own dynamics that were difficult to control. Yet it was imperative in Tompsett's procedures that resin flowed properly into and through vessels to ensure casting without blockages. Understanding and learning to manipulate this fluidity, then, was critical if the cast was to develop well.

The vivacity of resin, and its efficacy when cast as a model, was also suggested in reactions to its colour. Pigments added to resin before injection produced coloured casts that were appreciated for their intensity and brilliance, qualities that enhanced the casts' perceived beauty and capacity to educate: colour drew and engaged the observer's attention in anatomical displays. The cast in Figure 4.2, for example (although reproduced here in black and white), is in vivid, contrasting shades of red, blue, turquoise and yellow. Such colour provoked responses, it augmented the models' compelling quality. Further visual and tangible attributes of resin were suggested when Tompsett likened it to food – as a liquid it was 'indistinguishable in appearance from golden syrup' and when hardening its consistency was like 'Cheddar cheese' (1956: 104, 141). To inject the body or body part with this substance was thus to nourish it, as when alive. Resin was therefore both life-sustaining and animate; the life of the cast and that of the body from which it emerged were thoroughly entwined.

Resin also acquired positive cultural meanings that infused this substance with vigour. Tompsett's casting capitalized on the growth of the plastics industry and the take-up of plastics in many aspects of post-war life (see Küchler 2010, Fisher 2013, Mossman 2008). He obtained polyester resins in the relatively small quantities suitable for his work from the firm Scott Bader & Co. Ltd. which – usually supplying resins in bulk for industrial purposes, including boat construction – made

---

3   Although Tompsett focused on human anatomy, he continued to cast non-human organs for comparative purposes, especially the lungs, for example of horses, goats and toads.

up a 'special anatomical kit' for modelling (Tompsett 1956: 107, Scott Bader n.d.). In the 1950s, plastics were being channelled into a variety of experimental medical applications; they were explored for use in surgical dressings and in orthopaedic surgery, for instance. Such applications were discussed at a public exhibition and convention on plastics in Olympia, London, where Tompsett also presented his techniques for casting the bronchial tree and pulmonary blood vessels (Anon. 1951). This event was held during the 1951 government-sponsored Festival of Britain in which contributions by designers, architects and scientists highlighted post-war reconstruction and celebrated potential 'progress and modernity' in many facets of everyday life and work (Conekin 2003: 46). Here and more widely plastics accrued associations with health, optimism, brightness and vibrancy (see Fisher 2013).

Commenting on plastic as both a 'miraculous substance' and a 'prosaic' household material, Roland Barthes observed in 1957 that 'the whole world can be plasticized, and even life itself since, we are told, they are beginning to make plastic aortas' (1973 [1957]: 99). Barthes was presumably referring to the medical use of plastics in prostheses for the living, but it is his description of plastic's plasticity that is most pertinent in the context of anatomical modelling: 'it [plastic] is less a thing than the trace of a movement' (Barthes 1973 [1957]: 97). It was precisely this capacity for fluid movement through vessels, prior to setting, that Tompsett co-opted in the casting process. When injected resin moved through the vessels it took shape just as those parts of the body had grown: this equivalence between vital fluid (especially blood) or gas (especially oxygen) and resin lent the cast an animate quality. Each cast took the form of a deceased individual's anatomy at a particular moment in his or her growth. At the RCS numerous casts accumulated over time in an extended series, each successful cast acquiring post-mortem life as a model for learning. With blood – which often 'connotes kinship' (Carsten 2013: S7) – replaced by resin these casts became 'kin', sharing the same substance and general form as anatomical trees. This growth of casts contributed to the rejuvenation of museums at the RCS, and in this process Tompsett developed and grew as a skilled professional. In my final section I turn to the relationship between model and practitioner, highlighting aspects of growth in this shifting relationship.

**Pruning: Model as Plant, Prosector as Professional**

In a 1950s photograph Tompsett sits with a corrosion cast of the lungs and heart, holding a tool as he would when 'pruning' these finely worked models (Figure 4.1). Pruning – Tompsett's term for removing the outer parts of the cast so that deeper structures were clearly visible – was a laborious but important task, one with significant material, embodied and metaphorical implications for growing within this process of anatomopoeia. As in the earlier phases of a cast's production, pruning entailed a reciprocal relationship between practitioner and model that worked across distinctions between, and brought about changes in, both.

The cast in Figure 4.1 had already undergone resin injection, maturation and corrosion. According to Tompsett's directions on the injection of fluid resin, it was impossible to prevent resin travelling into the lung's most minute vessels and consequently, he explained, 'extensive pruning is necessary, as the cast of the fine branches obscures the view of the larger structures'. Out-of-control expansion or growth of the cast was thus cut back or pruned when it had hardened: 'twigs' were removed to display larger 'branches' of the tree (1956: 95, 120). This was done with dissecting forceps, slender probes and long, curved ophthalmic scissors (designed for delicate eye surgery).

In some ways, then, Tompsett's practices – including his writings – treated cast anatomical trees as living plants, merging his anatomical and botanical interests. The metaphor of anatomical parts as trees was familiar within anatomical discourse: late fifteenth-century anatomical explorations had described the 'tree of veins', for example (Leonardo da Vinci quoted in Bambach 2003: 408; see also Kusukawa 2012). Some late nineteenth-century scientists researching the nervous system preferred the organic metaphor of trees to the mechanical metaphor of the telegraph network in that it more appropriately conveyed the notion that nerves were not fixed structures but 'grew and changed throughout organisms' lives in response to ongoing activity' (Otis 2010: 574). Charles Darwin had envisaged life itself as a great tree (see O'Malley, Martin and Dupré 2010). Yet trees and pruning in Tompsett's casting practices were not only metaphors for highlighting the tree-like form of anatomical parts, they were also experienced in material and embodied terms.

The vitality of these trees was perhaps most apparent in lung casts, to which Tompsett devoted much time and effort. He explained that casts of dead, collapsed lungs would have 'little or no value' as they would not show the form of the bronchial tree as when alive. Therefore he devised a method for casting lungs in an expanded state: he filled them with warm gelatine solution and immersed them in warm water before injecting resin. Rather than showing the lungs of a 'cadaver', then, these casts were produced as though the body was still able to breathe (1956: 133). Becoming a living tree in this way, the deceased person's second body was valued for its distinctive features. As Tompsett emphasized, 'no part of the human body shows more important anatomical variations than the lung' (1956: 177); knowledge of how branching vessels could vary was needed to guide medical practitioners, especially surgeons, in their treatment of patients. The ritualized production of each cast – its making and growing – maintained the deceased's durable and educationally valuable second body as a particular instance of living anatomy, a tree with perceived potency as a source of knowledge regarding the living human body.

These were labour-intensive models in which practitioners invested themselves: in the casting process a resin anatomical tree became not only a trace of movement through the body of the deceased but also a trace of the interactions between the deceased and the practitioners who cast from that body. Thus the cast – like other products of anatomopoeia such as preserved specimens – incorporated aspects of both the deceased and the practitioners who participated in their post-mortem lives. Materialized as animate trees, casts were manifestations of the persons engaged in their production, and as such they were relational entities of epistemological and emotional import (see Hallam 2010). At the RCS, model production was a collective and collaborative process involving many people, yet it was Tompsett in particular who came to be associated with the corrosion casts discussed here.

This relation of practitioner and cast – in which each bore physical traces of the other – was generated through years of work during which Tompsett gained fluently embodied skills grown from countless hours of concentrated effort. The 1950s photograph (Figure 4.1) is a posed shot of just one stage in Tompsett's casting procedures which were often strenuous and 'messy', as outlined in his *Anatomical Techniques*. The fully embodied nature of the skills he developed, providing practical as well as anatomical knowledge, is evident in his references to the tactile, visual, olfactory and auditory training necessary in his working practices. He investigated and responded to the fumes and changing colours of fluids, the odour of decomposing flesh, the noises of procedures, the feel and temperature of organs undergoing treatment. The aesthetics of this labour were thus keen concerns to Tompsett – he noted what was 'pleasanter' or 'objectionable', for example – as was the enlistment of his own body in the laboratory, at the sink as well as the work bench. In the execution of this work there was an exchange between the body part being cast and Tompsett's own body, as he gained proficiency in casting. This engagement was at times too close for comfort: he applied an industrially manufactured 'barrier cream' to protect the skin of his hands and face from splashes of acid, and sometimes wore 'household' rubber gloves to guard against resin (Tompsett 1956: 107, 112, 118, 119, 179).

Manual dexterity was key in casting, which Tompsett developed especially by using, making and adapting tools. Those pictured in Figure 4.1 (forceps and probes) were suited to removing corroded tissue and to pruning, whilst avoiding damage to the cast. Tompsett's long-term work with these instruments rendered them as extensions of his own hands (Figure 4.4). Concentrated visual work was also required, for which Tompsett wore magnifying spectacles to enhance focus and precision. These reduced the 'risk of eye strain', he advised, and 'delay[ed] the onset of fatigue' arising from lengthy periods of work. Fatigue, Tompsett warned, along with impatience, are the 'greatest enemies' of the practitioner: stop working, he instructed in *Anatomical Techniques*, as soon as 'symptoms' of these conditions are recognized. Otherwise months of work could be wasted in half an hour of 'careless or hurried' activity that might cause damage either to the cast, or to the practitioner who was at risk, for example, when bits of cut-off twig fly into the eye (1956: 34, 36).

It was pruning, sometimes taking two weeks per cast, which appeared to push Tompsett to the limits of his patience. The latter quality he defined as 'a form of self-discipline' that was not easy for him to acquire, given his impatient 'temperament'. Delicate, sustained pruning required him, therefore, to work against what he saw as his own tendencies, thereby disciplining himself.

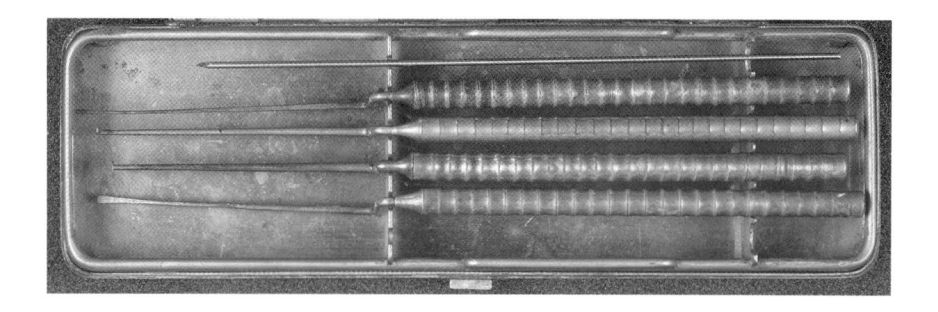

**Figure 4.4** Tools used by David Tompsett. Hunterian Museum at the Royal College of Surgeons of England

This seemed particularly difficult given that, from his point of view, symptoms of impatience and tiredness were hard to self-diagnose: although they were 'at once apparent to an experienced spectator', who could see the 'increasing violence with which the work is being tackled', he wrote, the practitioner 'himself is not always immediately aware when the time has come to take a rest'. By working through the difficulties posed by pruning, then, Tompsett learnt about himself, especially his 'feeling of impatience' and the 'strong desire' it created to persist with tasks, even when ill advised to do so (1956: vi, 121, 36). The cultivation of models cast as trees involved Tompsett's own development in terms of both skills and reflexive self-awareness: pruning was, at times, an inadvertently aggressive and fraught attempt to control anatomical trees' growth and a working out of Tompsett's own internal emotional tensions.

Growth as bodily and subjective enskilment in this context shaped the practitioner's sense self as he developed his expertise; Tompsett's techniques produced casts while also constituting aspects of his self-knowledge.[4] This growth intersected with that of his socially recognized identity and status as a successful professional prosector. His *Anatomical Techniques* was taken up, and found productive, in many medical schools throughout Britain – as David Sinclair (1971), professor of anatomy at the University of Aberdeen in north-east Scotland, for instance, confirmed. Practitioners adopted and disseminated his corrosion casting methods which became known as 'Tompsett's technique' (Edwards and Edwards 1959: 130). Medical visitors to the RCS museums viewed the 'beautiful and instructive' products of Tompsett's work, appreciating their 'effectiveness' in facilitating anatomical understanding of the vital organs (Anon. 1957a: 35, Anon. 1957b: 209). While acting as models of human anatomy, then, these casts were closely associated with Tompsett by his community of practitioners; it was through such casts that his professional standing was publically augmented.

---

[4] On the historically and culturally specific constitution of the self in scientific practices see Daston and Galison (2007), especially 191–251, 357–61.

This relation between model and practitioner was one of close identification based on the latter's care for, nurturance and cultivation of the former. In this respect, these models, through a ritualized process of anatomopoeia, became Tompsett's 'kin'. As resin replaced blood, the deceased's blood ties were displaced by the relations involved in institutionally based anatomical casting for medical teaching and learning.

## Conclusions: Life Writing and Rebirth

*Anatomical Techniques*, reviewed as a 'notable addition to the literature of craftsmanship', was in practice a work-in-progress – Tompsett referred to the 1956 edition as his 'interim report', published when he was about 46, and the second edition as his 'final report' at 60 (1970: vii).[5] This practical manual offered instructions on how to manipulate the working life of resin so that the deceased's second body could emerge as an effective, educational (and therefore health- and life-enhancing) model. Developing from interim to final report, *Anatomical Techniques* also documented aspects of Tompsett's own working life – his 'reports' were a form of life-writing even though far from intentional autobiography. The 1970 rewriting of his 1956 edition thus incorporated changes arising from developments in his practice.

Notable among these was his corrosion casting of blood vessels in stillborn babies, including arterial casts of whole bodies not practically possible in the much larger bodies of deceased adults (Figure 4.5). Here each baby's second body entered post-mortem life as an 'arterial tree' for anatomical study. Alive almost until born, these deceased babies were cast to enhance educational displays at the RCS, the development of which was central to the post-war museum rebirth at this institution. Vivid red resin flowed into even the finest of vessels, as the newborn's blood would have continued to do had he or she survived. In this plastic form such anatomical trees were initiated into a second life seemingly without end, they were intended to 'last indefinitely without deterioration' (Tompsett 1970: 94).

Just as medical practitioners sought to grow the 'tree of knowledge', so Tompsett and his colleagues participated in a process of anatomopoeia, as interrelated making and growing, which was both metaphorical and material. Deceased persons obtained for anatomical purposes became trees for generating and communicating knowledge of living anatomy, through modifications that relied on skilled attempts to manage decay as well as growth. These trees were models enmeshed in relations of 'kin' among materials, casts and practitioners; they materialized not only human anatomy but also connections between generations of experts – tree imagery having strong recognition as a means of visualizing relatedness (Bouquet 1996). Resin trees manifested relations and tradition through improvisation,

---

5  Tompsett's 'final report' was also provisional in that he continued to cast and publish journal articles on his techniques into the 1970s.

Cast of arteries of a still-born baby.

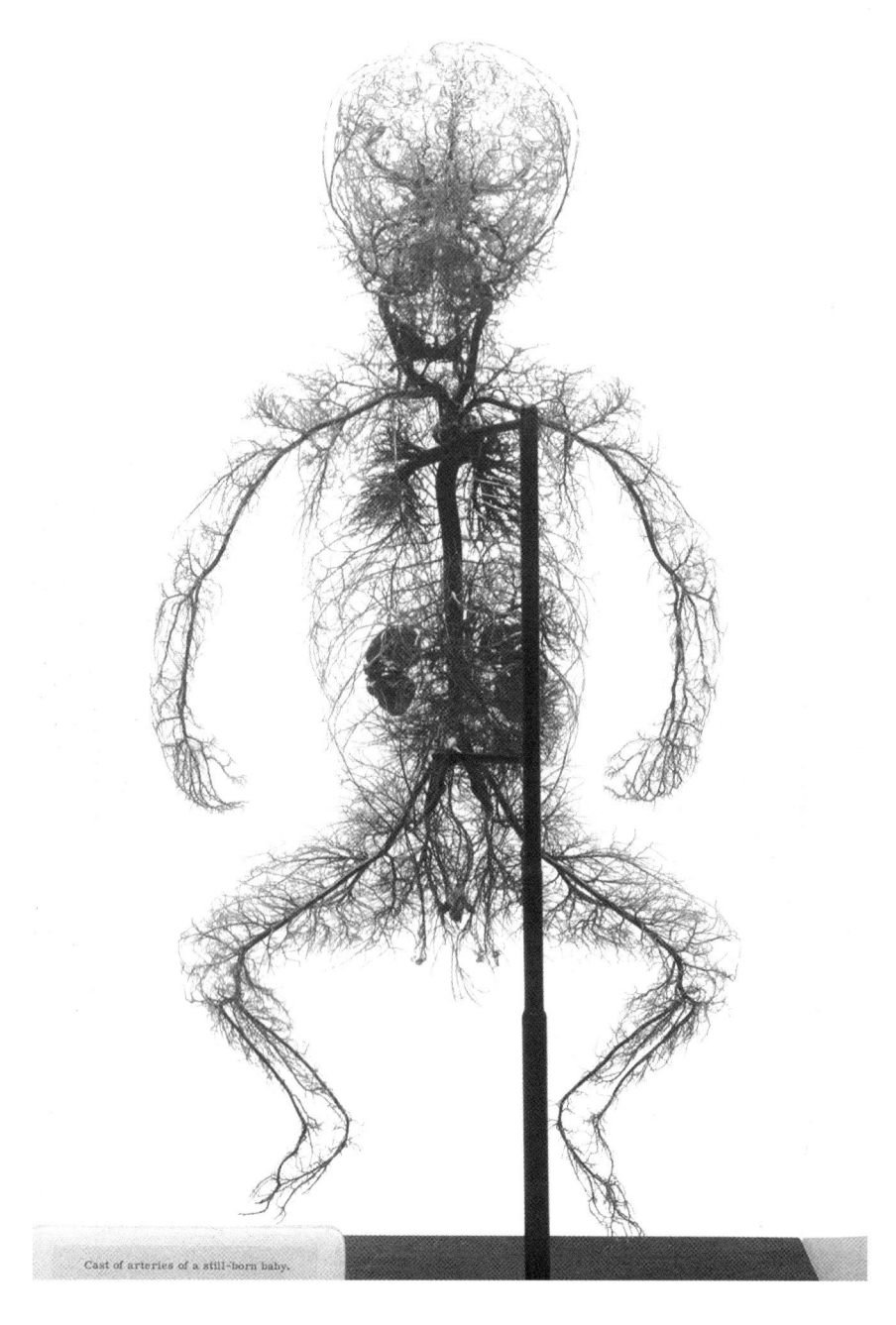

**Figure 4.5** Corrosion cast of the arteries of a child at birth, 1962. Hunterian Museum at the Royal College of Surgeons of England

and what were seen as pioneering methods and new substances. As both artefacts and organisms these anatomical trees, cultivated and crafted at the RCS for museum display, received Tompsett's energy and dedication, flourishing as did his skills and knowledge, enduring over time even as he aged, grew tired and left them behind.

**Acknowledgements**

Many thanks to Sam Alberti, Martyn Cooke, Milly Farrell and Kristin Hussey at the Royal College of Surgeons of England for their generous help with this research. I am also very grateful to Simon Chaplin who first alerted me to Tompsett's casts.

**References**

Alberti, S.J.M.M. forthcoming. Anatomical craft: A history of medical museum practice, in *The Fate of Anatomical Collections*, edited by R. Knoeff and R. Zwijnenberg. Farnham: Ashgate.

Anon. 1940. Battle-scarred London, *The British Medical Journal*, 2(4167), 678.

Anon. 1942a. Economy in the museum. *The Lancet*, 239(6183), 267.

Anon. 1942b. The Museum of the Royal College of Surgeons, London: dispersal of collections after air-raid damage. *The Museums Journal*, 41(12), 287–8.

Anon. 1945. Future of the medical museum. *The Lancet*, 245(6343), 376–7.

Anon. 1951. Plastics in medicine. *British Medical Journal*, 2(4722), 46–7.

Anon. 1957a. Review of *Anatomical Techniques* by D.H. Tompsett. *Postgraduate Medical Journal*, 33(375), 35.

Anon. 1957b. Review of *Anatomical Techniques* by D.H. Tompsett. *Proceedings of the Royal Society of Medicine*, 50(3), 209.

Anon. 1962. Twenty-five years' service at the College: Sidney Charles Bartlett, Charles George Bush, Edward John Noon. *Annals of the Royal College of Surgeons of England*, 30(3), 205–6.

Bambach, C.C. (ed.) 2003. *Leonardo da Vinci, Master Draftsman*. New Haven: Yale University Press.

Barthes, R. 1973 [1957]. Plastic, in *Mythologies*, translated by Annette Lavers, London: Granada, 97–9.

Bono, J.J. 2010. Making knowledge: history, literature and the poetics of science. *Isis*, 101(3), 555–9.

Brown, D. 1957. Review of *Anatomical Techniques* by D.H. Tompsett. *British Medical Journal*, 1(5020), 689.

Brown, D. 1971. Review of *Anatomical Techniques*, 2nd Edition, by D.H. Tompsett. *British Medical Journal*, 1(5746), 467.

Bouquet, M. 1996. Family trees and their affinities: the visual imperative of the genealogical diagram. *Journal of the Royal Anthropological Institute*, 2(1), 43–66.

Buzzard, E.F. 1942. Reconstruction in the practice of medicine. *The Lancet*, 239(6186), 343–7.

Carsten, J. 2013. Introduction: blood will out. *Journal of the Royal Anthropological Institute*, S1-S23.

Chaplin, S. 2009. *John Hunter and the 'Museum Oeconomy', 1750–1800*. PhD thesis, King's College London.

Conekin, B.E. 2003. *The Autobiography of a Nation: The 1951 Festival of Britain*. Manchester: Manchester University Press.

de Chadarevian, S. 2002. *Designs for Life: Molecular Biology after World War II*. Cambridge: Cambridge University Press.

Daston, L. and Galison, P. 2007. *Objectivity*. New York: Zone Books.

Degnen, C. 2009. On vegetable love: gardening, plants, and people in the north of England. *Journal of the Royal Anthropological Institute*, 15(1), 151–67.

Dezeuze, A. (2010) 'Open work', 'do-it-yourself' artwork and *bricolage*, in *The 'Do-It-Yourself' Artwork: Participation from Fluxus to New Media*, edited by A. Dezeuze. Manchester: Manchester University Press, 47–68.

Dobson, J. 1956. Historical introduction, in *Anatomical Techniques*, by D.H. Tompsett, London: E & S Livingstone Ltd, ix–xiv.

Dunglison, R. 1868. *Medical Lexicon: A Dictionary of Medical Science*. Philadelphia, PA: Henry C. Lea.

Edwards, J.J. and M.J. Edwards 1959. *Medical Museum Technology*. London: Oxford University Press.

Farquhar, J. and M. Lock 2007. Introduction, in *Beyond the Body Proper: Reading the Anthropology of Material Life*, edited by M. Lock and J. Farquhar. Durham, NC: Duke University Press, 1–16.

Fisher, T. 2013. A world of colour and bright shining surfaces: experiences of plastics after the Second World War. *Journal of Design History*, Advance Access published 18 March, doi: 10.1093/jdh/ept012.

Fitzgerald, M.J.T. et al. 1979. Purpose-made models in anatomical teaching. *Journal of Visual Commination in Medicine*, 2, 71–3.

Golinski, J. 2005 [1998]. *Making Natural Knowledge: Constructivism and the history of science*. Chicago: University of Chicago Press.

Good, B. 1994. *Medicine, Rationality and Experience: An Anthropological Perspective*. Cambridge: Cambridge University Press.

Goodman, N.M. 1944. The supply of bodies for dissection: a historical review. *British Medical Journal*, 2(4381), 807–11.

Hallam, E. 2007. Anatomical bodies and materials of memory', in *Death Rites and Rights*, edited by B. Brooks-Gordon et al. Oxford: Hart Publishing, 279–98.

Hallam, E. 2010. Articulating bones: an epilogue. *Journal of Material Culture*, 15(4), 465–92.

Hallam, E. 2013. Anatomical design: making and using three-dimensional models of the human body, in *Design Anthropology: Theory and Practice*, edited by W. Gunn, T. Otto and R.C. Smith. London: Berg, 100–116.
Hallam, E. forthcoming. *Anatomy Museum: Death and the Body Displayed.* London: Reaktion Books.
Hallam, E. and Alberti, S.J.M.M. 2013. Bodies in museums, in *Medical Museums: Past, Present, Future*, edited by S.J.M.M. Alberti and E. Hallam. London: The Royal College of Surgeons of England, 1–16.
Hallam, E. and Hockey, J. 2001. *Death, Memory and Material Culture*. Oxford: Berg.
Hamlyn, L.H. and Thilesen, P. 1953. Models in medical teaching with a note on the use of a new plastic. *The Lancet*, 262(6784), 472–5.
Keith, A. 1950. *An Autobiography*. London: Watts and Co.
Küchler, S. 2010. Materials and design, in *Design Anthropology: Object Culture in the 21st Century*, edited by A. Clarke. Vienna: Springer, 130–42.
Kuriyama, S. 2002. *The Expressiveness of the Body and the Divergence of Greek and Chinese Medicine*. New York: Zone Books.
Kusukawa, S. 2012. *Picturing the Book of Nature: Image, Text and Argument in Sixteenth-Century Human Anatomy and Medical Botany*. Chicago: University of Chicago Press.
Lawrence, C. and S. Shapin (eds) 1998. *Science Incarnate: Historical Embodiments of Natural Knowledge*. Chicago: University of Chicago Press.
Lewis, O.J. 1971. Review of *Anatomical Techniques*, 2nd Edition, by D. H. Tompsett, 1970. *Proceedings of the Royal Society of Medicine*, 64(5), 586.
Lock, M. and Nguyen, V. 2010. *An Anthropology of Biomedicine*, Chichester: Wiley-Blackwell.
Lockhart, R.D. 1960 [1948]. *Living Anatomy: A Photographic Atlas of Muscles in Action and Surface Contours*. London: Faber and Faber.
Marchand, T. (ed.) 2010. Making Knowledge, *Journal of the Royal Anthropological Institute*, 16, Siii–v, S1–S202.
Mossman, S. 2008. *Fantastic Plastic: Product Design and Consumer Culture*. London: Black Dog Publishing.
O'Malley, M.A., W. Martin, and J. Dupré 2010. The tree of life: introduction to an evolutionary debate. *Biology and Philosophy*, 25(4), 441–53.
Otis, L. 2010. Science surveys and histories of literature: reflections on an uneasy kinship. *Isis*, 101(3), 570–77.
Prentice, R. 2013. *Bodies in Formation. An Ethnography of Anatomy and Surgery Education*. Durham: Duke University Press.
Quirke, V. and Gaudillière, J-P. 2008. The era of biomedicine: science, medicine, and public health in Britain and France after the Second World War. *Medical History*, 52(4), 441–52.
Richardson, R. 2001. *Death, Dissection and the Destitute*. 2nd Edition. London: Phoenix.

Royal College of Physicians of London. 1944. *Planning Committee Report on Medical Education*. London: Harrison and Sons Ltd.

Scott Bader. n.d. *The History of a Future: Scott Bader Company, founded 1921*. Web pamphlet, www.scottbader.com. Accessed May 2013.

Seremetakis, C.N. 1991. *The Last Word: Women, Death and Divination in Inner Mani*. Chicago: University of Chicago Press.

Sinclair, D. 1971. Review of *Anatomical Techniques*, 2nd Edition, by D. H. Tompsett, 1970. *Journal of Anatomy*, 109(1), 182–3.

Smith, P.H. 2012. Workshop of history: making, writing, and meaning. *West 86th: A Journal of Decorative Arts, Design History, and Material Culture*, 19(1), 4–31.

Stewart, J. 2008. The political economy of the British National Health Service, 1945–1975: opportunities and constraints? *Medical History*, 52(4), 453–70.

Tansey, E.M. 2008. Keeping the culture alive: the laboratory technician in mid-twentieth century British medical research. *Notes and Records of the Royal Society*, 62(1), 77–95.

Tompsett, D.H. 1952. A new method for the preparation of bronchopulmonary casts. *Thorax*, 7(1), 78–88.

Tompsett, D.H. 1954. A method of making a cast in synthetic resin of the bronchial arteries. *Thorax*, 9(3), 229–32.

Tompsett, D.H. 1956. *Anatomical Techniques*. Edinburgh: E&S Livingstone, Ltd.

Tompsett, D.H. 1970. *Anatomical Techniques*. 2nd Edition, Edinburgh: E&S Livingstone, Ltd.

Tompsett, D.H. and S.C. Bartlett 1961. Improvements and additions to anatomical techniques: I. Mounting of specimens. *Annals of the Royal College of Surgeons of England*, 28(3), 189–94.

Turner, G.G. 1945. The Hunterian Museum: yesterday and tomorrow. *British Medical Journal*, 1(4390), 247–50.

Wakeley, C. 1956. Foreword, in *Anatomical Techniques*, by D.H. Tompsett. Edinburgh: London, v.

Wakeley, C. 1965. The Hunterian Museum today. *Annals of the Royal College of Surgeons of England*, 37(6), 329–45.

Wenger, E. 1998. *Communities of Practice: Learning, Meaning and Identity*, Cambridge: Cambridge University Press.

Chapter 5
# Artefacts and Bodies among Kuna People from Panamá

Paolo Fortis

This chapter focuses on the interrelations between the making of objects and the making of bodies among Kuna people in contemporary Panama. In doing so it builds on current debates on Amerindian notions of materiality and on the growing field in anthropology that deals with the study of native ontologies through a focus on material culture (Henare, Holbraad and Wastell 2007). As noted by Hugh-Jones (2009), Amerindian anthropology has only recently begun to contribute to discussions on the status of objects and material culture, since previous studies conducted in this region gave greater emphasis to the role of animals and plants in native ontologies. Recent works have nonetheless shown the richness of Amerindian thinking about artefacts, the place of objects in indigenous socio-cosmologies and their role in processes of creating human persons (Lagrou 2007, Barcelos Neto 2008, Santos-Granero 2009). In this chapter I analyze the making of particular objects among Kuna people and argue that this activity is best understood analogically as a process of making and growing human bodies. As the ethnographic and comparative material presented below shows, some Amerindian peoples do not distinguish between organisms and artefacts when they talk about bodies and material objects. What they instead emphasize are the capacities entailed in the making of artefacts and babies, the fertility that enables men and women to make both, and the qualities that the objects made transmit to human beings.

Alfred Gell's seminal work (1998) has stimulated anthropological analysis of artworks, their production and perception, and their place within peoples' worldviews. By considering objects *as* persons we de-objectify them, and by de-objectifying objects we gain better insights into their makers' ontology. For instance, in recent years scholars of Melanesia have explored the relations between persons and objects, highlighting native ideas of personhood by looking at the making, exchange and ritual use of specific objects (Battaglia 1983, Munn 1986). The main point that these scholars make is that objects are the analogical counterparts of persons. In this sense objects embody and propagate specific aspects of persons and, by the same token, enhance personhood and extend relations. Melanesian objects, therefore, comprise various elements, each refracting a specific relation, or an 'image of personhood – corporate or individual' (Battaglia 1983: 301). For instance, the external form of Gawan canoes (see Munn 1986: 138–47), produced by men, evokes the facial appearance of children, given by their fathers, in contrast to their bodily substance, given by their mothers. Men in Gawa acquire the capacity to give form from women, who provide them with the raw material to shape: blood in the case of foetuses, and red wood in the case of the hull of canoes (ibid.: 138). Form in this case is dependent on gendered substances.

Strathern explores ideas of personhood in relation to objects through her cross-cultural discussion of Melanesian ethnography (2004 [1991]: 63–76). Objects, she argues, are not just 'extensions integral to the relationships a person makes, and "instruments" in that sense'. Rather, 'the physical body is apprehended as composed of those instruments as it is composed of relationships' (ibid.: 76). Her argument provides an interesting counterpoint for my analysis here. While Strathern shows that some Melanesians consider the role of bodily *substances* to be crucial for body formation and making artefacts such as canoes (see Munn 1986: 138–47), Kuna people seem to concern themselves principally with *form* when thinking of bodies and artefacts. The difference of emphasis respectively on *substance* and *form* appears to be the main distinction between the ways in which the formation of bodies and persons and, by extension, the making and conceptualization of artefacts, are understood in these two regions of the world. For the Kuna, where both men and women are able to give form respectively to foetuses and to artefacts, what is at stake is the acquisition and mastering of plastic skill by Kuna men and of the capacity to create designs by Kuna women.

Santos-Granero argues that 'in Amerindian ontologies, it is craftsmanship rather than childbearing that provides the model for all creative acts' (2009: 8). However, Kuna ethnography shows that both childbearing and craftsmanship are processes that entail the manipulation of form. In this chapter I shall demonstrate that it is rather the making and growing of bodies that provides a model for material activities of giving form to objects. Kuna people use an idiom of birth to describe artefactual activities. In this sense, giving form is no more a way of *making* than a way of *growing*. Giving form is a process that entails the fertile capacities of persons. Fertility, for Kuna people, is a social praxis acquired by human beings through the mastering of non-human qualities, such as the predatory skills of particular animals and the blood strengthening property of some plant medicines (Fortis 2010). These qualities need to be channelled through shamanic practices in order to become productive for human sociality. Thus, giving form is to be understood as a social praxis emerging from the transformation of men's and women's bodily capacities. This transformation is itself the outcome of the interaction between different persons and between persons and the environing world. Moreover, far from being conceived only as the product of the creative human mind, form is better apprehended as a state of being within a network of relationships, including human beings, objects, animals and trees.

Ingold (2000) points out that the modern western distinction between *making* and *growing*, which rests on human transcendence and objectification of nature, carries the implication that the human capacity to make extends to the relations between people and living things. This allows human actions such as cultivation and animal breeding to be considered as forms of making, thereby extending the idea of making from inanimate to animate beings. Ingold further suggests that we can conversely extend the idea of growing from animate beings to artefacts, since people and materials are mutually involved in the growing of forms within a specific environment (2000: 347). Kuna people and other Amerindians understand human reproductive capacities as a form of *growing* that is akin to *making* (Viveiros de Castro 1979, Vilaça 2002); Cashinahua people say that bodies are 'made to grow' (Mc Callum 1996: 348). In what follows I argue, therefore, that artefacts, as bodies, are *grown* in this context as much as, or perhaps even more than, they are *made*.

## Amerindian Theories of Materiality

As described in myths currently told by different peoples across the Lowlands of Central and South America, objects used in everyday life were people in ancient times (Lévi-Strauss 1969, Viveiros de Castro 1977, Barcelos Neto 2008). These objects, along with animal and plant species, underwent processes of transformation and separation, thereby losing their appearance as persons. Thus it is not surprising that when nowadays indigenous people talk about the making of specific objects in their daily life they use idioms of birth and growth, and emphasize the human fertile capacities entailed in their production (Overing 1989, Fortis 2012a, 2012b).

People and objects are involved in constant flows of exchange whereby each party transmits qualities to the other. Some objects acquire their own independent subjectivity in relation to human beings and are imbued with human qualities, while human beings are strengthened, healed and made to grow by way of specific objects and bodily decorations, as in the carved wooden stools and body paintings used among the Cashinahua (Lagrou 2007). The ultimate goal of making objects seems always to be that of contributing to the creation and maintenance of healthy human bodies.

Taylor and Viveiros de Castro (2006) insightfully argue that Amazonian peoples, instead of creating what in the West is defined as 'figurative art', dedicate all their creative energies to the creation of human bodies. The real 'work of art' for Amazonians, they say, is the human body. The creation of bodies is indeed a long-standing topic in Amerindian ethnography. Many studies have focused on bodily decorations and the ways in which bodies are socialized and humanized through the use of decorations, painting and body marks (Seeger 1975, Turner 1995, Gow 1999, Lagrou 2007). More recently Ewart and O'Hanlon (2007) have brought the topic of body art into dialogue with notions of Amerindian perspectivism. These authors show how body decorations and clothing allow for specific bodily capacities to be activated and enable people to move within different social contexts. Santos-Granero, who addresses the interface between Amazonian notions of personhood and materiality, proposes the notion of 'constructional ontologies', arguing that many Amazonians conceive 'all living beings as composite entities, made up of the bodies and parts of bodies of a diversity of life forms, among which artefacts occupy a prominent place' (2009: 21).

Despite the analysis of notions of materiality among Amerindians the question of what counts as an object in native ontologies needs further ethnographic and comparative study. Here I draw on Taylor and Viveiros de Castro's point that the body is the real 'work of art' for Amerindians, to argue that for Kuna people making bodies is the prototype of making more generally. Next I consider a specific instance of Kuna woodcarving and its relation to the creation of bodies, which was made explicit to me by my Kuna informants in 2004. By focusing on this example as an instance of a more general model of making artefacts, I suggest a path for interpreting the analogy between making artefacts and making bodies in other Amerindian societies. I then compare Kuna ethnography with that of the Cashinahua living in the Acre state (Brazil) on the relation between making bodies and making artefacts, focusing on some key categories of Kuna aesthetic epistemology, namely, 'images', 'designs' and 'bodies' (Fortis 2012a).

**Kuna Woodcarving**

Kuna people use the verb *sopet* to indicate activities involving carving wooden objects such as dug-out canoes, building houses, weaving baskets, moulding clay and fermenting maize and sugar cane drink. The same verb is also used with reference to gestation, indicating the moulding of the foetus's body in the mother's womb. This last process is termed *koe sopet*, 'forming the baby'. Making objects and making bodies are thus thought of as similar processes by Kuna people. To better appreciate their understandings of such activities as carving a canoe, weaving a basket or carving wooden ritual figures, it is necessary to consider what Kuna people conceive of as 'form' (*sopalet*), and how forms are thought to be brought into being through different but interconnected processes that involve the complementary and coordinated actions of women and men.

Carved wooden figures, called *nuchukana* in Kuna language (singular *nuchu*), are small anthropomorphic figures between 20 and 30 cm tall, representing male and female persons. Sometimes these figures are carved to look like missionaries or soldiers, although mostly they appear as rough, generic figures of persons in an upright position. They all tend to have long, thin and prominent noses, and either a hat for male figures, or a headscarf for female figures. *Nuchukana* are kept in varying numbers in every Kuna household, and are assigned the role of protecting family members against illness and misfortune. Kuna people consider carving *nuchukana* the highest form of woodcarving, more difficult than carving a dug-out canoe, because it entails the creation of a new person that will be incorporated at home as a co-resident (Figure 5.1).

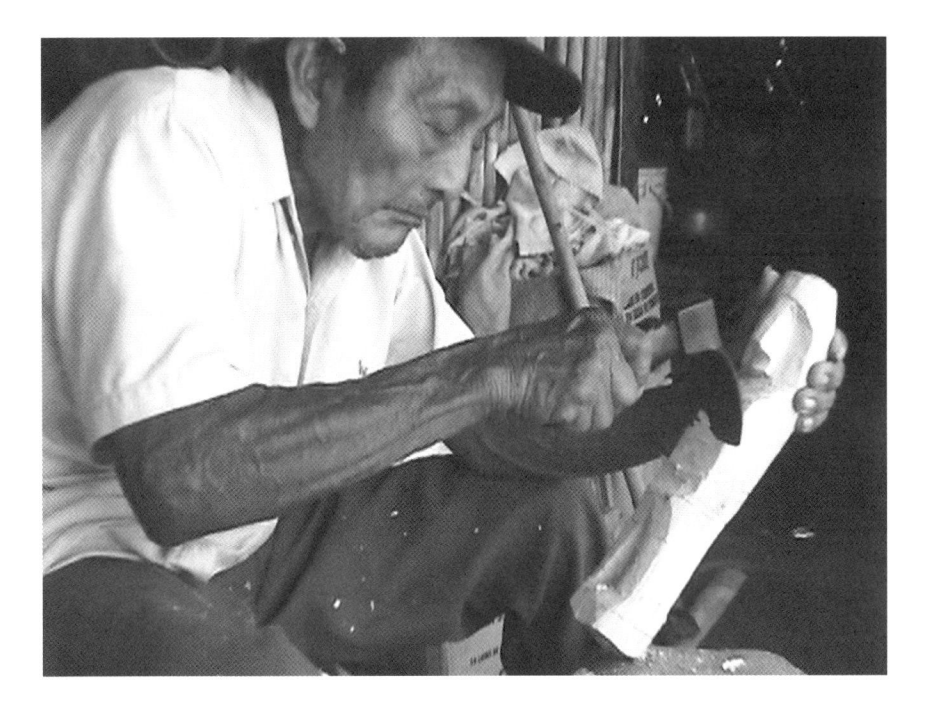

**Figure 5.1** Leopoldo Smith carving a female *nuchu*, 2004. Still from a video by Paolo Fortis

When an elder man goes to the mainland forest with the intention of making a *nuchu* he first finds an appropriate tree. Imposing emergent trees are mostly found deep inland, far from the coast, and reaching them requires a long walk in the forest. Once the appropriate type of tree, chosen from a restricted number of species used in woodcarving, has been found, the man sings a brief formula aimed at advising it that he is about to cut a part of its body. Normally the man would cut a small portion of a root and immediately make a small mark on one of its extremities with his machete. As Garibaldo del Vasto, a Kuna medicine man in his 60s, once explained to me while cutting part of a root of an incredibly tall and stout almendro (*Dipteryx panamensis*), the little incision is a reminder for later when, at home, he will start carving a stick from the portion of root. The mark will remind him where to carve the nose of the *nuchu*, starting from which he will then proceed to carve the rest of the figure. The nose is carved in the lower part of the stick, which was closer to the earth and facing eastward when still attached to the tree, that is, in the direction of the rising sun and where the souls of the dead reside (see Fortis 2012b). The position of the nose has to be remembered because, as Garibaldo and other Kuna men explained to me, *nuchukana* are born in the same way as human babies are, with the head positioned downwards.

The process of carving is normally completed without ceremony during spare time spent on the house patio where everyday activities are carried out by other members of the household. The last touches include inserting glass beads into small holes, for eyes, and painting the cheeks with red annatto (derived from the fruit of the achiote tree, *Bixa orellana*). Once the *nuchu* is carved it is the task of a ritual chanter, usually a different person from the carver, to sing it to life. The *nuchu* will then be given to the persons who requested the carver for it and incorporated into their household along with other pre-existing *nuchukana*. From that moment onwards it will start its life as a particular type of co-resident along with human beings.

## Co-residents

Almost every Kuna household keeps a box with several *nuchukana* in it. I have rarely seen boxes containing less than five or six figures, the usual number being between 10 and 20. These boxes are kept at the foot of one of the two wooden poles that support houses. It was my curiosity and insistence that brought Kuna men and women to pick up one particular *nuchu* to show it to me or to move the entire box outside the house so that I could better see the figures in it. Although people did not usually talk about *nuchukana*, when I asked about them they were adamant about one thing: *nuchukana* are 'persons' (*tulekana*) and need to be treated with respect, to be remembered. Kuna people explained to me that these figures are powerful 'seers' (*nelekana*), who can see and travel in the different layers of the cosmos, interact with different kinds of human and non-human beings and harm those who treat them badly. I also noticed that children never played with them or, indeed, dared to touch them. However some children were given, by their grandfather, wooden dolls to play with, which to my eyes closely resembled *nuchukana* (Figure 5.2).

Kuna people remember their wooden protector friends during daily life. To 'remember' (*epinsaet*) someone is an expression of love for one's kinspeople or of close amity towards one's friends. Kuna people remember their kin who live in other households by regularly sending them food. They remember the kin who have moved to Panama City or other destinations, and whom they have not seen for a long time, referring to them by name during daily activities. Acts of remembering are key to the everyday maintenance of kinship in the Kuna lived world, and food exchange is the main vehicle for creating and maintaining kinship relations (Margiotti 2010). Similarly, household members nurture their *nuchukana*. Adult men call them when they eat their daily meal, so that they can satisfy their hunger through the smell of food. Elder women, who enjoy smoking pipes or cigarettes at night-time, often puff tobacco smoke over the wooden figures, which provides them with refreshing unfermented 'maize drink' (*inna*). Young and pre-pubescent girls wash *nuchukana* every once in a while, bathing them in water perfumed with sweet basil leaves, the same bathing practice used by medicine men before going

**Figure 5.2** *Nuchukana*, 2004. Photograph by Paolo Fortis

to the forest to gather plant medicines. These are the ways in which Kuna people remember their powerful wooden friends and make sure that the latter remember them when illness and misfortune afflict a member of the household.

## Body and Form

The creation of new human bodies is paramount for most Amerindians and takes up much, if not most, individual and collective energies. Before further exploring Kuna ideas of 'form' or 'figure' (*sopalet*) in relation to the creation of bodies, I want to consider the connections between artefactual activities and bodily processes by presenting data from the ethnography of Cashinahua people, which points to similar analogies between making artefacts and making persons. In particular, I am interested in the relation between designs, images and the creation of bodies, which is key to Cashinahua ontology, as Els Lagrou suggests (2007: 108–37). This relationship is highly significant in Amerindian material and visual worlds, as becomes apparent with the comparative examination of specific features of Amerindian aesthetics.

Cecilia McCallum has argued that for the Cashinahua, 'making artefacts' and 'making babies' are similar activities. The verb, *dami va-*, meaning 'to transform', 'to make an image', is used to indicate the process of forming a foetus in the mother's womb through sexual intercourse; the noun *dami* denotes a 'drawing' or a 'doll' (McCallum 2001: 17). This has two main implications. The first is that the creation of human bodies is conceived as an active process of fabrication. The second relates to the status of artefacts as persons, endowed with agency and key in mediating relationships between human beings, animals and spirits (see Lagrou 1998). The creation of artefacts such as stools, woven hammocks and designs, either painted on bodies or woven, entails the skill and embodied knowledge of women and men. In particular, women master the creation of 'designs' (*kene*), while men learn to control hallucinogenic 'images' (*dami*).

As Cashinahua current myths explain, human beings learned to make designs in ancient time thanks to the encounter between a young woman and, depending on the version of the myth, either an old lady, or a young lover. Both the old lady and the young boy are incarnations of Boa, the mythical being and owner of all designs, which are visible on its skin. Designs on the boa's skin are in turn the origin of any kind of form, since the spots on the snake's skin, in the words of a Cashinahua man, 'open themselves and show a door to enter into new forms' (Lagrou 2009: 205). Designs, in Cashinahua exegesis, have therefore prior existence to images and forms. Designs originate forms. This is an important point to which I return below.

Another instance of this way of thinking, which sees designs as the precondition of form, is the link between the skin of the anaconda and women's menstruation. *Yube*, the mythological anaconda – which has all kinds of designs on its skin – is considered immortal because it sheds its skin. Women, Cashinahua people say, shed their internal skin during menstruation. Furthermore, the uterus is called *xankin*, which, as Lagrou notes, provides the root for the verb *xankeikiki*, meaning 'to weave designs' (2007: 113). Further, the uterus is thought of, by the Cashinahua, as a designed skin that filters communication between its inside, where the body of the foetus is being shaped, and the outside world beyond the mother's body.

The association between the skin of the anaconda and the 'internal skin' of women can be taken a step further. The designs on the skin of the mythical serpent open up, giving access to new forms (Lagrou 2009). Designs thus generate forms. When men and women look at the spots on the boa's skin in visions experienced during the ceremonial killing of this animal, they can enter into another world populated by images of persons, called *dami* (meaning 'images' or 'transformations)'. This is also reminiscent of Peter Gow's description of Piro people's *ayahuasca* visions (1989). When people ingest *ayahuasca*, a vine, their hallucinations begin with geometric patterns covering their visual field. Once they overcome this first stage, if they are able to cope with the intense fear caused by the visions, they will encounter the mother of *ayahuasca* in the appearance of a beautiful woman. But what the skin of the anaconda is also about for the Cashinahua is its shedding, a capacity that makes the snake immortal. The immortality of the mythical anaconda is connected with the infinite proliferation of forms that emerge from the designs on its skin.

With regard to the association between snake's skin and the uterus, for Cashinahua, it must be noted that the latter is seen as the container wherein new human forms are shaped. The womb epitomizes women's capacity to create new forms. Like the skin of the anaconda, women's internal skin can be shed, thus maintaining its powerful generative capacity. If shedding the skin gives the anaconda immortality, shedding the internal skin gives women the capacity to perpetuate human life, which is another form of immortality. Yet for Cashinahua there is an important difference between the creation of forms emerging from the designs on the snake's skin and the creation of bodies in women's wombs. As McCallum (2001: 52) notes, there is an association between procreating and cooking. Hence pots are analogous to wombs. Human bodies are made through a process similar to cooking food, *bava-* in Cashinahua, whereby female blood and male semen are mixed together to form the substance of a new body, which is cooked in the mother's womb. In addition to the process of 'cooking', bodies have to be made heavy in order to be made to grow and be healthy. This is achieved through naming, the feeding of proper food and other ritual actions (Lagrou 2007: 413–530).

**Body and Design**

Thus we can observe a series of connections between designs, skin (internal or external) and the creation of new forms and bodies. The idea that designs participate in the generation of forms and bodies is reinforced by a common feature of Cashinahua and Kuna ontologies, namely, that human bodies come to acquire their shape within a container covered in designs: the uterus. Kuna people describe the 'amniotic sac' (*kurkin*, which also means 'hat', 'brain' and 'intelligence') as constituted by several layers of tissue covered with geometric designs, which are drawn by non-human celestial entities referred to as 'grandmothers' (*muukana*). These designs are sometimes visible after birth on the remains of the amniotic sac covering the head of some newborns and are attentively scrutinized by Kuna midwives, the main interpreters of amniotic designs. Those babies who are born showing amniotic designs are considered destined to be particularly intelligent and skilled in socially valued activities, such as making clothes, carving canoes, and learning healing chants, botanic medicine and foreign languages.

The presence of designs at birth provides a powerful means to enhance the future capacities of the person-to-be. Amniotic designs are the visible sign of the animal side of newborns, and indeed of the common humanity of animals and humans. By showing the link with a particular predatory species, each amniotic design represents both a danger and a gift. In its initial state the design is the visible manifestation of an illness caused by the animal. However, if properly treated with plant medicines, for newborns with amniotic designs the dangerous consubstantiality with animals can be turned into much prized human praxes when they grow into adult persons (Fortis 2010: 488–9). Thus animals for Kuna people are both a cause of illness and death, and the source of knowledge. However, cutting this initial link to animals, manifested in amniotic designs, is a precondition for the fabrication of human bodies. Amniotic designs are a means to form human bodies, insofar as they provide a guide for adult people to choose the best medicine to ensure that their young kin lose those animal habits that they might have acquired in their pre-natal life, and to strengthen the bodies of those kin.

**From Body to Artefacts**

Amniotic designs signal a further overlap between the creation of bodies and that of artefacts. Kuna people regard the amniotic sac (*kurkin*) as the first clothing of babies (see Gow 1999: 236), and described it to me as several layers of tissue that contain the foetus in the mother's womb. *Kurkin*, as noted above, also means 'hat', and this refers to both the hat that men wear in everyday life and that which some babies are born with, in the form of layers of amniotic membrane. After birth, amniotic designs turn into bodily capacities that, if properly mastered and channelled, when adult people teach their young kin, will help develop social praxis. Each person develops the gendered skills that make him or her into an adult person in the eyes of the other adults. Men learn to garden, fish and hunt, and some specialize in ritual knowledge. Women learn to cook food, make maize drink and sing lullabies, and some specialize in birth medicine. In this context, young children's amniotic designs guide adult people in making the bodies of their young kin grow to become healthy and skilled.

Among the gendered social praxes that men and women acquire throughout their lives are the skills involved in making artefacts. The development of such skills depends on personal inclinations, which, as Kuna people explained to me, are in some cases a 'gift' that a person receives from birth. This gift takes the form of the aforementioned amniotic designs which signal the newborn's attachment to a particular animal species, and thus make visible the predisposition of some children to become skilled persons. Indeed, those born showing their amniotic designs have the advantage of receiving further medicinal treatment that will increase their capacity to learn specialist skills. Men can learn to carve canoes, stools and other objects, to build houses, and to weave baskets. Women learn to design and sew their colourful blouses, make beadworks and mould clay braziers.

Design *is* praxis for Kuna people, insofar as it is a constitutive part of the person (i.e. *kurkin*) and it makes visible a person's capacity to learn socially recognized knowledge (Fortis 2010: 491). The capacity that Kuna people have to carry out particular activities in their daily life, or indeed their individual skill in creating what are regarded as beautiful artefacts, derives from the transformation that each person's amniotic designs undergoes during his or her life. Furthermore, amniotic designs are both bodily features and artefacts. They are drawn by the celestial grandmothers and consequently undergo manipulation through the healing practices of Kuna specialists. They are thus fabricated and transformed by both human and non-human agencies. As such, they blur the western distinction between organisms and artefacts. Amniotic designs, therefore, force anthropologists to rethink what they have so far assumed an object to be for Amerindians.

## Layering and Immortality

Besides covering the amniotic sac, designs assume other forms in the Kuna lived world. As with the Cashinahua and most Amerindians, it is Kuna women who make designs. They spend most of their spare time in sewing their elaborate blouses, called *molakana* (singular *mola*). The technique that they employ involves the use of two or more layers of poplin fabric in different colours. They draw designs with a pencil on one layer of fabric, then cut along the drawn lines and stitch each layer onto the one below. Adding more layers on top of each other, they increase the complexity of designs and the number of colours, thereby creating beautiful patterns that are subsequently sewn together with yoke and sleeves to form the blouse. Each seamstress then typically wears her own blouse (see Salvador 1978, 1997).

*Mola* and *kurkin*, blouse and amniotic sac, have two features in common: they are both constituted by several layers of either fabric or amniotic tissue and they are covered with designs. The layering of *mola* and *kurkin* is reminiscent of the shedding of snakes' skin. As noted earlier, for Kuna people, snakes are immortal thanks to the shedding of their skin, as for the Cashinahua who, in addition, suggest a similarity between women's menstruation and the shedding of snakes' skin. Moreover, for them, women are fertile because they shed their internal skin (Lagrou 2007: 113). Immortality and fertility are therefore linked. Furthermore, Kuna people's description of the amniotic sac is not entirely dissimilar to the Cashinahua description of the shedding of women's internal skin. Although my Kuna informants never stated this explicitly to me, I suggest that there might be a connection between the amniotic sac and the skin of snakes (Figure 5.3).

Constituted by several layers of tissue that come off one after the other, the amniotic sac is like the petals of a flower, as a Kuna woman told me. This layering also provides the amniotic sac with characteristics similar to the skin of snakes. This connection between amniotic sac and snake is perhaps the reason why, as Kuna people explained to me, persons who have been bitten by a snake are cured in seclusion, taking particular care not to get close to pregnant women. Even brief physical proximity to an expectant mother could aggravate the condition of the person bitten by a snake and even cause their death. The illness caused by a snake bite is said to be particularly difficult to cure since it keeps changing its form inside the victim's body. For this reason, at the time of my fieldwork few healers could master the song to cure snake bites. This song is said to be one of the most lengthy and difficult to learn, and the images it evokes are particularly complex since their purpose is to counteract the constantly changing forms that the snake's soul, which causes the illness, assumes once inside the victim's body.

**Figure 5.3** Nixia Pérez sewing a *mola*, 2003. Photograph by Margherita Margiotti

The task of the healer is to stop these transformations and pin the snake's soul down to then expel it from the sick body (see Chapin 1983: 112, 284–96). It therefore makes sense that the creative power of a pregnant woman, who is in the process of producing a new human form, poses a threat to the healing of snake bites, which aims at stopping the transformations of the snake's soul.

If layering stands for shedding skin, then what is the link between layering, shedding skin and immortality? I suggest the link is the production of new forms. In the case of the Cashinahua mythical anaconda the new forms are immaterial images that populate the cosmos. In the case of the shedding of the internal skin, and indeed of the layered *kurkin*, the production of new forms amounts to the creation of new bodies. And women's fertility, the capacity to produce new human bodies, is connected with their bodily capacity to create designs.

Kuna people explain that within the womb, male and female sexual fluids are moulded like an alloy in a cast that gives it a human shape. To ensure the safe creation of their child's human body both parents have to follow several dietary and behavioural restrictions, including the avoidance of eating, or even physical or visual proximity to, a number of animal species considered dangerous due to their predatory attitude (Margiotti 2010). During pregnancy, and for a few days just after birth, taboos are at their strictest as these are considered the most dangerous periods. There is usually close scrutiny of the neonate's body, as form and visual appearance are the first signs of humanity and of the successful work of both parents. Thus *kurkin*, and its outward analogue, *mola*, stand in comparison with the Cashinahua uterus and with the skin of the mythical snake. For the snake's skin, layering and designs are connected to immortality. For *kurkin*, layering and designs are connected to the reproduction of human life – perhaps, then, another form of immortality.

**Origin of Designs and Forms**

According to the Kuna myth of origin of designs, in the ancient time a woman called Nakekiryai – in some versions the sister of a powerful shaman, in others a powerful shaman herself – travelled to the underworld village of Kalu Tukpis, where she observed all types of designs covering tree trunks and leaves. When she returned to her village she taught other women how to make such designs. In this way Kuna women learned to decorate their clothing and to make beadworks (see Méndez in Wakua, Green and Peláez 1996: 39–43, Perrin 1998: 19). In the village of Ustupu I asked the man who told me this myth what Kuna women wore before they had access to western goods. I also asked whether the layered reverse-appliqué technique currently used for *molakana* is a recent invention, given that women's attire since the end of the nineteenth century has been entirely made out of material obtained from non-Kuna people in Panama and Colón. He answered that *molakana* were made long before the arrival of Europeans. Ancient Kuna people, he said, made *molakana* using tree bark.

Tree bark is *ukka* in Kuna language, which means 'skin', and Kuna people say that trees are immortal because they shed their skin, like snakes (see Rivière 1994: 260). That Nakekiryai saw the first designs on the bark of trees, in Kuna myth, is therefore particularly telling, since this would close the circle of associations between snake skin, amniotic sac and *molakana* via tree bark. Thus tree bark can be seen as another type of skin that is shed and which, like the skin of snakes and the uterus, generates new forms. But how is this so?

Returning to Cashinhua ethnography, the connection between tree and uterus stands out clearly. In one myth about the origin of humanity it is narrated that the 'first people were created in a hole in a tree; and in the transcription the term used for this hole (*xankin*) is that normally used to refer to a womb' (McCallum 2001: 52). This provides interesting cross-cultural support for my argument, which could be extended to other Amerindian societies. Trees are often seen as containers either for primordial spirits, as in the case of the Kuna, the Emberá (Vasco 1985: 38) and the Wauja (Barcelos Neto 2002: 115), or for the souls of the dead, as in the case of the Cashinahua (Lagrou 2007: 348–9), or for the souls of sick persons, as for the Emberá (Vasco 1985: 80). Furthermore, in Kalapalo and Yanomami mythology the first human beings were carved out of the wood of specific trees (Basso 1987, Rivière 1994).

The interior of a tree, its hardest part, its core, is called *kwa* in Kuna language. To my knowledge there are only two ways in which the *kwa* of trees is used by Kuna people. One is to make house posts, in which case the core of the trunk is stripped of the softer external parts. Another is to carve *nuchukana*. *Nuchukana* are best understood as 'figures of interiority', which stand in a metonymic relation with the invisible and immortal component of persons, *purpa*, or 'soul', or 'image' (Fortis 2012b). As noted by Rivière (1994) for the Trio, by Lagrou for the Cashinahua (1998) and more recently by Miller for the Mamaindê (2009), Amerindians associate hardness, instantiated by hard wood, rocks, or glass beads, with permanence, immortality, souls and the spirit world. Since many Amerindians regard trees as containers of 'soul images', the association between hollow tree and uterus assumes new connotations. The process of 'forming the baby' in the mother's uterus for the Kuna is akin to the proliferation of soul images inside trees. As trees for Kuna people host infinite primordial souls, when an elder man carves a *nuchu* he facilitates, as it were, the birth of a new subjectivity. As the Kuna myth of the origin of designs suggests, in accordance with Cashinahua exegesis, trees are therefore analogous to design-covered uteruses.

The ethnography analyzed in this chapter shows that trees and wombs share the capacity to create forms. Furthermore, as shown above, designs are associated with the generative capacities of the maternal womb, snake skin and trees. Since design for Kuna people instantiates the capacity to act skilfully in their lived world and facilitates the growth of healthy and intelligent persons, it is not surprising that it is primarily associated with the creation of bodies, and of forms such as *nuchukana* and *molakana*.

## Conclusions

When a Kuna man carves a *nuchu* his activity is similar to that undertaken when a woman gestates a child. He carves a wooden form to host the invisible soul of primordial beings. By doing so he effectively creates a new subjectivity out of the multiplicity of primordial souls, thus creating the conditions for their interactions with human beings. But whereas human beings acquire the capacity to reproduce themselves, *nuchukana* lack that capacity. They lack the generative capacity that human beings acquire through their design-covered *kurkin*. Lacking designs, *nuchukana* are sterile beings, incapable of generating new forms and so, in this respect, they are incapable of growing. By contrast, human beings develop the praxis to grow and reproduce themselves, and to create beautiful and powerful objects. Learning to sew *molakana* and wearing them in everyday life, Kuna women effectively make their fertile capacities visible to other people. Women make *molakana* in adulthood and when they have children. During pregnancy a woman dedicates the time freed from heavier domestic chores to sewing *molakana* (Margiotti 2010). *Molakana* are conceived, then, as manifestations of both the preconditions and the fulfilment of women's capacities to make babies (Figure 5.4).

*Artefacts and Bodies among Kuna People from Panamá* 103

Figure 5.4 **Mikita Smith posing with her *nuchukana* and one of her nephews, 2004. Photograph by Paolo Fortis**

The material activities described by Kuna people as 'giving form' (*sopet*) should be understood as transformations of processes of making bodies. The basic element in this process, form, is what matters when new babies and objects are created. It is through the human praxis of giving form that Kuna women and men create bodies and artefacts. For Kuna people there is no opposition between making and growing; bodies and objects are equally the outcome of processes of making and growing. Most importantly, the human capacity to make is understood as an ongoing transformation of fertility emerging and developing during a person's life cycle, from birth to death. Being able to create human bodies epitomizes artefactual processes in general. What is at stake is clearly not a distinction between organisms and artefacts, but the capacity to generate forms as the precondition of existence in a human lived world.

Human beings possess *purpa*, or soul, which renders them alive. They receive the *purpa* when the body first forms. Similarly, giving form to particular objects makes them alive, it endows them with *purpa*. Carving *nuchukana* is a case in point, where their aliveness is conveyed by their visual resemblance to human persons. These Kuna wooden figures are just one instantiation of a more general principle, according to which artful activities are understood in relation to processes of procreation, and procreation is understood as an artful process.

## Acknowledgments

Fieldwork in Panama (2003–4) was funded by the University of Siena and the Smithsonian Tropical Research Institute. I am thankful to the people of Okopsukkun who have generously shared their daily life and knowledge with me. An initial version of this chapter was written during a Visiting Research Fellowship at the Sainsbury Research Unit (University of East Anglia) and also benefited from comments of the participants at the workshop 'Power, Materiality and Objectification in Lowland South America' at the University of Oxford. I thank Anne-Marie Colpron, Els Lagrou and Margherita Margiotti for their insightful comments.

## References

Barcelos Neto, A. 2002. *A Arte dos Sonhos. Uma Iconografia Ameríndia*. Lisboa: Museu Nacional de Etnologia/Assírio & Alvim.
Barcelos Neto, A. 2008. *Apapaatai. Rituais de Máscaras no Alto Xingu*. São Paulo: EDUSP.
Basso, E. 1987. *In Favor of Deceit. A Study of Tricksters in an Amazonian Society*. Tucson: University of Arizona Press.
Battaglia, D. 1983. Projecting personhood in Melanesia: the dialectics of artefact symbolism on Sabarl Island. *Man*, 18(2), 289–304.

Chapin, M. 1983. *Curing Among the San Blas Kuna of Panama*. PhD thesis, University of Arizona.
Ewart, E. and O'Hanlon, M. 2007. *Body Arts and Modernity*. Wantage: Sean Kingston Publishing.
Fortis, P. 2010. The birth of designs: a Kuna theory of body and personhood. *Journal of the Royal Anthropological Institute*, 16(3), 480–95.
Fortis, P. 2012a. *Kuna Art and Shamanism: An Ethnographic Approach*. Austin, TX: University of Texas Press.
Fortis, P. 2012b. Images of person in an Amerindian society: an ethnographic account of Kuna woodcarving. *Journal de la Société des Américaneistes*, 98(1), 7–37.
Gell, A. 1998. *Art and Agency: An Anthropological Theory*. Oxford: Clarendon Press.
Gow, P. 1989. Visual compulsion. Design and image in Western Amazonia. *Revista Indigenista Latinoamericana*, 2, 19–32.
Gow, P. 1999. Piro designs: painting as meaningful action in an Amazonian lived world. *Journal of the Royal Anthropological Institute*, 5(2), 229–46.
Henare A., M. Holbraad, and S. Wastell (eds) 2007. *Thinking Through Things: Theorising Artefacts Ethnographically*. London: Routledge.
Hugh-Jones, S. 2009. The fabricated body. Objects and ancestors in Northwest Amazonia, in *The Occult Life of Things: Native Amazonian Theories of Materiality and Personhood*, edited by F. Santos-Granero. Tucson: University of Arizona Press, 33–59.
Ingold, T. 2000. *The Perception of the Environment: Essays on Livelihood, Dwelling and Skill*. London and New York: Routledge.
Lagrou, E. 1998. *Cashinahua Cosmovision: A Perspectival Approach to Identity and Alterity*. PhD thesis, University of St Andrews.
Lagrou, E. 2007. *A Fluidez da Forma: Arte, Alteridade e agência em uma Sociedade Amazônica (Kaxinaua, Acre)*. Rio de Janeiro: Topbooks.
Lagrou, E. 2009. The crystallized memory of artifacts: a reflection on agency and alterity in Cashinahua image-Making, in *The Occult Life of Things: Native Amazonian Theories of Materiality and Personhood*, edited by F. Santos-Granero. Tucson: University of Arizona Press, 192–213.
Lévi-Strauss, C. 1969. *The Raw and the Cooked. Introduction to a Science of Mythology: 1*. London: Jonathan Cape.
McCallum, C. 1996. The body that knows: from Cashinahua epistemology to a medical anthropology of lowland South America. *Medical Anthropology Quarterly*, 10(3), 347–72.
McCallum, C. 2001. *Gender and Sociality in Amazonia: How Real People are Made*. Oxford: Berg.
Margiotti, M. 2010. *Kinship and the Saturation of Life Among the Kuna of Panamá*. PhD thesis, University of St Andrews.
Miller, J. 2009. Things as persons: body ornaments and alterity among the Mamaindê (Nambikwara), in *The Occult Life of Things: Native Amazonian*

*Theories of Materiality and Personhood*, edited by F. Santos-Granero. Tucson: University of Arizona Press, 60–80.

Munn, N. 1986. *The Fame of Gawa: A Symbolic Study of Value Transformation in a Massim (Papua New Guinea) Society*. Cambridge: Cambridge University Press.

Overing, J. 1989. The aesthetics of production: the sense of community among the Cubeo and Piaroa. *Dialectical Anthropology*, 14(3), 159–79.

Perrin, M. 1998. *Tableaux Kuna. Les Molas, un Art d'Amerique*. Paris: Arthaud.

Rivière, P. 1994. WYSINWYG in Amazonia. *Journal of the Anthropological Society of Oxford*, 25(3), 255–62.

Salvador, M. 1978 *Yer Dailege! Kuna Women's Art*. Albuquerque: Maxwell Museum of Anthropology.

Salvador, M. 1997. *The Art of being Kuna. Layers of Meaning among the Kuna of Panama*. Los Angeles: UCLA Fowler Museum of Cultural History.

Santos-Granero, F. 2009. Introduction: Amerindian constructional views of the world, in *The Occult Life of Things: Native Amazonian Theories of Materiality and Personhood*, edited by F. Santos-Granero. Tucson: University of Arizona Press, 1–29.

Seeger, A. 1975. The meaning of body ornaments: a Suya example. *Ethnology*, 14(3), 211–24.

Strathern, M. 2004 [1991]. *Partial Connections*. Updated Edition. Walnut Creek: Altamira Press.

Taylor, A.-C. and E. Viveiros De Castro 2006. Un corps fait de regards, in *Qu'est-ce qu'un Corps?*, edited by S. Breton. Paris: Musée du Quai Branly/Flammarion, 148–99.

Turner, T. 1995. Social body and embodied subject: bodiliness, subjectivity, and sociality among the Kayapo. *Cultural Anthropology*, 10(2), 143–70.

Vasco, L. G. 1985. *Jaibanás: Los Verdaderos Hombres*. Bogotá: Banco Popular.

Vilaça, A. 2002. Making kin out of others in Amazonia. *Journal of the Royal Anthropological Institute*, 8(2), 347–65.

Viveiros de Castro, E. 1977 *Individuo e Sociedade no Alto Xingu. Os Yawalapíti*, Masters thesis, Museo Nacional, Universidade Federal do Rio de Janeiro.

Viveiros de Castro, E. 1979. A fabricação do corpo na sociedade Xinguana. *Boletim do Museu Nacional*, (n.s.) 32, 40–49.

Wakua, A., A. Green and J. Peláez 1996. *La Historia de mis Abuelos. Textos del Pueblo Tule*. Panama – Colombia: Associación de Cabildos Indígenas de Antioquia.

## Chapter 6
# Designing Body-Pots in the Formative La Candelaria Culture, Northwest Argentina

Benjamin Alberti

**Like Marble or Myrtle?**

On attempts to convert the natives of South America, the seventeenth-century Jesuit Antônio Vieira had the following to say:

> You who have travelled through the world, and have entered into pleasure-houses of princes, will have seen on those lawns and along those garden-paths two very different types of statues, those of marble and those of myrtle. The marble statue is quite difficult to make, because of the hardness and resistance of the material; but, once the statue has been fashioned, one no longer needs to put one's hand to it again: it always conserves and sustains the same shape. The statue of myrtle is easier to form, because of the ease with which the branches are bent, but one must always keep reshaping it and working on it in order for it to stay the same. (Quoted in Viveiros de Castro 2011: 1–2)

Vieira went on to compare native Brazilian 'nations' to statues of myrtle, describing them as docile and compliant in instruction but impossible to keep in shape. More than a simple simile, this observation suggests a way to rethink how we approach archaeological material – its nature or materiality – when considering issues of constancy and inconstancy. Viveiros de Castro (2011) argues that what prompted the statues of myrtle imagery was an ontology (a theory and experience of what exists) in which transformation was the rule and not the exception and where form and stability were to be constantly worked at rather than assumed. The strange fusions and excessive bodily forms of a class of ceramic vessels from the first millennium AD northwest Argentina recall Vieira's statues of myrtle, despite their petrified state (Figure 6.1). The pots – diagnostic of the La Candelaria archaeological culture – have been pulled out of ancient burials since the mule trains of early archaeologists traversed the *yungas* of Salta and Tucuman provinces in the late nineteenth century (Alberti 2007). There are several hundred known pots, either hurriedly excavated in the 1960s from sites subsequently flooded by the El Cadillal dam, or in private collections. Derived from a liminal geographical region between the Andes and the lowlands, many of these body-pots are striking in their hybrid anthropomorphic and zoological forms as well as in their reference to themes of volatility, growth and life.

**Figure 6.1** La Candelaria body-pot. Museo Arqueológico El Cadillal, Tucumán, Argentina. Photo: B. Alberti

The question I focus on in this chapter is why the La Candelaria pots also appear to be bodies. The equivalence established between body and pot produces interesting effects, whether we consider them to have been made or grown, as artefact or organism. I argue that archaeologists understand the relationship between pots and bodies on the basis of weak or strong equivalence. Weaker versions are predicated on a hylomorphic model of production or making which assumes that form is inscribed onto passive matter (Ingold 2010). Archaeologists commonly work from the assumption that bodies and persons are somehow constructed and that pots accrue meaning through their processes of manufacture and role in social relations

(Hurcombe 2007, Sofaer 2006). I present a critique and alternative centred on the concept of growth, which seems to better fit the La Candelaria material. Rather than resting on representation and analogy, the relationship between bodies and pots concerns their processes of formation where the equivalence is ontological. Instead of pots standing for bodies, both can be understood as subject to the same processes of growth. Amazonian perspectivist theory – defined as 'the conception according to which the universe is inhabited by different sorts of persons, human and non-human, which apprehend reality from distinct points of view' (Viveiros de Castro 2012: 83) – provides a further necessary step in my argument by challenging any presumption of universality implicit in the concept of growth. Even though the materials are found in a region with geographical and historical links to the Amazonian lowlands, I use perspectivism as a theoretical resource rather than a model for past societies (Alberti and Marshall 2009). Interestingly, perspectivism prompts notions of bodies as artefacts, and artefacts are as likely to be the sites of subjectivity as are bodies. In archaeology, stronger versions of the equivalence of pots and bodies posit their co-constitution via the development of skills within material environments. Thinking about design in this context sheds light on why La Candelaria potters drew an equivalence between bodies and pots. I argue that design in relation to La Candelaria body-pots was neither a matter of making an intentional image into a realized product, nor the reflex of a generalized process of growth, but rather a process that crucially entailed inconstancy, a continuous creative response to the exigencies of somatic uncertainty and ontological risk.

**Constructed and Performed Bodies and Pots**

Conceptualizing bodies, on the one hand, and pots, on the other, establishes a framework for thinking about body-pots. Whether regarded as organisms or artefacts, both bodies and pots could be analyzed in terms of how they acquire cultural meaning through their involvement in human relations. The logic of cultural construction that underwrites this way of understanding bodies and pots and their relationship, however, is ultimately circular. In such a scheme, body-pots are conceived of as artefacts that incorporate meanings about bodies into pots; and those meanings reflect that very idea – that the body is fabricated, just like the pot.

In archaeology, the equivalence between bodies and pots is often treated as an issue of form or of process: pots are like bodies because they look like them or because they are treated as such. The function of pots as containers also frequently suggests a metaphorical relation to the body, especially when the latter is considered the 'biological container par excellence' (Knappet, Malafouris and Tomkins 2010: 584). The vessel metaphor is widely acknowledged and supported by reference to ethnographic or historical accounts (Crossland 2010, Fowler 2008). Knappett, Malafouris and Tomkins (2010) have even reversed the usual relationship, by which pot is likened to body, arguing that the advent of practices of containment in the 'resilient' medium of ceramics catalyzed the metaphor such that body was likened to pot. Furthermore, pots can stand in for bodies and persons, and surfaces can be equivalently inscribed. For example, in an exhaustive survey, Gosselain (1999: 212) demonstrates that pots in sub-Saharan Africa are 'frequently associated with human beings' and decorated or treated as bodies. Blacksmiths among the Kapsiki of Cameroon perform work with both pots and bodies, grinding shards from old ceremonial pots to be included in new ones and also taking responsibility for funerals (Gosselain 1999).

These types of equivalence rest on archaeologists' understanding of what bodies and artefacts are. In bioarchaeology bodies are treated as sources of raw data; while in much theorizing of the body they are regarded as fully social (Sofaer 2006, Joyce 2005). In the latter, the body can be a metaphor for society or social relationships. Theories regarding the social construction of the body have come under considerable criticism for reducing the body to a passive carrier of social meanings. Phenomenological theories of embodiment respond by attending to active, sensing subjects (Crossland 2010). The body as 'lived experience' performs, communicates and extends personhood through inscriptive and representational practices that fully incorporate material culture and the surrounding world (Joyce 2005: 139).

Approaches in material culture studies that highlight social and cultural construction explore how artefacts take on cultural meaning through complex processes of manufacture and circulation. Hurcombe (2007) explains that artefacts as material culture embody social relations, encode social information and communicate meaning. Sofaer, however, goes further to suggest that bodies too are shaped by practices; as such, developmental plasticity allows discourse to penetrate the body through 'the incorporation of cultural norms' (2006: 79). La Candelaria pots appear to have been both similar to, and treated as, bodies, as is evident in their form and in the markings on the vessels (Alberti 2007, Alberti 2012) (Figures 6.1, 6.2, 6.4). It can be argued that where a pot was regarded as analogous to the body, bodies were considered amenable to cultural fabrication. The pots were thus a form of material discourse on the body, acting as metaphors for features of bodies such as containment and processes of transformation.

This equivalence posited between bodies and pots is, however, a weak one, based as it is on analogy. It is problematic in that it is premised on a concept of material culture in which 'brute matter' is shaped by cultural agency (Ingold 2012: 431). The formulation rests on a hylomorphic model in which form is brought to matter by an agent with a design in mind (Ingold 2010). In this way, material things are regarded as repositories or products of mental activity (Thomas 1998: 149). This is also evidenced in Hurcombe's definition of materiality as the transformation of the 'properties of raw materials' through their involvement in human relationships (2007: 13, 109). Gosselain's analysis of pots, which draws on the notion of the *chaîne opératoire*, rests on the same foundation: 'Every single part of a technical process', he writes, is symbolically saturated as people '"invest" meaning in clay' (Gosselain 1999: 218). Gosselain's conclusion that pots and the processes associated with them can act as metaphors for transformations in peoples' physical and social states tends to reiterate the assumption that matter is simply manipulated for social and cultural purposes. Similar problems are apparent in studies of embodiment in which lived bodies are tethered to a relatively stable biological substratum. Thus, for instance, sex and aging, defined as the real 'physical characteristics of the body that underpin … human experiences', remain unaltered (Sofaer 2006: 66). The active material make-up of the body is formulated as a problem of 'material culture', which then reinforces the premise of the body's 'dual character as biological and cultural' (ibid.: 2006: 78).

A further related issue for material culture theorists is how to conceptualize things as active agents, especially when their position attributes genuine agency exclusively to humans and artefacts are only assigned secondary agency. In such cases animacy is not considered an inherent attribute of the artefactual (Gell 1998). Items of material culture are thus theorized as meaning-laden artefacts produced by people from raw matter. With regard to La Candelaria body-pots, both bodies and pots can be conceived as products of social action; both are therefore fabricated. The concept of social construction, when applied to body-pots, results in their being conceptualized as material discourses on *themselves* – as the materialization of ideas about the socially constructed nature of bodies in ceramic form. To escape this circularity we need to look for resources that allow the 'myrtle-like' character of the pots to be grasped. Instead of regarding the pots as reflections on the constructed nature of bodies we can reverse the formulation and conceptualize the pots as living organisms subject to processes of growth.

**Growing Body-pots**

La Candelarians were clearly concerned to present their natural environment in their ceramics, including peccaries, amphibians, water fowl, foxes, vines, water, exuberant forms that seem to grow (Figure 6.1). But more than crafted versions of nature, are these pots – closer to myrtle than marble – themselves better understood as organisms? Can we, with Ingold (2012: 431), raise 'artefacts to the status of things that, similarly to organisms, both grow and are grown'? Ingold's (2012) ecology of materials is characteristic of work that focuses on the inherent vitality of things (Barad 2007, Bennett 2010), on an ontology in which primacy is given 'to the processes of formation as against their final products' (Ingold 2010: 92). Production, rather than a crafting of mental representations out of matter, is an on-going process that produces both maker and object. By attending to the inherent vitality of materials, it is possible to explain the movements of things without having to rely on notions such as agency which theorists, having started their analyses with ready-formed objects, are inclined to introduce *post hoc* in order to re-animate the world (Ingold 2010, 2011).

A change in focus from 'stopped up objects to leaky things' encourages a view of objects and bodies as emergent and never complete, never free from the materials and processes that give rise to them (Ingold 2012: 438). In this argument, objects are only ever apparently solid images of things. For example, in the process of metallurgy, a maker appears to take clear steps in the transformation of matter from one distinct state and form to another. Understood as a process of growth, however, metallurgy concerns matter in movement. Metal must be hammered, heated and finally quenched – all in response to conditions as they emerge, and thus the work flows rather than proceeding in transformational steps. The metallurgist must follow this 'matter-flow', as maker and materials respond to each other (Ingold 2012: 213). Rather than action taking place between the metal and the mind of the maker, these processes involve a 'vital principle' which is the process of metallurgy itself (Conneller 2011: 13). As such, form is ever-emergent, not pre-determined.

The sense of emergent forms is strong in La Candelaria pots. Traditional descriptors such as coil construction, firing in a reduced atmosphere, and rough stone inclusions all apply but only tell half the story. In addition, the pots' fractured, friable, uneven, rushed work suggests that they were unfinished, still in motion rather than completed and static. Many of the smaller, anthropomorphic pots were made in a hurry or carelessly. Cracks appeared upon firing, vessels were unsteady or lopsided; incised marks were left rough, showing the traces of the rapid gestures used to execute them.

**Figure 6.2**  **Detail of roughly incised lines. Museo Arqueológico El Cadillal, Tucumán, Argentina. Photo: B. Alberti**

When analyzed according to the hylomorphic model, such details of process are incidental to the form and its meaning because the material substratum is always mute. Traces of action are simply more or less skilled means of representing a mental image. Thinking in terms of growth, however, means that we can imagine a world in which materials, bodies and pots were experienced quite differently. Conneller (2011) has shown convincingly that the properties of materials and their relationship to form only ever emerge relationally. For example, in the case of Middle Magdalenian *contours découpés* from the Pyrenees (pendants carved predominantly into the shape of horses' heads from the hyoid bone of horses), their form was suggested by the materials. Importantly, however, this form only emerged for people '*who knew how to see it*' – that is, those who had the specialized knowledge earned through practices of predation and butchery (Conneller 2011: 36). Thus Conneller argues that 'the techniques selected for working a material are inseparable from broader understandings of the workings of natural processes' (2011: 7).

Ultimately, the key question here is whether the ceramic materials of body-pots can be understood in ways that are substantially different from the presuppositions of the substance ontology that underlies the hylomorphic model. If not, then body-pots remain projections – of a local interest in the natural world – onto the material. The alternative is that La Candelaria experienced everything about the world at its most fundamental as growth, including bodies and pots. This sets up a much stronger notion of equivalence between body and pot, one that rests on an ontology in which matter is not a passive substratum for the external imposition of form but, rather, is thoroughly caught up in processes of formation (Ingold 2010: 92). Nevertheless, simply positing a theoretical framework that emphasizes growth is too general to account for the pots. In order to explain these body-pots in particular, I argue that within the specific La Candelaria ontology processes of growth crucially involved matter which was radically inconstant and unreliable, continually threatening to transform.

## Perspectivism and the Mutability of Form

One unsettling element of the La Candelaria corpus is the presence of pots that resemble each other closely in form yet differ unexpectedly in anthropomorphizing details. 'Faceless' pots appear when a face is looked for; bulges replace arms or legs. Thus, pots not only force a comparison with bodies; they also deliberately stage the absence of specific bodily features. Most noticeable is the lack of faces on pots with a form that commonly includes them (Figure 6.3). Some have bulges for limbs and some have appendages of frogs, foxes or human bodies, while others have these parts missing.

How does the notion that these pots have grown help us understand the specific processes that lead to features such as facelessness? In answering this question, to which I return in the conclusion, theories such as Amazonian perspectivism can help challenge the over-generalization that might happen if the pots and their makers were taken to exemplify a universal ontology (Alberti and Marshall 2009).

**Figure 6.3** Faceless body-pot. Museo Histórico Municipal de Rafaela. Photo: B. Alberti

For Conneller, Ingold is guilty of precisely this when he treats technical processes such as weaving as the foundation for a meta-theory for material relations in general: in her view every entity (such as a pot) should be taken in its own 'ethnographic moment' (2011: 30). In Amazonia growth entails practices of care within an all-encompassing sociality that includes people, animals and plants, appearing in its most pronounced form in rituals surrounding the manufacture and use of certain artefacts (Overing and Passes 2000, Santos-Granero 2009).

Reciprocal relations of care are part of a world that sees humans as active and responsible players in processes that are regarded as both natural and cultural. The Wari', for example, pay much attention to human bodies to ensure proper growth, which is regarded as a collective responsibility: they are moulded and shaped by kin from foetus through to adult (McCallum 2001). Actions carried out on the body, such as massage, painting and piercing, are seen to have profound and lasting effects (Lagrou 2000: 160–61, Vilaça 2002).

Among Amazonian groups, however, it is the artefactual mode of production – not growth or reproduction – which is regarded as paradigmatic of creative acts (Santos-Granero 2009, see also Fortis, Chapter 5 in this volume). People are made; bodies are composite transformations of artefacts from the time of myth. Thus babies, for example, are fabricated according to the Cashinahua and are 'made things' for the Wayana – as are artefacts, hunted animals and enemies (Santos-Granero 2009: 17). Terence Turner's (1980, 2009) analysis of 'social skin', influential in archaeology (Joyce 2005), proposes that Amazonian peoples work on the surface of the body in multiple ways through, for instance, scarification, tattooing and dress, to fabricate a thoroughly social body. Such surface modifications regulate internal bodily powers, thus shaping 'the social meaning of the physical body' (Turner 2009: 31).

Perspectivism suggests, however, that the fabrication of bodies in Amazonia is not fully explained by such an analysis. Vilaça (2009: 129) argues that the concept of the phenomenological body that underlies Turner's analysis has been imposed wholesale on the region precisely because of the apparently close fit between phenomenological and local ideas. The analysis treats Amazonian bodies as exemplary of the 'mindful body', a notion which has developed in the industrialized West but which has no counterpart in the Amazon. By contrast, according to perspectivism, many beings can be subjects (Viveiros de Castro 2010, 2012). Their visible bodily form is merely an envelope or clothing that hides (but does not imprison) an anthropomorphic 'essence' or soul (Viveiros de Castro 2012: 83). Each being sees itself and its kind as human. The variable appearance of bodies differentiates species, whose bodies are not inherently stable. Rather, they are stabilized through acts of care. Bodies are not organisms, as conceived in western theories, but 'bundles of affects' (ibid.: 125). Affects are understood as 'dispositions or capacities which render the body of every species unique: what it eats, how it moves, how it communicates, where it lives, whether it is gregarious or solitary' (ibid.: 113). Such practices ensure that individuals act and see in the same ways as their kin or conspecifics. Strathern explains that perspectivism is not simply a metaphor for perspective; it implies a 'specific material habitat and … the body that goes with the habitat' (2009: 159). Different sets of relations do not, then, produce different objects in a singular world, but 'different bodily constitutions of the subject' and hence different worlds (Vilaça 2009: 136). Practices of care are not examples of 'social construction', the making cultural of a natural substrate as Turner has it, but rather 'the production of a distinctly human body, meaning *naturally* human'

(Viveiros de Castro 2012: 121). But intrinsic to bodies is also the ability or threat of transformation; 'soul' designates the ability to change, to lose one's perspective and therefore body. Bodies and worlds are inherently unstable.

In the La Candelaria material, human skeletal bodies show evidence of having been worked on in life and death: traces of piercings, cranial modification, disarticulation, and secondary burial indicate a desire to ensure that certain transformations and states were achieved (Alberti 2007). Perspectivism suggests that there is no interior space to the body, only superposition of body and soul: 'The human form is, as it were, the body within the body, the naked primordial body – the "soul" of the body' (Viveiros de Castro 2012: 123). Bodies and souls eclipse one another (Vilaça 2009). Perspectivism is based on the radical and infinite superposition of states; insides and outsides are simply figure and ground to each other (Viveiros de Castro 2010). As such, bodies cannot contain, in the sense of *constraining* what lies within, and pots cannot therefore convey the notion of body as container in this sense (see Viveiros de Castro 2012: 133). Rather, the pots suggest a concern with instability and the inability of matter and form to remain fixed. In this respect it can be argued that the body-pots participated in the same processes as did bodies. Both were marked and moulded, broken, buried, mended and re-used. The incised marks on pot bodies recall tattoos or scarification of the flesh; pot faces were frequently pierced and adorned.

The actions performed upon bodies are ontologically equivalent to those directed on pots. To mark a body was the same act as to mark a pot in that the desired outcome was the same: such acts can be taken as practices of care that fortified bodies and pots against the chronic instability of a world constantly at risk of transformation.

**Organs of Knowledge**

> 'Si todo puede ser humano, entonces nada es humano en forma clara y distinta'.
>
> [If everything can be human, then nothing is human in a clear and distinct way.]
> (Viveiros de Castro 2010: 52)

Perspectivism has been accused of an overemphasis on human–animal relations, paying little attention to the importance of objects, artefacts or things (Santos-Granero 2009). In fact, as Stephen Hugh-Jones concludes in a study of Tukano body objects, 'not just humans and animals ... are undifferentiated in Amerindian mythology; this lack of differentiation can apply equally between humans, animals, and objects' (2009: 56). Viveiros de Castro (2010) has gone so far as to argue that there is no logical reason why anything can't be a person. Objects of personal use can gradually become 'ensouled' and artefacts can be considered the children of their makers, sharing their subjectivity (Santos-Granero 2009: 12,

Figure 6.4   Pierced nose of pot. Museo Arqueológico El Cadillal, Tucumán, Argentina. Photo, B. Alberti

see also Viveiros de Castro 2010: 34–5). The process is reversible: powerful objects can be de-subjectivized by being removed from active relations – hidden and left to rot in the case of Urarina hammocks (Walker 2009), or by the removal of mouths and eyes in the case of Wauja masks (Barcelos Neto 2009). Ensoulment is not adequately analyzed as the transference of something like agency to an object. Subjectivity is a condition and outcome of all affective relations rather than a capacity that can be awakened in a seemingly inert thing.

There is, however, something unsatisfactory about the conceptualization of materiality in these object-oriented accounts. For instance, when it is argued that hammocks and masks are simply left to rot, the materials themselves are not conceptualized by ethnographers as active components. I suggest, to the contrary, that materials can and should be theorized as fully implicated in the play of perspectives. Erikson (2009: 187) writes that the Matis mark pots with incised parallel crisscrossed lines, called *musha*, and these he interprets as tattoos, or '*Mushabo*', meaning 'bearers of face tattoos', so that pots are marked as people. The clay, temper and water are not merely the supports or props for this personhood but are themselves fully active. If actions of piercing, feeding and painting human bodies differentiate them from animals by producing affects, or capacities, then when bodies of clay are pierced, pinched, shaped and scarred, they too develop affects. Any resiliency in the pots lies in the care and attention, the marks left, and not in the presumed inherent qualities of the ceramic medium. Materials are not conceptualized as already endowed with qualities or properties that will ensure they take a given shape. Rather, piercing skin or clay partakes in a natural process in which the materials are active participants. The active nature of materials refers to their recognized capacity to escape form, their untrustworthiness. Action done to them is done in full consciousness of these capacities. As such, materials are known to be active in the same way humans are active. In Ingold's terms, they are co-respondents (Ingold 2011); in perspectivist terms, they are part of natural processes and therefore always potentially involved as active subjects in relations with other beings (Viveiros de Castro 2012).

In perspectivism, bodies, as bundles of affects, have the ability to acquire knowledge and see the world in a specific way. The body, not the mind (or 'soul'), is the seat of knowledge (Lagrou 2000: 159). Different parts of the body know in quite distinct ways. For example, Lagrou reports that the Cashinahua have 'hand knowledge (*meken una*), eye knowledge (*bedu una*), ear knowledge (*pabinki una*), liver knowledge (*taka una*) and skin knowledge (*bitxi una*)' (2000: 158). Knowledge of sun, rain and wind, for instance, is acquired through the skin. Painting can also facilitate the absorption of knowledge into the body (Lagrou 2009). Ear piercing is associated with the ability to receive knowledge among the Canela (Crocker and Crocker 2003). Eye knowledge for the Cashinahua allows people to see the true nature of people and things (Viveiros de Castro 2012).

Similarly, La Candelaria body-pots may have been provided with bodies as a means to acquire and communicate knowledge. Sensing organs are common on the pots. They appear on a general body form that consists of two volumes separated or related by cinching, often into a body and a neck (Figures 6.1, 6.3). Moulded bulges are also incorporated into this form; appendages are applied, and bulges and marks are often then incised into both. These incisions and appendages perhaps endowed pots with affects associated with specific body parts and organs of knowledge. Eyes were particularly prominent, as were mouths and chins. Ears, lips and noses were explicitly pierced – care was taken to puncture even the smallest feature through-and-through (Figure 6.4). Parts of pots, like bodies, could thus become loci or organs of knowledge and subjectivity not only via these practices but also by virtue of their materials. In line with my argument that it makes no sense in this context to simply repeat form in new media, the properties and possibilities of these materials can be conceptualized as practices in themselves. For instance, the production of *curare* (poison) is a fraught process because materials are potent and never passive in the light of human action. Working with materials is, therefore, a matter of intervening in processes in an attempt to pre-empt or promote a response.

**Skill and Ontological Risk**

Attending to growing as a generalized ontology of materials and practices, in relation to all bodies, recasts the relationship of potter to pot. Budden and Sofaer address the equivalence or co-constitution of potters and pots at the Bronze Age tell of Százhalombatta, Hungary, where 'potters and pots [were] physically created through the act of potting' and socially created by the performance (Budden and Sofaer 2009: 211). Potters' bodies were shaped irrevocably by their skilled practice. Moreover, as they improved, their changing relationship with materials and the way they were thus judged by audiences constituted their social identities. Furthermore, the objects they made were never complete. When they were brought into use – for instance, when they were aligned with others' concerns, and when they became fractured or broken – they were drawn into potters' social identities and into the category of potter in general. Budden and Sofaer argue persuasively that makers are involved in the process of making at a fundamentally embodied level, becoming *subject to* the processes they are involved in. This total commitment involves them in both the task and its ongoing material consequences.

Budden and Sofaer claim that potters 'literally came into being' through potting (2009: 203), but they tend to refer to the body's development on the one hand, and to social identity on the other, with skilled practice situated as the mediator between one realm and the other. In Amazonia, however, where natural and cultural processes are not distinguished in the same way, skill is conceived far more broadly and is not an exclusively human capacity. In the case of the Kuna, for example, skill is a mark of the maker's openness to alterity; skills are learned in dreams from animals that lost the ability to perform those activities in mythic times (Fortis 2010). Skill not only acts upon surfaces or moulds forms; it also transfers qualities. For instance, among the Matis, the practice of '*curare* watching' –

the hours spent observing the process in excess of practical necessity – is fundamental to the efficacy of the poison. For the Matis 'the physical and mental experience of making something has an impact on its ultimate properties' (Erikson 2009: 176). Such material–conceptual properties are therefore relational and practice is a conduit for their emergence. Moreover, if artefactual production is the paradigm for creative acts, then all actions – human authored or not – are potentially creative. Hence there is skill in the work of the tiny *ciê* crustaceans (*Goniopsis cruentata*) that bring sediment to the surface and so alert the Tremembé Indians to the presence of red and yellow ochre that they collect and use as pigment (Marques and Meneses Lage 2011).

'Skill matters', as Bleed (2008: 155) argues, but not only as a gauge of technical action applied to raw material. Applying these perspectives, then, La Candelaria potters may have worked in a context in which all skilled action was considered natural and all natural acts considered potentially skilled. Skill was the means for all beings to bring forth qualities or properties. The potter would bend over a pot, working quickly, pushing and pinching shapes into the material. Tools were selected from bird or other small bones and drawn through the clay. Edges of incised lines remained ragged, uneven (Figure 6.2). These tool marks were themselves signs of natural processes, as was the skill of detecting when a response from hand and eye, arm, skin and thought required the movement or piercing of another part of the material. If my argument is accepted, that potters intervene in materials considered active in their own right, then what was their aim when they deftly moved a sharp edge or point against a clay body?

Potters' identities were vulnerable, stress Budden and Sofaer (2009) with regard to Bronze Age Százhalombatta. They were at risk because they were dependent on the audiences who judged each potter's skill; their performance was thus 'socially sanctioned' (Budden and Sofaer 2009: 214). La Candelaria potters' identities were at risk too. But it was not as if the potter's social self was buoyed up by a physical body shaped by skill. The potter's self was quite literally their body. And their performance had to be naturally sanctioned because sociality included a much broader audience of beings. To maintain their identity and bodies as human was to do things as humans do. If they did not convince their audience of their skill they would not only lose their identity; they would also lose their perspective and therefore their selves to a different world. If performances were not maintained, then the results were immediate and potentially catastrophic, resulting in transpecific transformation. While Budden and Sofaer's argument relies on a separation of the natural from the cultural, reflected in the language of social identity versus embodied skill, I argue that local ontology was a process of growth involving (what a western view would regard as) both natural and social processes. La Candelaria potters conceptualized and experienced their activity as growth, within the very particular context of an inconstant world in which materials were lively and equally capable of subjectivity. The risks were therefore ontological because to fail at an embodied task could result in the dramatic transformation of a human being's world.

**Design and Inconstancy**

Contrasting conventional notions of design with the notion of improvisation opens up the question of why La Candelaria potters made body-pots. Design, as conventionally conceived, follows the hylomorphic model. By contrast, Ingold (2010: 97) characterizes improvisation as a fluid, 'forward movement' which does not 'project' future states but 'follows the paths along which such projections take shape' (Ingold and Hallam 2007: 15). Similarly, La Candelaria potters' concern was not with reproducing or representing a mental image of a completed body-pot. It seems likely that the notion of a finished object was anathema to a world conceptualized as one in continual growth. Furthermore, as Overing and Passes (2000) argue, in Amazonia no distinction is made between thoughts, feelings, body and mind; since 'thoughts and actions happen in the same ontological space' (Viveiros de Castro 2012: 124). Thus, as Fortis has argued with regard to the Kuna, 'design is not conceptually separated … from the surface on which it appears' (Fortis 2010: 491). In the process of making the pots there was no separation of material from conceptual design. For La Candelaria potters, thought was coincident with their embodied knowledge of materials.

Taking this line, La Candelaria potters did not represent but rather participated in their high-stakes world. By making body-pots La Candelaria potters took part in an aesthetics of care that was also a response to the threat of the inconstancy of all forms. Rather than making a mental image into an object, potters may have been responding to perturbations in the movement of materials. According to Ingold, makers' skill 'lies in their ability to find the grain of the world's becoming and to follow its course while bending it to their evolving purpose' (2010: 92). Engaged in their tasks, potters would indeed have wanted to bend materials to their purpose, acting in relation to the material-conceptual movements which they encountered. The grain of their world, moreover, included knowledge of its inconstancy and of materials always capable of subjectivity.

La Candelaria potters' awareness developed with the flow of materials and was directed at ongoing relationships, at the potential subjectivity of all beings, including the materials they worked with. Rather than just a matter of artistic convention, it made a significant difference whether a body-pot was fully equipped with a face and organs of knowledge. Faceless pots were not part of a repertoire of forms potters drew upon but were rather partial subjects that made possible certain kinds of relations and hence knowledge. The bodies of body-pots did not need to be complete in a biological sense because they were not representations of complete bodies. Materials and body parts combined in the pots to produce possibilities for communication and knowledge between disparate subjects. Pots without faces were responses to a situation in which the organs of the face were not called for or were deemed too dangerous, as in the case of the Wauja masks that can turn predatory if relations with them are not properly maintained (Barcelos Neto 2009).

Given these design processes in such an inconstant world, the alterity embodied by these pots cannot be fully captured from a 'social construction' perspective. Body-pots were ambivalent responses to the threat of inconstancy in a world wherein forms, like statues of myrtle, were only ever apparent. As Budden and Sofaer (2009) demonstrate, each making of a pot is a performance and an improvisation. This process is unscripted and can therefore go wrong (Ingold and Hallam 2007). In a world of growth in which all materials were active, design did not produce fixed forms but was rather a continuous, ongoing response to a world in which ontological transformation was an ever present danger.

**Acknowledgments**

Research for the chapter was partially funded by a Fulbright Lecturing and Research in the Social Sciences Award. My thanks to the staff at the Museo Arqueológico El Cadillal and the Museo Histórico Municipal de Rafaela. I am grateful to Sr. Carlos Weiss for permission to publish photographs I took of the Arminio Weiss collection. Andres Laguens, Marcos Gastaldi and Francisco Pazzarelli contributed to ideas that made their way into this chapter. All translations are my own.

**References**

Alberti, B. 2007. Destablizing meaning in anthropomorphic forms from Northwest Argentina. *Journal of Iberian Archaeology*, 9/10, 209–29.

Alberti, B. 2012. Cut, pinch and pierce: image as practice among the Early Formative La Candelaria, first millennium AD, Northwest Argentina, in *Picture This! The Materiality of the Perceptible*, edited by I.-M. Back Danielsson, F. Fahlander Y. and Sjöstrand. Stockholm: Stockholm University, 23–38.

Alberti, B. and Marshall, Y. 2009. Animating archaeology: local theories and conceptually open-ended methodologies. *Cambridge Archaeological Journal*, 19(3), 344–56.

Barad, K. 2007. *Meeting the Universe Halfway: Quantum Physics and the Entanglement of Matter and Meaning*. Durham and London: Duke University Press.

Barcelos Neto, A. 2009. The (de)animalization of objects: food offerings and subjectivization of masks and flutes among the Wauja of southern Amazonia, in *The Occult Life of Things: Native Amazonian Theories of Materiality and Personhood*, edited by F. Santos-Granero. Tucson: The University of Arizona Press, 128–51.

Bennett, J. 2010. *Vibrant Matter: A Political Ecology of Things*. Durham and London: Duke University Press.

Bleed, P. 2008. Skill matters. *Journal of Archaeological Method and Theory*, 15(1), 154–66.

Budden, S. and J. Sofaer 2009. Non-discursive knowledge and the construction of identity: potters, potting and performance at the Bronze Age Tell of Százhalombatta, Hungary. *Cambridge Archaeological Journal*, 19(2), 203–20.

Conneller, C. 2011. *An Archaeology of Materials: Substantial Transformations in Early Prehistoric Europe*. London: Routledge.

Crocker, W.H. and J.G. Crocker 2003. *The Canela: Kinship, Ritual and Sex in an Amazonian Tribe*. Belmont: Wadsworth.

Crossland, Z. 2010. Materiality and embodiment, in *The Oxford Handbook of Material Culture Studies*, edited by D. Hicks and M. Beaudry. Oxford: Oxford University Press, 386–405.

Erikson, P. 2009. Obedient things: reflections on the Matis theory of materiality, in *The Occult Life of Things: Native Amazonian Theories of Materiality and Personhood*, edited by F. Santos-Granero. Tucson: The University of Arizona Press, 173–91.

Fortis, P. 2010. The birth of design: a Kuna theory of body and personhood. *Journal of the Royal Anthropological Institute*, 16(3), 480–95.

Fowler, C. 2008. Fractal bodies in the past and present, in *Past Bodies: Body Centered Research in Archaeology*, edited by D. Borić and J. Robb. Oxford: Oxbow Books, 47–58.

Gell, A. 1998. *Art and Agency: Towards and Anthropological Theory*. Oxford: Oxford University Press.

Gosselain, O.P. 1999. In pots we trust. The processing of clay and symbols in sub-Saharan Africa. *Journal of Material Culture*, 4(2), 205–30.

Hugh-Jones, S. 2009. The fabricated body: objects and ancestors in Northwest Amazonia, in *The Occult Life of Things: Native Amazonian Theories of Materiality and Personhood*, edited by F. Santos-Granero. Tucson: The University of Arizona Press, 33–59.

Hurcombe, L.M. 2007. *Archaeological Artefacts as Material Culture*. London: Routledge.

Ingold, T. 2010. The textility of making. *Cambridge Journal of Economics*, 34(1), 91–102.

Ingold, T. 2011. *Being Alive: Essays on Movement, Knowledge and Description*. Abingdon: Routledge.

Ingold, T. 2012. Toward an ecology of materials. *Annual Review of Anthropology*, 41, 427–42.

Ingold, T. and E. Hallam 2007. Creativity and cultural improvisation: an introduction, in *Creativity and Cultural Improvisation*, edited by E. Hallam and T. Ingold. Oxford: Berg, 1–24.

Joyce, R. 2005. Archaeology of the body. *Annual Review of Anthropology*, 34, 139–58.

Knappett, C., Malafouris, L. and Tomkins, P. 2010 Ceramics (as containers), in *The Oxford Handbook of Material Culture Studies*, edited by D. Hicks and M. Beaudry. Oxford: Oxford University Press, 588–612.

Lagrou, E.M. 2000. Homesickness and the Cashinahua self: a reflection on the embodied condition of relatedness, in *The Anthropology of Love and Anger: The Aesthetics of Conviviality in Native Amazonia*, edited by J. Overing and A. Passes. London: Routledge, 152–69.

Lagrou, E. 2009. The crystallized memory of artifacts: a reflection on agency and alterity in Cashinahua image-making, in *The Occult Life of Things: Native Amazonian Theories of Materiality and Personhood*, edited by F. Santos-Granero. Tucson: The University of Arizona Press, 192–213.

Marques, M. and M.C.S. Meneses Lage 2011. La tinta y la tela en el arte rupestre del Sertão Central de Ceará, nordeste de Brasil, in *Biografías de Paisajes y Seres: Una Visión Sudamericana*, edited by L. Miotti and D. Hermo. Buenos Aires: Editorial Brujas, 20–30.

McCallum, C. 2001 *Gender and Sociality in Amazônia: How Real People are Made*. Oxford: Berg.

Overing, J. and A. Passes 2000. Introduction: conviviality and the opening up of Amazonian anthropology, in *The Anthropology of Love and Anger: The Aesthetics of Conviviality in Native Amazonia*, edited by J. Overing and A. Passes. London: Routledge, 1–30.

Santos-Granero, F. 2009. From baby slings to feather bibles and from star utensils to jaguar stones: the multiple ways of being a thing in the Yanesha lived world, in *The Occult Life of Things: Native Amazonian Theories of Materiality and Personhood*, edited by F. Santos-Granero. Tucson: The University of Arizona Press, 105–27.

Sofaer, J.R. 2006. *The Body as Material Culture: A Theoretical Osteoarchaeology*. Cambridge: Cambridge University Press.

Strathern, M. 2009. Using bodies to communicate, in *Social Bodies,* edited by H. Lambert and M. McDonald. New York and Oxford: Berghahn Books, 148–70.

Thomas, J. 1998. Some problems with the notion of external symbolic storage, and the case of Neolithic material culture in Britain, in *Cognition and Culture: The Archaeology of External Symbolic Storage* edited by C. Renfrew and C. Scarre. Cambridge: McDonald Institute for Archaeological Research, 149–56.

Thomas, J. 2002. *Understanding the Neolithic*. Abingdon: Taylor and Francis.

Turner, T. 1980. The social skin, in *Not Work Alone*, edited by J. Cherfas and R. Lewin. London: Temple Smith, 111–40.

Turner, T. 2009. The crisis of late structuralism. Perspectivism and animism: rethinking culture, nature, spirits, and bodiliness. *Tipití*, 7(1), 3–42.

Vilaça, A. 2002. Making kin out of others in Amazonia. *The Journal of the Royal Anthropological Institute*, 8(2), 347–65.

Vilaça, A. 2009. Bodies in perspective: a critique of the embodiment paradigm from the point of view of Amazonian ethnography, in *Social Bodies*, edited by H. Lambert and M. McDonald. New York and Oxford: Berghahn Books, 129–47.

Viveiros de Castro, E. 2010. *Metafísicas Caníbales: Líneas de Antropología Postestructural*. Buenos Aires: Katz Editores.

Viveiros de Castro, E. 2011. *The Inconstancy of the Indian Soul: The Encounter of Catholics and Cannibals in Sixteenth-Century Brazil*. Chicago: Prickly Paradigm Press.

Viveiros de Castro, E. 2012. Cosmological perspectivism in Amazonia and elsewhere. *HAU: Journal of Ethnographic Theory*, Masterclass series, 1, 45–168.

Walker, H. 2009. Baby hammocks and stone bowls: Urarina technologies of companionship and subjection, in *The Occult Life of Things: Native Amazonian Theories of Materiality and Personhood*, edited by F. Santos-Granero. Tucson: The University of Arizona Press, 81–102.

Chapter 7

# Stitching Lives: A Family History of Making Caribou Skin Clothing in the Canadian Arctic

Nancy Wachowich

**Introduction: The Intimate Stitching of Lives**

Stitches are what drew the women together in their seats, stitches that held the backing of a mitten to its palm and thumb pieces, sewn into delicate tucks. It was an ordinary scene in the airport at Iglulik (Igloolik), an Inuit community in the northern Foxe Basin region of the Canadian Eastern High Arctic, on a November afternoon in 1997.[1] The light outside was fading, so the two women, second cousins Lily Taqaugaq Tongak and Leah Aqsaajuk Otak, leaned in closer, so as to better admire the seams on Lily's caribou skin mittens. The mittens were a plain pair, with no decorative ornamentation, made of de-haired, and bleached caribou skin. They were the handiwork of Lily's mother, Damaris Ittukusuk Kadlutsiak. Damaris was born in 1943 in a camp called Nalluaq near Mittimatalik (Pond Inlet) on the northern tip of Baffin Island. She was of the last generation of Inuit in this region to have spent her childhood and early adulthood following a semi-nomadic, hunting-trapping lifestyle on the land, prior to the 1960s establishment of settlements. Damaris had died unexpectedly just a few months previously. The final time we met, in the spring of 1997, I sat opposite her at a bingo night in the Iglulik Community Hall. A friendly, redoubtable woman, of slight build, with cropped hair, she wore a signature homemade parka made of beige cotton. Damaris was well known in town for her industriousness, talent as a seamstress, devotion to the Christian faith and to her family as a loving mother and grandmother, and for a fiercely competitive streak when it came to bingo. That afternoon in the airport, the two younger women brought the mittens to their faces, feeling the texture of the hide against their cheeks. They ran fingers across the waxed thread stitches, showing hushed admiration for the precision of Damaris' handiwork, remarking on how skilled their mothers, aunties and grandmothers had been at processing

---

1  There are different designations and spellings of settlement names in the Canadian Arctic. I use Inuktitut (Inuit language) designations Iglulik and Mittimatalik rather than the English designations Igloolik and Pond Inlet.

furs and sewing skin clothing. Leah slipped one of the mittens on, still warm from Lily's hand. And they fell silent, lost in memories.

Waiting for my flight departure, sitting alongside Lily in the airport lounge, I was moved by this shared moment of tenderness, captivated by the small gestures and all that was left unsaid between the women as they handled an unassuming garment. Fifteen years on, this chapter is an effort to understand this act of homage, the materials and processes of manufacture, and the life histories being paid tribute. It is concerned with how relationships are made and grown through the making of skin garments. Different telling episodes from Damaris' life history are spliced into a social biography of a pair of mittens she made to protect the hands of her fourth child Lily from the biting cold. It considers the social and material processes that went into the mittens' making and their particular placement in the socio-material worlds constituting Arctic colonialism during the twentieth and twenty-first centuries. Through this analysis, I contend that the making of skin garments generates social relationships between family members and with people's cultural past, present and future. This making also draws connections with the animal world once crucial to survival in the past, now missed and mourned for, and latterly sought out once again.

By tracing social relationships through skin garment production, and documenting the materiality of meaning-making in this process, it is possible to reconsider what it is to make things. Careful analysis of the social lives of this pair of mittens highlights the difficulty of distinguishing making from growing, artefact from organism. In the process of hunting animals and making their skins into garments there seems no clearly identifiable threshold at which the organism takes the status of inanimate artefact. As I shall show, the reason for this is that hunted animals are said not to die. If, in an animal's killing, butchering, and the processing of its skin, a hunter and the seamstress demonstrate respect for the animal and follow appropriate rituals and observances, the animal's spirit is said to remain in the garment after death, helping the hunter successfully to kill the physical bodies of its reincarnated self, and its fellow creatures, again and again. Thus the manufacture of skin garments is understood as part of a cycle of regeneration. New caribou could be envisioned as being grown in this process, alongside the people who rely on caribou meat for sustenance and whose social identities (as hunter, wife, mother) are forged through the making of garments and through the particular design of clothing they wear. Skin garment manufacture therefore draws human persons into a wide set of generative social relationships, eschewing any strict demarcation of humans from animals, or animate being from inanimate manufactured garment.

Before the move into settlements and the availability of industrially produced clothing in the North, the abiding work of Inuit women was to foster and strengthen this regeneration and renewal process through the careful processing of animal skins into garments. Today, many Inuit women sew skin clothing but, unlike before, this activity must be made to fit around schooling and employment. If only during fleeting moments in these women's busy lives, tactile memories emerge from the handling of a mitten, reconnecting them to their family histories and an ecology of relations fundamental to life in the Arctic.

In what follows, I describe this ecology of relations, presenting the manufacture of caribou skin clothing as a social practice tying together seamstresses and their families, humans and animals, combining oral histories and present day activities. I begin with my own introduction to this generative and transformative practice of garment making. Five thematic sections then follow. 'Caring' considers the mittens as a keepsake, and a means to remember appreciatively a mother's skills of making. In 'protecting', insulating properties are described, uniting caribou and human skin, and elder and apprentice seamstresses. 'Processing' explains the sequence of operations and the practical wisdom required to turn animals into garments. In 'sewing', an Inuit ecology of relations is described, one that simultaneously makes people and grows animals. 'Fracturing' examines damage done to these social and material relations when conditions for reciprocity are destabilized. Finally, I consider how in items of skin clothing there exists the potential for social resilience and renewal despite the many vicissitudes faced by Inuit communities. I draw throughout upon a series of episodes from the life of Inuit seamstress Damaris Ittukusuk Kadlutsiak, and from her family history, thereby combining life stories with social analysis as well as technical explanation of sewing and the skin processing to which it is intimately related.

**Personal Connections and Skin Stories**

This analysis emerges from long-term fieldwork with women in the Canadian High Arctic communities of Iglulik and Mittimatalik: anthropological research that was often, especially in the early years, articulated through the coordinated activities of garment and narrative production. In the autumn of 1992, I was hired by the Canadian Government's Royal Commission on Aboriginal People (RCAP) to coordinate two oral history projects with women storytellers in Mittimatalik, a settlement of then about 1,000 people where I had spent the previous two summers.[2] Interviewing can be an awkward exercise in Canadian Arctic communities, places where asking directed questions is generally considered a marker of self-importance, laziness or rudeness: the clumsy imposition of one agenda over another. Instead, people learn by carefully observing and by attuning their behaviour to the fluctuating world around them (Briggs 1991). The women elders I interviewed, perhaps in an effort to temper this interrogatory practice – or perhaps like many a mother who recognizes opportunities to multitask – would often schedule my interview requests for times when seal or caribou skin needed processing.

---

2 The first oral history project was part of the five-nation women's governance research project where I worked with a team of Inuit researchers interviewing 18 women in Mittimatalik. The second was a three-generation life history project (Wachowich, in collaboration with Awa, Katsak and Katsak 1999).

During this time in Mittimatalik, it became evident that storytelling and sewing, while creatively distinct, served as complementary forms of social action, both offering a way for women to articulate their realities and to nurture people as social beings (Cruikshank 1998, Jackson 2002). Historically, in the days before television, Internet and gaming consoles, storytelling and sewing were closely interrelated. In much the same way that northern indigenous hunting and wayfinding practices incorporate narrative elements (Ridington 1990, Kwon 1998, Ingold 2000), women elders in Mittimatalik would tell stories as they sewed, so stitching narrative threads into their garments. Though made to be functional for the hunt, clothing was sewn with design and decorative features that were meant to relay cultural, familial and biographical details, thereby affording social status to the wearer. When worn correctly, garments could authorize and engender social relationships.

My early fieldwork rarely involved me in the skilled, physical work of scraping and stretching skin, and sewing. The risk of tearing a valuable skin was too great. Instead, I initially came to appreciate this skill from a distance, often with a tape recorder in hand. Both sewing and storytelling demanded concentration and an intimacy of treatment on the part of the women. Physical force was applied to the animal skins, scraping, soaking, rolling, stretching and chewing them in parts so they might be cut to fit and fall just right on the wearer's body. This multisensory, intimate activity brought about narrative recollections more vivid than those recorded in the formalized settings of oral history interviews. Often synchronized with the sound and rhythm of a scraper blade stroking against the animal's flesh, stories of lives in the past spent travelling between hunting camps were set against the backdrop of contemporary life in town. Through such narrative practices women's social realities were articulated and internalized in the act of processing skins.

In 1997 an opportunity arose for me to undertake a more hands-on apprenticeship in skin processing. In Iglulik (a community 398 km away but nevertheless regarded as the neighbouring settlement to Mittimatalik) I participated in weekly women's caribou skin processing workshops organized by a local elders' group, the Inullariit Society. Iglulik is a fly-in Inuit settlement, at the time with a population of 1,200. On Wednesday nights during that winter, women gathered in a community garage and were tutored by their elders in the techniques of stretching, scraping, softening and sewing skins. This work requires precise climatic conditions: it must not be too cold lest skins freeze, but nor must it be too warm, as heat dries out the skins, making them too brittle to process. In the garage, amongst stored boats, snowmobiles and heavy machinery, women sat together on the floor in pairs or small groups working on caribou skins provided by the Inullariit Society hunters.

Funding for the workshops was from a 'community wellness' grant, specifically intended to teach adult women skin processing skills while serving as a support group for individuals with personal or relationship problems. This was one of a raft of government initiatives established in communities across the Canadian North in the late 1990s and early 2000s, where the teaching and learning of skin garment manufacture were seen to provide a supportive environment for women suffering from cultural isolation or undergoing difficulties expressing themselves. Despite the winter chill in the garage, the atmosphere was warmly welcoming. As a novice, I was given a caribou leg skin to scrape, chew and soften, a task that I had not yet finished when the funding ran out and the workshops dissolved. My piece was taken home by a fellow participant and sewn into her son's boot. A few months later, a friend's elderly mother taught me the local mitten pattern by cutting a pattern for me out of duffle, a material, I was told, which was easier to work with and which would wear better in southern cities.

It was made clear to me through these early fieldwork experiences that skin clothing manufacture is often as much about nurturing social relationships as it is about making the garment itself. Neither the skills of making nor the relationships they foster should be diminished but nor should the one or the other be overplayed. As a model of such seamless entwining of material and social lives, Damaris' caribou skin mittens made for her daughter, Lily, are exemplary. My 2012 correspondence with Lily, which attempted to uncover the mittens' material and social lives, also activated an expanding network of family and friends in Arctic settlements and of scholars further afield. Through this network, memories of nurturing and mother-love were brought into dialogue with ancestral histories, as well as further Inuit material, environmental and colonial histories. A social biography emerged in this process, one grown and made through collective efforts to document a life and art form, but also one sustained by social relationships that reached into centres beyond Iglulik, as well as towards the animal whose hide was used to make the mittens.

**Caring: On Mother-love and Mitten-making**

Lily lost her mother suddenly, not long after receiving the mittens as a gift. Damaris' premature death, aged 54, pained her nine children and her many grandchildren. The loss was felt bitterly by people in Iglulik, where she spent her married life, and in the Mittimatalik region, which was her childhood home. In the months following, caribou clothing she had made the previous year started to show signs of wear. Caribou skin and hair has very little oil content compared with other mammal skins. It becomes dry and brittle, and decomposes easily.

Fifteen years after first seeing the mittens in the airport, I asked Lily whether she still owned them. 'Yes', she confirmed, 'I've kept them'. Even as the skin became distressed, as the stitching started to wear and as the trim frayed, she held on to them as a memento of her mother's love. 'They tear easily', she wrote in an email, and then went on to describe how, in 2010, they had been damaged in a house fire. Lily had retrieved the mittens from the debris the next day, charred but still intact. 'They are still dear to me', she wrote, and sent me photos of the mittens taken from various angles. While they have aged since the time I first saw them, Damaris' meticulous stitching is still visible in the photos along with the print of Lily's hand, the template from which the pattern piece was cut (Figure 7.1).

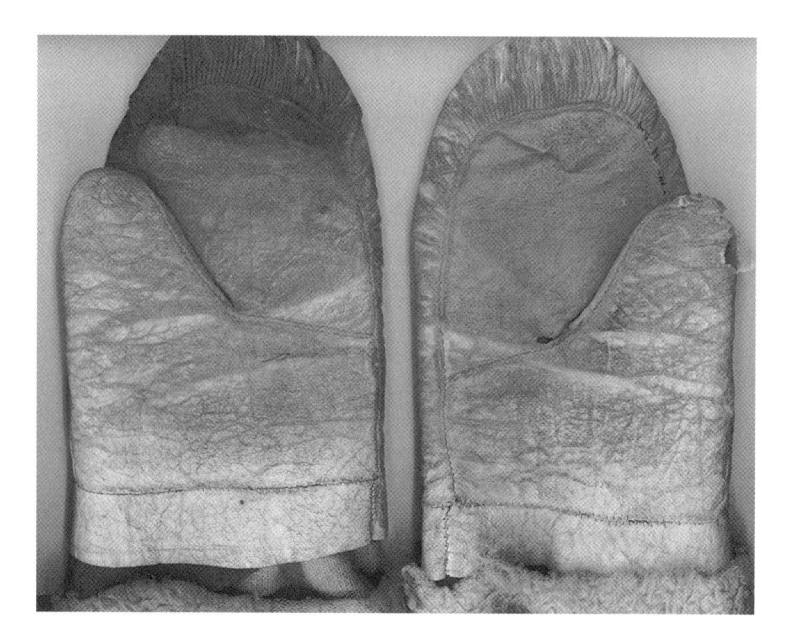

**Figure 7.1** Caribou skin mittens made by Damaris Ittukusuk Katdlutsiak. Photograph by Lily Taqaugaq Tongak in Iglulik Canada, September, 2012

Damaris sewed Lily's mittens from the standard four-piece pattern (thumb piece, palm piece, back mitt and wrist strip), a design common throughout the Arctic (Issenman 1997: 47–50, Oakes 1991: 235–7, Null and Manning 1944: 165–6). She chose caribou skin, a warmer, softer and more pliable, though less resilient material than its traditional alternative, sealskin (used for spring and summer hunting). Caribou hind leg skins are customarily used for mittens as they are durable and their relatively short hairs prevent moisture build up (Issenman 1997: 49). The pelts of caribou taken in the autumn, once the new hair has started to grow, are preferable (Null and Manning 1944: 156). It takes three leg skins of an adult caribou to make one pair of mittens (Oakes 1991: 235, Null and Manning 1944: 160). Most mittens are made wrist length, with a short cuff, to fit inside the sleeve of the *atigi* (or outer parka).

Lily's mittens are of the summer (or settlement) style: depilated, and lined with fabric. She remembers her mother often using the bathtub to wash blood and dirt from unprocessed furs. Damaris then soaked skins in warm water before rubbing off the hair and epidermis (the outermost layer of the skin). Timing is crucial in this process, as skins must soak and fester just long enough to dissolve the protein substance (or membrane) between the epidermis and the next layer of skin, the dermis (Stambolove 1969, cited in Oakes 1991). When families still lived in camps, this slight rotting of the skins was done in a summer lake or rock pool, or by leaving the skins in a bag. Once the skins for Lily's mittens had the hair rubbed away, they were scraped, stretched and left outside for several days to be bleached white by the sun. They were then softened again by stretching and chewing, cut to fit her hand size, then sewn, trimmed with sheepskin and lined with fuchsia wool serge that Damaris purchased from a store.

## Protecting: On Insulation, Design and Practical Wisdom

Damaris was renowned locally as a skilled and productive seamstress. The attention and care she invested in Lily's mittens was characteristic of her overall work, and for very good reason. Caribou skin clothing has ever been crucial to human survival in arctic conditions, where temperatures and wind chills often dip to -50°C, rendering high-tech synthetics impractical and uncomfortable (Oakes et al. 1995). Caribou fur is lightweight and easy to move in with thermoregulation properties attributable to the structural properties of the skin and hair fibres. Caribou hair is almost twice the width of human hair, with grooved surfaces and an internal cellular structure consisting of cubical cells that fill with air (Klokkerness and Sharma 2005, Meeks and Cartwright 2005). Short, fine hairs trap air close to the skin and long coarse guard hairs grow out parallel to the skin to provide additional layers of insulation (Stenton 1991, Issenman 1997). When caribou fur is worn against human skin in frigid conditions, warm air pockets develop between and within the hairs, generating a 'bubble wrap' effect insulating the wearer in layers of warm air (Meeks and Cartwright 2005: 43).

This insulating effect is augmented by the traditional Inuit design for winter outfits, consisting of inner and outer layers of caribou fur: the inner sewn so that the fur turns inwards against the naked body and the outer sewn so that the fur faces outward. These outfits are still worn today by hunters going out in winter. All but the soles of the boots are made from caribou skin. Garments are designed to fit loosely, with overlapping layers, thus keeping warm air inside the parka but also allowing for ventilation at the neck, with the removal of the hood, at the wrists and waist, and with the removal of the outer parka (Hatt and Taylor 1969: 7, Issenman 1997: 38–40). The ability to adapt clothing layers while perspiring is crucial for survival, for if the warm air around the body were to become saturated by water vapours, the parka would freeze on the body (Stenton 1991: 9).

For Damaris, the process of learning the skills and techniques of skin clothing manufacture began early. Inuit elders describe how, from a very young age, girls watched mothers and female relatives at work, handled tools for their feel, and were given tiny pieces of skin to sew together. However, seamstress skills are not limited to manual dexterity. As with many craftspeople, assessing the potentiality of social and material environments, and of a person's place and practice within it, 'is an integral part of the process of learning and improving one's craft' (Portisch 2010: 564). For Inuit women, learning how to process skins thus meant learning how to perceive and to conduct oneself in the world as a seamstress.

Girls were taught how to think about the animals being hunted and strategies to best draw these animals to the group through their sewing and overall comportment. So girls became versed in the zoological nomenclature of animals in relation to humans (Randa 2002) and learned the lexicon for parts of a caribou skin (Oakes 1991: 206), for different pattern pieces and for designs. Perceiving the world as a seamstress also meant developing multisensory skills to assess the material qualities of fur, and to recognize the effects of an animal's age, health and sex, in addition to seasonality, on the density, length and colour of its pelage. The look, smell, and feel of an animal pelt could determine a skin's use, for instance as a mattress, or as a man's, woman's or child's garment. Animals were always eyed and evaluated for their potential later incarnation.

As surviving siblings recollect, Damaris was trained by her mother, Qaumayuq, and her great-grandmother, Maikpainnuk. This careful tuition was said to have prepared Damaris, like many women of her generation, for the arduous task of outfitting hunters in her extended family, a task she would perform throughout her life. With the movement of Inuit into permanent settlements in the 1960s and 1970s came the introduction of mandatory school laws and full-time employment opportunities. Financial demands and time constraints on young women meant that significantly fewer were apprenticed in skin clothing manufacture, a skill that takes years to acquire, and a lifetime to hone. Today, relatively few young women are knowledgeable about skin processing. But with the rising prices of staple foods in settlement stores, extended families must rely upon full-time hunters to provide meat all year round, and upon elder women seamstresses to outfit them for this task. Damaris is well remembered for having spent much of her time processing and sewing skins (Figure 7.2).

## Processing: On Turning Animals into Garments

The need for meat and for skin clothing generates a delicate ecology of relations between animals and humans in the Arctic. Hunters are said often to set out travelling and scouting with a thought for their family's wardrobe needs. Whether it is caribou or some other animal, its sex and age, the colour and texture of its pelage, and seasonality will be considered before the kill; and carcasses will be butchered in anticipation of the garment a seamstress might make from its fur. Of course, such a close monitoring of resources is not always feasible. A young caribou buck is not always available when a parka is needed and other animals – seals, bears, wolverines, hares, whales, walrus and birds – make irregular and unexpected appearances. In pre-settlement times, it was understood that an animal would present itself to the well-dressed, generous and courteous hunter who was then tasked with its careful and dutiful killing, and its respectful treatment during the curing of its skin (Driscoll-Englestad 2005: 38). Infractions on the part of the seamstress who had dressed the hunter – not keeping skins clean or disposing of bones properly – would interfere with the family's relationship with the animal.

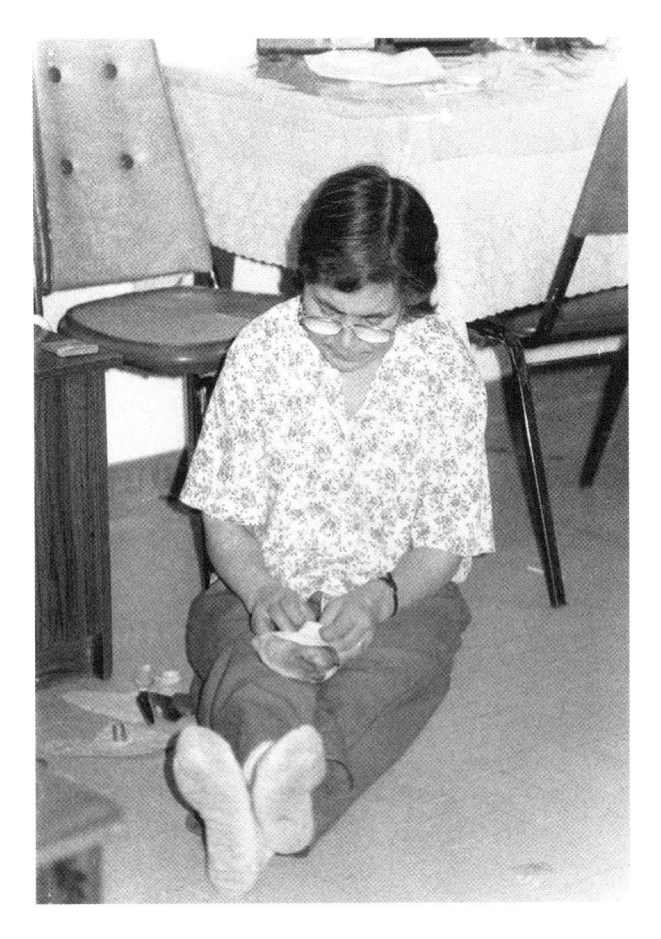

**Figure 7.2** **Photograph of Damaris Ittukusuk Katdlutsiak sewing a pair of mittens, taken in Iglulik by Nancy Katdlutsiak, c.1992**

However, if the animal was treated well, the family would have its good will, and therefore could carry hopes of its catch or kill over and over again.

Skin clothing manufacture can be understood, then, as women's indirect participation in the hunt (Bodenhorn 1990). Pelts were regarded as pre-shaped by an animal and charged with its identity. Given the duty of care for these most precious properties, it was the seamstress's role to manage the delicate transition of animal persons from live creature to animate thing. This transition, when handled properly, appeased and welcomed the animal so it might pass on part of its spirit to the wearer through the finished garment (Chaussonnet 1988: 212). Endowed with the spirit of the animal, the hunter could successfully hunt the placated animal again and again.

**Figure 7.3** Close-up of the back of a caribou skin parka. Photograph by Jayson Kunnuk. Isuma Productions, 2005. Permission by Isuma Productions

Making animal furs into garments is complex, ritually significant, time-consuming and arduous work. It takes up to eight hours of labour, spread out in stages over several days, to transform the skin of a freshly killed animal into one that it is suitable for clothing (Figure 7.3) (Oakes 1991: 104, Otak 2005: 74). Usually this is considered women's work, though men help occasionally with the most physically demanding tasks.

Given the cyclical and generative nature of Inuit hunting, it is difficult to identify a point when a woman's skin processing work begins. Caribou are normally skinned and butchered on site, where they are killed. Skins are transported directly back to the hunting camp or settlement for women to process. Dirt, blood, meat particles, fat and subcutaneous tissues must be washed, scrubbed and scraped from the skins within a few hours or a day of the animal being taken. If left untreated the skins will rot.

Once cleaned, the caribou skins are then dried. Where and how this happens depends on the historical period and the season. Winter skins in pre-settlement times were dried indoors in a sodhouse over a seal oil lamp. In contemporary times, heated areas in a settlement house work well to dry these thick, coarse skins. The highly valued, thinner, late summer skins used for clothing are laid out flat on dry ground outside so that the fascia is exposed to sunlight and the skins are ventilated while drying (Otak 2005: 75). Under ideal conditions, these skins dry within a day but in changeable weather, or during rain and snow, skins are moved indoors and then moved back out again with the sun's return. When Inuit were still semi-nomadic, following migrating caribou herds in the summer months, drying could be done on poles (Boas 1888, cited in Hatt and Taylor 1969: 13). If the relocation of a family was necessary, and they could not wait for skins to dry on the ground, wet skins were strung across backpacks using large poles and air-dried during the walk (Jenness 1946, cited in Oakes 1991: 106).

When half-dry, the skin side is worked with a blunt tool made from bone, antler, stone or metal, concentrating on any areas that may have dried more than others and become rigid (Otak 2005: 75). Before its second scraping, the dried and partially softened skin is either left outside to freeze, or it is heated if the skin is intended for clothing and needs to be extra soft. Before people lived in centrally-heated (or furnace-heated) settlement houses, families would heat the skins by using them as bedding, sleeping with the flesh side against their naked skin (Boas 1964 [1888]: 114, Amundsen 1905, cited in Klokkernes and Sharma 2005: 93). Smaller skin pieces could also be put inside clothing worn during the day (Otak 2005: 76). Leah Aqsaajuk Otak – another of the mitten admirers on that day at the airport in 1997 – recollects this now largely abandoned, but most intimate, stage in skin processing. She describes cherished memories of her grandfather curing the belly portion of a caribou skin 'by wrapping it round his back, under his clothing, while scraping a previously cured skin' (Otak 2005: 75). Exposure to freezing temperatures or to prolonged body heat, in the family bed or slipped under a person's clothing, weakens the epidermis of a caribou skin, partially fracturing it so that it becomes more pliable (Klokkernes and Sharma 2005: 93).

The next stage of skin processing involves a forceful, repetitive scraping of the hide using dull, blunt tools made of antler, scapula bones, brass, iron, or steel to more deeply fracture the epidermal layer (Oakes 1991: 107, Otak 2005: 74). The length, intensity and duration of these scrapings are determined by the physical properties of each individual skin. Variables such as the season in which an animal is caught, its age and health, and the particular body part, all affect the density of the fibre bundles, and thus the relative stiffness of the skin. The more compact the fibre bundles, the more scraping is required to break them down. With a dull scraper, the seamstress uses slow, firm, criss-crossing strokes until she hears a crackling sound (Otak 2005: 76), indicating the breaking up of tissue connections in the animal skin. When this sound is no longer audible – which could take several hours of effort – the hide is ready for the next stage in the curing process (Otak 2005: 76, Oakes 1991: 107, Klokkerness and Sharma 2005: 94).

The seamstress dampens the skin 'by sprinkling it liberally with water and then rubbing the water over and into the skin with the palm of the hand' (Null and Manning 1944: 157). It is then rolled into an airtight bundle (with the skin side inwards) and left for several hours. The quantity of water needed for each skin is precisely gauged. Too much water rots the skin and loosens the hair (Null and Manning 1944: 157 Otak 2005: 76), and not enough leaves it brittle.

When the dampened skin is unrolled, it is then stretched or scraped repeatedly with a blunt instrument until dry, using short, slow, even strokes in all directions, so as to rupture skin cells in the dermis and create spaces between each small cluster of hair (Oakes 1991: 110). Women and girls then chew parts of the pliable skin to remove excess membrane, especially around the head, eyes and ears where it is difficult to remove with a tool (Otak 2005: 77). The skin is then scraped again, with a sharpened metal scraper, to remove the hypodermis (tissue beneath the skin). This continues until 'the high-pitched scratchy sound of the scraper against the skin becomes low and resonant' (Oakes 1991: 111). The soft and velvety skin is then either placed outside again where frost crystals are left to accumulate on it or it is rubbed with water. It is then stretched one final time to align the sides with each other, before it is cut into a pattern.

In pre-settlement times, never during this extended processing of skin was the animal spirit said to have left that skin. At no stage was the skin ever seen to have been made into an inanimate object. Before explaining this meaningful connection between spirit and skin further, I move from the technical to the personal and return to Damaris' training as a seamstress.

## Sewing: On the Making of People and the Growing of Animals

Damaris was the first child of Arnakallak and Qaumayuq, and three years older than the next eldest of seven siblings. Lily describes her mother's accelerated entry into the world of women's work. Damaris' skills were crucial for outfitting her parents' expanding family of growing children. As the couple had more children, Damaris accompanied her father, Arnakallak, on overnight hunting trips. A successful hunter required a wife travelling along with him (Bodenhorn 1990: 62) and when a wife was unable to travel a daughter or another woman from the camp might fill in. Women would be charged with such tasks as keeping the snow-house warm, helping to tend the dog team, processing the skins of freshly butchered animals, drying the hunters' wet clothing upon their return, repairing seams and holes in garments, chewing stiffened boot soles and softening other hardened clothing to have them ready for the next day.

Damaris' mother Qaumayuq was born in 1926. She died of lung cancer in the early 1960s, a few years before Lily was born. Lily's younger brother, Bobby, was given Qaumayuq's name. In Inuit society, children are gifted the names of recently deceased relatives or friends, and are said to inherit the characteristics of that person; in many respects they are said to become that person again. Since the diffusion of Christianity in the Canadian Arctic in the 1920s and 1930s, Inuit have also been customarily given Christian names or, more recently, secular English names. A few photographs of Lily's grandmother Qaumayuq have survived. In one family photograph, from the 1950s, Qaumayuq stands with her husband Arnakallak, their five children, and Arnakallak's, grandmother, Makpainnuk (Figure 7.4).

*Stitching Lives* 139

**Figure 7.4** Qaumayuq and her family. From left to right. Back row: Qaumayuq, Arnakallak, Rhoda, Maikpainnuk, Damaris. Front row: Timonie, Pheobe, Jonathan. Photograph taken at Nunaviniq, Ellesmere Island, possibly by Akpaliapik or Tatiga, the other family residing there at the time, c.1955. Pond Inlet Archives

Qaumayuq's right hand is clad in a de-haired caribou skin mitten, very similar to Lily's mittens later made by Damaris. Qaumayuq's left hand is bare and her index finger is gently positioning her toddler son, Timonie, for the camera. Damaris is also present, a timid-looking 10-year old, slightly offset from the other family members, to the far right edge of the image, standing beside her great-grandmother, Maikpainnuk.

As Rhoda Arnakallak, Damaris' younger sister by three years, remembers, the photograph was taken at a camp called Nunaviniq, between Craig Harbour and the Royal Canadian Mounted Police (RCMP) post at Grise Fiord on Ellesmere Island. Damaris' family was one of six (two from the Mittimatalik region, and four from Inukjuak, formerly known as Port Harrison) who were relocated to a previously unoccupied region of the High Arctic as part of a Canadian government programme to populate the region and so secure claims to territorial sovereignty.

The geopolitical motivations behind this scheme, its many misjudgements, its bureaucratic failures, and its effects on Inuit have been well documented in academic research (Marcus 1995) and more popular accounts of the period (McGrath 2006). The relocation programme was the subject of a three-volume report by the Royal Commission on Aboriginal Peoples (RCAP 1994a, 1994b, 1994c), resulting in a $10 million dollar (CAD) compensation payment made by the Canadian government in 1996.

That life for these 'arctic exiles' (as they later came to be known) was difficult is a serious understatement. Broken promises over government support left the families under-provisioned and impoverished, without the material tools or knowledge of the landscape necessary for survival. Here there were no established hunting paths or customary routes. Indeed, according to Damaris' brother Morgan, there is no Inuktitut place name for Craig Harbour. It translates into Kuriik Haapa, the Inuktitut pronunciation of the English name, because it was neither a traditional camp nor a hunting spot. The barrenness of this place was so very different to Qaumayuq's family's previous home near Mittimatalik. In the 1950s the latter region had been rich in caribou, a marker of wealth in Inuit society. When the RCMP service ship docked in Mittimatalik on 28 August 1953 to pick up the families recruited to travel to Craig Harbour, the officer noted in his report how well dressed the Mittimatalik people seemed in their caribou skins (McGrath 2006: 113).

Hunting this animal had been a key part of Damaris' family's yearly cycle before they were relocated to the High Arctic. Traditionally, once the break-up of sea ice was complete, young families were dropped off by boat at nearby inlets, where they tracked caribou herds, hunting, skinning and caching meat as they went. Skins were carried back to the coast, where they would await the arrival of the elders to transport them back to larger family walrus- and seal-hunting camps where winter wear was manufactured during the wait for sea-ice to form again. Climatic and environmental cues influenced these cycles of movement, harvest and making (Awa, in Wachowich 1999: 124). Therese Qillaq Ijjangiaq, one of Lily's relatives, recollects how, for example, snow buntings were used to assess the readiness of caribou for making into clothing:

> We started for the interior when the small fledglings [birds] had started to walk around. It was said that at this particular period the caribou skins would have become just right for the clothing material ... It was also said [that] when the chicks' feathers had turned reddish, the caribou calves' furs would also have turned reddish in colour at which time they were just right to be used for a qulittaq [outer parka]. So the snow buntings were used to determine when the caribou skin was right for clothing material. (In Bennett and Rowley 2004: 307–8)

At the coastal walrus- and seal-hunting camps elder women allocated skins to younger seamstresses who went about processing and sewing for their family's winter season. Through this manufacturing process, young girls grew into adults: they acquired social recognition as adults by becoming proficient in skin processing and sewing.

It was imperative that a camp should have enough skins to clothe everyone for the winter and that the clothing was made with care and precision. It took eight caribou skins to outfit a man with inner and outer parkas, trousers, stockings, boots and mittens (Mathiassen 1927: 159). To clothe an average family of five, a hunter had to take 30 caribou, at the very least (Vézinet, cited in Issenman 1997: 71). The Arctic climate and weather made slipshod sewing a dangerous practice. Seamstresses were taught to sew stitches less than half a millimetre apart (Issenman 1997: 14) and they became adept with different types. Morality tales emphasized the harm that might come to idle hands making loose stitches, as in the story of a hunter whose trousers were poorly sewn told by Emile Immaruittuq (a relative of Lily's, on her father's side). Clad in poorly made trousers, this man's sex organs froze, so the story goes. Rendered immobile, he 'did not wish to be a burden and he wanted [the rest of his hunting party] to survive, so he asked to be left behind. ... He only cared that someone would tell his family of his fate' (Immaruittuq, in Bennett and Rowley 2004: 329).

Skin clothing production was critical in protecting people's bodies from the wind and cold, but it also served broader social purposes: making visible and nurturing relations between animals and humans. Clothing production transformed an animal's skin into a second skin for humans, one that through its design features 'still maintained its animal identity' (Chaussonnet 1988: 212). Caribou skin parkas, hoods, trousers and leggings are tailored so that the parts of the animal cover the corresponding parts of the human body (Chaussonnet 1988: 213, Driscoll 1987). The neck and shoulders of the caribou enclose the neck and shoulders of the wearer; the head becomes the hood (sometimes with ear flaps left on); the thicker rump skin of the caribou becomes the seat of the trousers; and the legs become boots and mittens. Garments are sewn so that the direction of the fur corresponds to the way it would grow on an animal. The skins of young and baby caribou are made into children's and infants' clothes respectively.

For a seamstress, the fact that unprocessed skins were seen as 'pre-shaped and charged with animal identity stimulated her creativity and guided her work towards a distinctive cut, according to which particular character of the animal she wished to emphasize' (Chaussonnet 1988: 216). Clothing thus facilitated a hunter's imitation or embodiment of his prey (Willerslev 2007). Yet tails inserted into a man's caribou hunting parka (in the back panel) and other design features could also make metaphoric reference to the wolf, the predatory enemy of the caribou thus allowing the hunter to mimetically allude to prey and predator simultaneously (Driscoll-Engelstad 2005: 37). This symbolic mediation enacted in parka designs sustained the cycle of regeneration and renewal of animal spirits (Driscoll 1987). Furthermore, by donning skin clothing 'humans take on the form of animals and express their bond with the rest of the animal domain. They acquire the strength, knowledge and powers of the animals' souls' (Issenman 1997: 181). Seamstresses facilitated this transfer and worked together with hunters and animals to grow new animals through the hunting cycle.

**Fracturing: On Exile, Estrangement and Re-settlement**

Damaris' intimate understanding of the animal realm and of skin garment production is credited by surviving siblings to the singular training she received from Maikpainnuk, her paternal great-grandmother. In a 1993 testimonial for the RCAP about the colonial relocation exercise, Damaris' father, Arnakallak, recounted how, when he was first recruited by the RCMP to move his family to the High Arctic, 'he wanted to bring his grandmother along, but he was told that she was too old. He became very angry and said that if she was not allowed to go, he would not agree to go so the police allowed him to take his grandmother along' (In RCAP 1994a: 81).

They may have needed her, but Maikpainnuk's environmental skills and knowledge base were ill suited to the new landscape in Craig Harbour. This relocation was disorienting for even this most experienced elder. After only a week in Craig Harbour, the Inuit families were transported to a different location, Lindstrom Peninsula (about 64 km away), ostensibly so that they would not grow reliant on the RCMP for trade goods or relief. Here too, traditional hunting paths were almost non-existent and the mountainous terrain was mostly impassable by dog-team (Marcus 1995: 108). In his RCAP testimony, Arnakallak recalled having been told that they would be moving to a place where wildlife and game were plentiful, yet this proved wholly inaccurate (1994a: 81). Government officers had not carried out preparatory wildlife distribution studies, and land resources proved scarce (Marcus 1995: 109). To make matters worse, efforts to feed and clothe the families were hampered when the area was designated as a game reserve. Inuit were prevented by law from taking muskoxen and polar bear, and, critically, caribou hunting was tightly regulated. As Arnakallak stated:

> The police and the commissioners were the only ones allowed to actually kill the caribou. The police had the attitude that the people did not know the difference between female and male caribou so they were the ones who shot the caribou. The people were told not to kill any caribou from that area. (In RCAP 1994a: 80)

Faced with a scarcity of supply, and prevented from hunting those caribou that were available, people suffered great hardships. Remembering events 40 years earlier, Arnakallak described the effects on his aged grandmother: 'Tired of eating the same food', she 'hungered for fish and other wild game' (Arnakallak, in RCAP 1994: 80). In later years, caribou skins were flown into the settlement for the Inuit women to sew, but this was not the same as selecting animals by hunting. The cycle of regeneration was broken. Unsurprisingly, bison skins transported from the Prairies proved to be unusable.

Arnakallak and Qaumayuq's family endured life on Ellesmere Island for four years, until they were finally permitted to return to Mittimatalik, in August 1957. But Maikpainnuk had contracted tuberculosis while in the High Arctic and when the ship docked in Mittimatalik she was not allowed to disembark. Instead she was transported south to a sanatorium in Hamilton, Ontario, where she died on 2 October 1957. By Lily's reckoning, the cause of her great-great-grandmother's death was not contagious disease but the heartache, loneliness and depression of exile. Having returned from Ellesmere Island, Damaris and her family resettled in their home camp, Nalluaq. On 28 June 1958, aged 15, she was married to Josiah Kadlutsiak, son of an Inuit Anglican lay preacher. Lily remembers her mother's description of events, of how her husband was unknown to her before their wedding day and of how, following custom, she had little say in the arranged marriage that took her to live with in-laws in the Iglulik region, far from her birth family. By the time of Damaris' marriage, Maikpainnuk had already died, and a few years later Damaris lost her mother, Qaumayuq.

During the 1960s the Canadian government increased colonial pressures on Inuit to settle permanently into communities where they could be more easily administered. Damaris and her new family joined others moving from their outpost camps to live year-round in Iglulik. These settlements were run as microcosms of southern society (Brody 1975), and adapting to these new dynamics proved difficult for these formerly hunting and travelling families. Yet through all the hardships, Damaris maintained an intimacy with the earlier phase of her life, and with animals, through her manufacture of skin clothing.

Lily remembers her mother reflecting on her life, and reminiscing with her daughter about her time on Ellesmere Island. People suffered terribly during those years. Without proper food and housing, and with the cold, dark winters, illnesses flared, and people died. Paradoxically – according to Lily's account – Damaris grew nostalgic about this time in her life, despite the hardships endured, to such a degree that she longed to return to places inhabited during the time before her marriage. Today, Lily (now working full time as an administrator in a government office) explains with some regret that she had always planned to take her there. But Damaris died before this could be arranged. The mittens, the memories, and her adopted son, whom she named after her mother, are what Lily has left.

## Conclusion: The Material Emergence of Lives

In pre-settlement times, before the advent of arctic colonialism, Inuit were part of a cycle of regeneration and renewal, born of an intimate ecology of relations between hunters, seamstresses, animals and skins, and one where new persons were born and reborn, produced and reproduced. This intimacy of relation found expression at every stage in skin processing: from an animal giving itself to a hunter, to butchering, the manipulation of skin, and fabrication into a garment that resembled the animal's former self. The engagement between people and animals was at once multi-sensual, intimate, and mimetic, as humans sewed themselves into animals to ensure their nourishment through the hunt. Animals and people were made and grown in this process. With the move into settlements in the late twentieth century came a period of dislocation and coercion as Inuit families were resettled in unsuitable environments, and in such a way as to threaten traditional relations with the land. Skin clothing manufacture has persisted in the Canadian Arctic, albeit in a more limited way, and in the context of the distractions, social problems and despair that often characterize contemporary life in settlements. The procurement of hunting and sewing materials, access to tools and the acquisition of skills are now highly dependent on a person's socio-economic status. Many contemporary women simply do not have the income or the time to sew. Estrangement is now as powerful a motif as engagement.

In the tension between engagement and estrangement, people have found possibilities for resilience, resistance and renewal. Fifteen years after the tender handling of the mitten witnessed at the airport in 1997, this garment is now tattered and worn. Yet it continues to form a focus for the generation of new social lives. The ethnographic research on which this chapter is based has stimulated a collaborative effort to explore Damaris' artistry – her sewing – and through this exploration localized forms of history and meaning-making are emerging as Lily draws her father's, sister's, aunts', uncles' and cousins' stories of Damaris into this project of recovery. In the process, homage paid to creativity and strength crosses generations from daughter to mother, grandmother and great-grandmother. Memories of mother-love embodied in a pair of mittens come to enrol all those who participated in their making, traversing different material, animal, and human lifeworlds.

**Acknowledgments**

My deepest gratitude goes to Lily Tauqaugaq Tongak in Iglulik for her friendship and for sharing with me stories and photographs of her late mother's artistry. I also want to thank Phillipa Ootoowak, Rhoda Arnakallak, and Morgan Arkakallak for their family history research in Mittimatalik. I thank Apphia Agalakti Awa and Leah Aqsaajuk Otak for teaching me about skin sewing, and Nancy Kadlutsiak and Jayson Kunnuk (Isuma Productions) for sharing their photographs with me.

**References**

Bennett, J. and S. Rowley 2004. *Uqalurait: The Oral History of Nunavut*. Montreal and Kingston: McGill-Queens University Press.
Boas, F. 1964 [1888]. *The Central Eskimo*. Lincoln: University of Nebraska Press.
Bodenhorn, B. 1990. I'm not the great hunter, my wife is: Inupiat and anthropological models of gender. *Etudes Inuit Studies*, 14(1–2), 55–74.

Briggs, J. 1991. Expecting the unexpected: Canadian Inuit training for an experimental lifestyle. *Ethnos*, 19(3), 259–87.
Brody, H. 1975. *The People's Land*. Vancouver: Douglas and MacIntyre.
Chaussonnet, V. 1988. Needles and animals: women's magic, in *Crossroads of Continents: Cultures of Siberia and Alaska*, edited by W. Fitzhugh and A. Crowell. Washington, D.C.: Smithsonian Institution Press.
Cruikshank, J. 1998. *The Social Life of Stories: Narrative and Knowledge in the Yukon Territory*. Lincoln and London: University of Nebraska Press.
Driscoll, B. 1987. Pretending to be caribou: the Inuit parka as an artistic tradition, in *The Spirit Sings: Artistic Traditions of Canada's First Peoples*, edited by The Glenbow Museum Toronto: McLelland and Stewart/Glenbow Museum.
Driscoll-Engelstad, B. 2005. Dance of the loon: symbolism and continuity in Copper Inuit ceremonial clothing. *Arctic Anthropology*, 42(1), 33–47.
Hatt, G. and Taylor, K. 1969. Arctic skin clothing in Eurasia and America: an ethnographic study. *Arctic Anthropology*, 5(2), 3–132.
Ingold, T. 2000. *The Perception of the Environment: Essays on Livelihood, Dwelling and Skill*. London: Routledge.
Issenman, B.K. 1997. *Sinews of Survival: The Living Legacy of Inuit Clothing*. Vancouver: UBC Press.
Jackson, M. 2002. *The Politics of Storytelling: Violence, Transgression and Intersubjectivity*. Copenhagen: University of Copenhagen, Museum Tusculanum Press.
Klokkerness, T. and N. Sharma. 2005. The Roald Amundsen collection: the impact of a skin preparation method on preservation, in *Arctic Clothing of North America: Alaska, Canada, Greenland*, edited by J.C.H. King, B. Pauksztat, and R. Storrie. Montreal and Kingston: McGill-Queens University Press.
Kwon, H. 1998. The saddle and the sledge: hunting as comparative narrative in Siberia and beyond. *The Journal of the Royal Anthropological Institute*, 4(1), 115–27.
Marcus, A.R. 1995. *Relocating Eden: The Image and Politics of Inuit Exile in the Canadian Arctic*. Dartmouth: University Press of New England.
Mathiassen, T. 1928. *Material Culture of the Iglulik Eskimo (Report of the Fifth Thule Expedition 1921–24, Vol. 1. No.1)*. Copenhagen: Nordisk Forlag.
McGrath, M. 2006. *The Long Exile: A Tale of Inuit Betrayal and Survival in the High Arctic*. New York: Vintage Books.
Meeks, N.D. and C.R. Cartwright 2005. Caribou and seal hair: examination by scanning electron microscopy, in *Arctic Clothing of North America: Alaska, Canada, Greenland*, edited by J.C.H. King, B. Pauksztat and R. Storrie. Montreal and Kingston: McGill-Queens University Press.
Null, T.H. and E.W. Manning 1944. The preparation of skins and clothing in the Eastern Canadian Arctic. *Polar Record*, 4(28), 156–69.
Oakes, J. 1991. *Copper and Caribou Inuit Skin Clothing Production*. Ottawa: Canadian Museum of Civilization.
Oakes, J. et al. 1995. Comparison of traditional and manufactured cold weather ensembles. *Climate Research*, 5(1), 83–90.

Otak, L.A. 2005. Iniqsimajuq: caribou-skin preparation in Igloolik, Nunavut, in *Arctic Clothing of North America: Alaska, Canada, Greenland*, edited by J.C.H. King, B. Pauksztat and R. Storrie. Montreal and Kingston: McGill Queens University Press.

Portisch, A.O. 2010. The craft of skilful learning: Kazakh women's everyday craft practices in western Mongolia. *Journal of the Royal Anthropological Institute*, S62–79.

Randa, V. 2002. Qui se ressemble s'assemble: logique de construction et d'organisation des zoonymes en langue inuit. *Etudes Inuit Studies* 26(1), 71–108.

RCAP [Royal Commission on Aboriginal Peoples]. 1994a. *The High Arctic Relocation: Summary of Supporting Information*. Ottawa: Canada Communication Group Publishing.

RCAP. 1994b. *The High Arctic Relocation: Summary of Supporting Information*. Ottawa: Canada Communication Group Publishing.

RCAP. 1994c. *The High Arctic Relocation: Summary of Supporting Information*. Ottawa: Canada Communication Group Publishing.

Ridington, R. 1990. *Little Bit Know Something: Stories in a Language of Anthropology*. Iowa City: University of Iowa Press.

Stenton, D.R. 1991. The adaptive significance of caribou winter clothing for arctic hunter-gatherers. *Etudes Inuit Studies*, 15(1), 3–28.

Wachowich, N. in collaboration with Rhoda Kaukjak Katsak, and Sandra Pikujak Katsak. 1999. *Saqiyuq: Stories from the Lives of Three Inuit Women*. Montreal and Kingston: McGill-Queens University Press.

Willerslev, R. 2007. *Soul Hunters: Hunting, Animism, and Personhood among The Siberian Yukaghirs*. Berkeley: University of California Press.

# Chapter 8
# Gardening and Wellbeing: A View from the Ground

Anne Jepson

## Growing Plants and People

*I watch as my one-year old explores her world. She applies all her senses to new objects: what they feel like in her mouth, what they do if shaken or banged against something. A few months on from her seeming indifference to objects, she is now utterly absorbed in every material she encounters. Her curiosity is in her discovery and mediation of (or negotiation with) whatever she crawls near to, or is given to her. In the winter she stared for ages at snow on the doormat from my boots before tentatively touching it. In the summer she sat repeatedly putting stones in her mouth. As she did, I knew, in my own mouth, exactly the texture, the sound and feel of tooth on pebble, the grittiness of soil. I had done the same at her age. My mouth remembered.*

*I have been a gardener since I was a child. Then, with only nascent self-consciousness, my favourite activity was pruning; not topiary, but the containment of a shrub alongside others that had been deliberately placed and organized according to their characteristics and particular requirements. The growing was not of immediate interest; it was the controlling, the making, and the sensual elements of our garden in southern England that attracted me.*

*I remember the plants – I can visualize their positions and remember rolling the strange names – Philadelphus, Phlomis, and Chaenomeles – around my tongue in that garden that I left when I was 12: the feel of the leaves, the pungency of aromatics, the thorns, the flowers that had a head-filling fragrance. Only 20 years later did I realise that not all of us have similarly intimate memories of our childhood gardens.*

*As a child I was merely rehearsing a slightly more sophisticated version of what my one-year old is doing now. Our involvement with the world was totally sensual from the start. As a 'grown-up' gardener and anthropologist of gardening I have struggled with the 'being and doing' in both realms: I have internalized aspects of anthropology as a discipline, but the practice of it both profoundly engages with and influences the world around me. As a gardener, practice too becomes embodied, and my interaction with the soil, with the garden and its various elements is something of a dialogue.*

*I am also the parent of two grown-up children. They were produced from the very stuff of myself, but from the moment of birth, their journey away from me has been inexorable and inevitable. With children, as with gardens, questions emerge about where making ends and growing begins as we nurture, protect and guide them towards independence.*

*In the garden I am involved in an endless process of making, in which growing is merely one aspect. I might be trying to make something beautiful or functional, something that reflects my personality and ideals. In all the activity my mind and body are focused, but my activity is also greatly influenced by the garden around me. The weather, the soil, the plants themselves can change without input from me. A created garden alters continually as, for example, plants grow ever larger, some are smothered by other plants and seeds blow in from elsewhere. The gardener has no exact mental picture of how a garden will develop, just a hunch. What is regarded as 'nature' proceeds and the gardener intervenes with more or less ferocity. The same might be said of parents raising human beings.*

## Therapeutic Horticulture

There is, I suggest, an equivalence between the production of a person and the production of a garden; the processes for both are sensual as well as unpredictable. In this chapter I argue that in gardening, growing and making are as inseparable as they are in the rearing of a child. I discuss these processes with reference to a recent gardening project in Scotland which offered a therapeutic avenue for people seeking to enhance their wellbeing, or for people who felt alienated in some way, or for those whose self-perception, as indicated in their personal narratives, had become negative or destructive. Drawing on my work in this garden project, I argue that gardening can allow people to feel that they have reconnected with significant sensual aspects of being human, through interactions with earth or soil, plants and tools. Such experiences of reconnection can be perceived as therapeutic, as can the growing of food that can be directly eaten and the sharing of experience with others.

Such aspects of gardening tend to go unrecognized in studies of therapeutic horticultural projects which, for the most part, have failed to take account of the contexts in which they have been developed (see Bhatti 2006, Milligan et al. 2003, Sempik et al. 2003, Parr 2007). Yet therapeutic horticulture has existed for centuries across the world, and more particularly in Britain, from the havens that were medieval monastery gardens, to post-World War rehabilitative projects for injured veterans. My experience of therapeutic horticultural projects over the last 25 years has been that they tend to form secluded gardens and sanctuaries of escape and quiet recovery, or explicitly rehabilitative units within hospitals. For instance, many institutions which had initially opened as large Victorian asylums (and later became psychiatric hospitals) retained their fruit and vegetable gardens until they were closed down during the early 1990s, the therapeutic value of the garden continuing to be recognized until then.

Despite the long-term uses of gardens in therapeutic practices, there has been little attempt to establish empirical links between gardening and the prevention or curing of disease. Extensive literature reviews on therapeutic horticulture in 1978 (Markee and Janick 1979) and 2003 (Sempik, Aldridge and Becker 2003) found few such studies, although this has been partly redressed since (see Gonzales et al. 2010). The flourishing fields of positive psychology (Thin 2011) and happiness and wellbeing studies (Thaler and Sunstein 2009) now provide a backdrop that fits well with the therapeutic benefits of gardening described in qualitative studies, many of these 'benefits' being fairly inchoate and difficult to quantify. These studies suggest that gardening can provide an escape from a difficult life or experience (Kaplan 1995), that it can stand as a metaphor for life and its cycles (Relf 1981), and also that it provides a structured arena for nurturing and social interaction (Neuberger 1995, Sempik et al. 2003).

A further benefit that, as Sempik notes, has been under-explored, is the production of food. Indeed, the direct connections between growing, cooking and eating together emerged as central to the garden project I describe in this chapter. Although eating together in the garden did not extend to creating kin (Carsten 1995), it did become the very heart of the enterprise, as I discuss later. The wider political and cultural context of the garden project was also significant and in what follows I briefly allude to a range of organizations and practices which informed the project, such as government, funders, policy, health propaganda and bureaucracy, which seek to 'make' virtuous, self-disciplined, healthy citizens through therapeutic means. While identifying these factors my argument builds on those of Relf (1981), Neuberger (1995) and Sempik et al. (2003), regarding the constructive and therapeutic aspects of being and working in a garden.

This chapter draws on five years that I spent working in a particular kind of garden, from 2006 onwards. The garden project, located on the outskirts of Edinburgh, was supported by the National Health Service (NHS) and the City Council and its functions extended beyond that of growing food or providing a recreational and relaxing space with ornamental plantings. The project developed in the context of large bureaucracies and amidst emerging discourses around healthy eating, obesity (Cordain et al. 2005), environmental change, biodiversity and the local food movement. I was employed as the project's founding manager and my job description stated that the project must engage with these issues as well as with ethnic minorities and with problems surrounding disability, mental health and social exclusion. It is preposterous to imagine that this small project was going to achieve all of this, but the project was situated in a bureaucratic and political environment where 'outcomes' had to be demonstrated.[1] Such expectations were cascaded down from policy makers and funders. As Lock and Nguyen (2010: 4)

---

1   The Scottish Government produced a set of 15 'Single Outcome Agreements' in 2007, see: http://www.scotland.gov.uk/About/scotPerforms/outcomes. Accessed October 2011.

point out, 'the health of people everywhere is inextricably entangled with global politics, social issues, and economics'.

It is important to note that I was not employed as an anthropologist to research the garden project. My remit as the project's manager was to create a successful therapeutic gardening project on a new allotment site within a year. This chapter is an anthropological reflection on those years, rather than a report of research findings. Yet my training and work as an anthropologist, together with my previous experience in therapeutic horticulture and other care settings, informed all the important decisions I made about how the project should run. I am also a life-long gardener, and have developed anthropological analysis of gardening in terms of knowledge which is embodied and often unarticulated (Jepson 2006). With this background of interrelated gardening and anthropology in practice, I discuss the garden project, analyzing it in retrospect. The account that follows is not derived from research data collected through methods such as participant observation. Rather, it draws on my recollections of my work and involvement in the garden project. All personal names and some details have been changed to respect the anonymity and privacy of staff and participants involved in the project. My discussion of their activities and views rests on my own interpretations and does not necessarily claim to be in accord with the views of participants themselves.

The garden project attempted to provide its participants with an uncomplicated and unfettered experience of growing food. It aimed to provide therapeutic benefit while not being prescriptive or assumptive. This allowed people simply to 'be', to develop relationships with others in an open environment, and to explore or rediscover encounters with non-human life through the activities involved in gardening, cooking, and eating together (Figure 8.1). In this process there was both a growing and a making of the garden and of a community of participants in a wider context of limited funding and amidst broad swathes of social and health policies.

**Cultivating the Garden, Creating Relationships**

Biomedicine, which guides conventional approaches to health in the UK, has been criticized for narrowly targeting diseases and conditions (Lock and Nguyen 2010), and for being predominantly concerned with directly observable results, rather than considering the whole person in their wider environment. Although many conditions, such as heart disease, poor mental health and obesity, are now strongly linked with economic deprivation (see Marmot and Wilkinson 2005), biomedical practices still tend to focus on the illness rather than the person (or community). The garden project was a different enterprise. Through a description of the project and some of those involved with it, I aim to show how growing things was perceived to help resolve difficulties in some participants' lives, not only because it provided an escape from stress and anxiety, but also because people seemed to feel benefits from their integration within an environment of soil, cycles of growth and decay,

**Figure 8.1    View of the garden project, 2006. Photo: Anne Jepson**

seeds, worms, weeds and dirty vegetables. Involvement in the garden was a fully embodied experience for participants, such that many gardening practices seemed to be internalized. Given that our influence in the garden was inevitably tempered by the vagaries of weather, plants, garden pests and diseases, among many other factors, our approach had to be one of flexibility and creative response: disasters and crises were not features of project life.

The project's staff (none medically trained) sought to ease participants' feelings of alienation – whether caused by personal crises and medicalization (Conrad 2005, 2007) or the industrial processing of food – in an uncomplicated, non-directive way through embodied experiences of growing plants, harvesting, cooking and eating together. In sharing their horticultural knowledge and experience, staff were committed to practising and promoting respect, tolerance, compassion, nurturance and empathy. While cultivating the garden, therefore, they were also helping to cultivate particular values, kinds of relationships and ways of interacting. Through bodily engagement in gardening and cooking activities, people became involved in basic provisioning and started to take care of themselves and each other, as well as the plants. They also adopted a different perspective on time. Annual cycles of growth, decay and re-growth suggested an alternative to participants' narratives of their lives as linear – narratives in which their lives had been disrupted by crises that overshadowed everything that followed (see Gell 1992, Ingold 1993). Participants' perspectives on their own lives could therefore subtly and beneficially alter through their involvement in the garden.

**From Seeds**

The idea for this garden project, or allotment health project, was first proposed in 2005 by an NHS public health policy officer whose area of expertise was diet and healthy eating, and who was also on the City Council's Allotment Strategy Group. After a short time in gestation within the Council's parks department, an area was identified for a new, flagship allotment site. Funding was sought by the Council for the infrastructure – fencing, water, access roads, paths, and so forth – and the Strategy Group planned the set-up of Scotland's first 'organic' allotment. Issues and agendas regarding sustainability, biodiversity, social inclusiveness and conservation, as well as health, were embedded from the outset in the planning of the allotment site. The ambition was to create an exemplar for a new wave of allotment sites, incorporating a clear health message – that growing your own food is good for you, for your families, and for your community (Scottish Government 2008a, 2008b, 2008c, 2008d, 2008e, 2009, 2011).

The site for the allotment was close to several areas on the city's outskirts where social and economic deprivation was a significant and entrenched problem. Integral to plans for the site was the aim to address poor physical and mental health through the communal growing of food, in a project where support and training would be available. The project's hub was to be set up on four contiguous plots on the site, each covering just over 150 m$^2$, which were leased from the Council. This hub was to be the initial focus of activity, with the aim that satellite growing projects would begin to emerge in the surrounding areas of deprivation. The project hub would offer support, advice and training to these emerging projects.

In January 2006, before the allotment site was set up, two of us were initially employed part-time: myself as manager and my colleague Stella as a project officer. As time went on we took on a number of part-time staff, and with further funding we were able to employ more full-time workers. At the outset we had funding for only a year, so part of our remit was to raise the funds to enable the project to continue. From January to the end of March, all we could create was a virtual place because the contractors who were preparing the field were behind schedule and did not leave the site until April, giving us just eight months to establish the project. During the first three months we were involved in a mix of tasks to assemble the project site: installing a polytunnel and a Portakabin; seeking planning permission; grappling with the different systems of the NHS (including finance, estates and human resources); and ordering materials, plants and seeds. We also decided on how the project was going to operate, given its very broad remit, the limited staff time, and its short timeframe.

The day after the last of the contractor's diggers left the site we launched the project with an open day. There were various family and food-growing activities, information about the health project and stalls about composting and healthy eating. There was a good buzz of curiosity and within a short time we had a committed core of people, with others blowing in and out according to their own needs and timetables. The working week was organized into two flexible day-long drop-in sessions. There was no pressure on anyone to commit to any day or time slot. The idea was to attract people, especially those who rarely participated in local projects and who found it very difficult to go out due to severe anxiety or depression.

**Working the Soil and Opening Up**

Little by little a garden started to emerge, with vegetable beds, paths, fruit trees and bushes alongside a 'biodiversity' strip of birch, rowan, wild flowers, brambles and wild strawberries. Stella and I wanted to introduce visitors to the notion that the distinction between what is cultivated and what grows wild is quite arbitrary, and that these categories have a history of their own. We encouraged children (who visited the garden with their schools, or with parents) to forage for the wild strawberries and blackberries amongst the grass and wild flowers, as well as to help themselves to crops from the vegetable beds.

Often children, and some adults, were reluctant to eat food directly from the bushes, pea vines or ground because they believed it was dirty (see Douglas 1966, Campkin and Cox 2007). They often referred to the earth or soil as 'dirt' and recoiled initially from handling it. The staff endeavoured to show participants how soil life (such as the worms and beetles that children collected) was involved in the production of the soil itself. We had wormeries set up in an old bath and an old tractor tyre where project participants and visitors could see the process of humus production close up, feeding the tiger worms with food scraps and peelings. The rich brown humus could be seen emerging after a few weeks, and people eventually felt happy to handle it; they helped to incorporate it into the vegetable beds, and understood that this was precious food for the growing plants. Staff also often highlighted parallels between human health and plant health. Children could more easily understand processes of growth and health in plants when analogies with their own experiences were used. For example, we explained that plants 'breathed' (respiration), that they 'sweated' (transpiration) and that they too needed healthy food to grow strong. Such analogies and metaphors became more sophisticated with adult participants, as they projected some of their personal views and feelings onto the plants themselves.

This was noted by a University of Edinburgh anthropology undergraduate who approached me in the garden project's second year. She wanted to visit the project as her fieldwork site, and she attended as a participant. Her dissertation discussed how participants formed relationships with the plants they were growing, projecting onto and borrowing from the processes of growth and nurturing (Blezard 2007). Drawing on Csordas (1994), she examined embodied experiences of working with plants and soil as well as the associations that participants made between human bodies and behaviour and those of plants – associations which emerged as participants relaxed and felt part of the process of the garden and the project.

It was remarkable how the layout of the garden changed over the years as staff and participants worked in it. At first it was quite formal, with an area of small, square raised beds where Stella wanted to try growing vegetables intensively, subdividing the plots and allowing each participant to have his or her own space. After one season these subdivisions were removed and replaced with larger beds, giving more growing space. Participants didn't want their own micro-plots; they came to work with and alongside others, growing for the project rather than just for themselves (Figure 8.2). Their social collaboration therefore became embedded in the collective areas for growing plants within the garden. Participants also came to see how differently the land itself could be inscribed from one season to the next, and that things which might at first appear immutable were actually alterable.

Latterly this area was dug out into a spiral garden with a pond at its centre and also seating. Re-designs like this were initially discussed over lunch in the polytunnel, and later in our regular 'pie and planning' days for which we used a nearby community centre. Staff and participants brought food to share, supplemented by produce from the plot. One skilled staff member had carved a beautiful huge wooden salad bowl that became the centrepiece for most mealtimes. Incrementally, growing and eating food, in step with the strengthening social relationships of staff and participants, became more central to the project.

Through the fluidity and openness that were founding principles of the project, a vibrant, ever-evolving, if sometimes anarchic, community grew around the project in which people felt a degree of freedom to explore their relationships with their environment as well as with each other. People arrived with very different life experiences, finding common ground in gardening. As they collaborated, they forged relationships whilst developing as gardeners and as people. For instance, Marion, an elderly woman, was very diffident and unconfident as a gardener, but eager to learn. She had been an activist with various campaigns and was strongly opposed to today's manufactured and over-processed food. Alec, a taciturn man remained quiet but clearly gained confidence as he learned and got involved with the heavy tasks of digging, constructing compost bays and creating vegetable beds. Over the years we discovered that he struggled with literacy and was also taking anti-psychotic medication. What participants disclosed of their situation was left entirely up to them. They talked about themselves as they wished, while they gardened. In the latter they had varying levels of skill: a young, very shy and frightened man who had never gardened before came along and learned how to hold and use tools, such as a garden fork, while Jock, a retired miner, was already a skilled grower. Desperate for an allotment of his own, Jock became an active participant in the project. Ken, probably a veteran of the first Iraq War (from 2003) who always attended the project in military style fatigues, helped to make food itself central to the project. He brought boxes full of apples from trees near his home and suggested we make chutney. He took charge of the process and produced delicious pickle.

**Figure 8.2** Pumpkin in the garden. Awaiting Hallowe'en and pumpkin soup, 2007. Photo: Anne Jepson

## Making Food, Eating Together

The project gradually changed from one where lunch was incidental to the day's tasks, with people bringing their own, to one where lunch became the main focus as staff and participants gathered food to create a communal meal. We cooked on 'rocket stoves', rudimentary cookers made from metal catering oil containers, and also in an outdoor clay oven, made by project staff, which was lit daily. In this we cooked bread, pizzas and even cakes when it was someone's birthday. Many project participants lived alone, and for some, eating together was initially difficult. Eating lunch together at the project transformed, for some participants, what was sometimes a problematic relationship with food, or a lonely functional activity, into one that valued food as an unremarkable yet important aspect of social interactions and connections with others.

Even though lunch started out merely as a break in the day, it was the only time that everyone at the project gathered together as we sat in the polytunnel to eat. It became the arena where information, recipes, chat about food, and ideas for the garden and future plans were aired and disseminated. Growing food became a primary function of the project, and since the polytunnel was in the middle of the garden there was a seamless progression from one activity to another – from growing to eating and vice versa. For participants to connect these activities was, in itself, a positive experience for them in a society where the relationship between growing food and eating is often ruptured due to the prevalence of industrialized food processing. Initially people brought their own food to the garden – anything from instant noodles and canned drinks to macrobiotic dishes. These were supplemented by produce from the garden as soon as crops became ready, and people added the fresh greens, salads and fruit to their meals.

Over time, the practice and significance of lunch changed dramatically, becoming central to our activities. One of the catalysts for this development, in addition to the 'pie and planning' days and the chutney making, was the arrival of two groups of women whose families were originally from Bangladesh and Pakistan. They were part of a group being encouraged by the NHS to become more involved in physical activity as a means to address diabetes.

Their interaction with the project was haphazard and intermittent, and some participants and staff struggled with their very different approach to the allotment site and the project. During the women's visits they seemed, to some participants, to be acquiring food from the project without appreciating the codes of conduct often expected at allotments (Crouch and Ward 1988). From the outset the women noticed a 'weed' growing across the site, known locally as 'Fat Hen', and they eagerly gathered it. This caused more lunchtime discussion on the definition of weeds and their historic use and value. Significantly, it led us to gather more weeds – nettles and ground elder – from which we made soup. The women treated Fat Hen as a vegetable, rather like spinach, and offered to make a curry with it on the barbecue. Tuesdays quickly became curry days. The women brought chapattis and home-made dishes, and cooked on site with produce they harvested, and everyone then sat around sharing and discussing the food. Some regular participants remained unconvinced that they would like the food, but most tried it. The women's participation prompted the installation of an outside kitchen, including the clay oven, and thus cooking and eating together became one of the main pillars of the project.

For some participants, however, food and eating together were not unmitigated social pleasures, especially when they had difficult relationships with food, or problems with eating in front of other people. An early participant, Kathy, had initial difficulties with the communal lunchtimes. But as lunch was simply treated as part of the day, with people seamlessly moving from growing activities to eating in the same space, it had become easier for her to deal with. Jenny, from the young persons' unit at the city's psychiatric hospital, who had been diagnosed with anorexia, wanted to come to the project precisely because it involved food. She frequently brought in food to share, and took on the task of compiling a project recipe book. Again, she found the seamless transitions, from growing to making food and eating, helpful in building a less problematic relationship with that food.

**Emotional Growth**

A number of people came to the project more for social reasons than, necessarily, to learn to garden, although gardening seemed to encourage participants to return to the project instead of joining a different project with a social focus. Jack, an ex-offender, was one of these: he valued the social contact at a place which welcomed him without judgement. Participants came to the garden for varying lengths of time. For some, it didn't suit and they quickly stopped visiting, but it was often hard to predict who would stay and who would leave. John participated for about two years. The staff knew little about him other than that he had been receiving treatment through the city's psychiatric hospital. Like other participants, he slowly disclosed aspects of his life history as we gardened together. Sometimes people spoke about themselves in conversation, while at other times they rolled up their sleeves to reveal the scars of self-harm. Sharing personal details in this way was regarded as a display of trust and an indication that the person felt accepted by others at the garden, not as a cry for help.

The histories revealed were often shocking and upsetting. Initially I questioned my responsibilities regarding participants at the project and the information they shared about themselves. But along with the other staff, I soon realized that our usefulness lay in providing uncomplicated opportunities for people to garden. We hoped participants would derive benefits through the absorbing and rewarding activities of gardening, as well as from their relationships with other participants within a community with a shared purpose.

Being witness to participants' retold experiences that could now be voiced was humbling, and exposed the personal vulnerabilities and strengths of the staff, who had themselves to learn to deal with these stories. The garden as therapeutic process was rooted in activities during which people spoke of their different experiences. Embodied engagement in the garden, cooking and eating together were crucial to these emerging narratives (see Skultans 2007). Carol, a quiet young mother, came to the project with her son, Ben, a bright two-and-a-half-year old. At first they would work closely together, but as he became more confident he was happy to be further away from her. He learnt quickly, and was articulate and sharp. Over the months, gardening with others, she revealed that she had suffered severe post-natal depression and alcoholism, and her arms bore the evidence of self-harm. Her relationship with her son was recovering from the traces left by that phase of depression, and this was an intense experience for both of them. She said that the garden project gave her the space to breathe, and yet also to be with her son in a mutually gratifying activity. They quickly started to garden together at home, and every week they told stories both of their successes and of the home-grown food presented to Daddy. Happily, Carol told us that Ben now refused shop-bought vegetables, insisting on eating only those that they had grown (Figure 8.3).

**Figure 8.3** **The youngest project participant watering his transplants, 2007. Photo: Anne Jepson**

This emotional attachment to what had been grown was even clearer with another participant, Muriel, who had never gardened before and who had suffered a life of abuse at home and at work. On her first visit, in the small staff office, she described her many experiences, problems and medical diagnoses relating to abuse, depression and anxiety disorders. She became visibly distressed as she spoke about these, but it was clear that she was accustomed to doing so. For it seemed that they had come to define her. They offered her an identity, fully endorsed by an authoritative institution, the NHS. Her story of illness had become a familiar and, paradoxically, a safe narrative for her. Yet I never saw anyone so transformed by their experience of growing plants. She cried on seeing the seeds she had sown germinate and grow. She said that she couldn't believe that she could bring something to life like that.

Several themes recurred in participants' descriptions of the gardening project. One was of escape – from the pressures of everyday living, or from more specific and personal stresses. Further themes centred on learning, on not being judged but accepted, on getting to know people otherwise difficult to meet because of social barriers, and on having purpose. However, some participants said they sometimes felt invisible. Staff were aware that they were too few to give each of the participants the attention they sometimes needed. Problems and tensions were not therefore absent from the garden as therapeutic process. This became especially apparent when participants wrote about their experiences of the project in terms not only of what was good but also of what was not. One participant conveyed both positive and negative aspects, for example, when he wrote that at times he felt like a child, asking constant questions during what was for him an intense experience of learning.

**Towards Wellbeing**

There are very real and pressing issues – political as well as financial – facing such projects, even as participants see them as havens of escape. Although sometimes fraught with difficulty, and dealing with deeply-felt distress, the garden project nevertheless became a source of wellbeing. While as noted earlier, an ethos of freedom and space for people to relax was encouraged at the project, the staff nevertheless aimed gently and indirectly to challenge some of the unhelpful dispositions that participants had taken on, and which seemed related to their difficulties. They did this by encouraging participants to experience and, indeed, to embody aspects of the garden – the soil, plants and produce – through involvement in practical tasks which entailed the forging of new relationships with each other and with food (Figure 8.4).

**Figure 8.4** **Working together, digging, 2006. Photo: Anne Jepson**

Staff passed on knowledge, and gained knowledge themselves, working alongside participants and encouraging them to consider alternative perspectives in the relatively unstructured context of the project. Participants learned that to grow something from seed is to nurture it. This requires a return to the basic elements of soil, water and air. Connections with these at the garden were fundamental, in a wider social and economic context in which many people have lost these connections, or in which they have been overlain by more complex concerns. Some people at the project had never had a positive experience of nurturing, and at the garden they responded overwhelmingly to their successes in the nurturing of plants, as when they raised a tray of seedlings. I interpreted in their responses an implicit recognition of their own positive power to transform, to care and to reconnect with something other than their despair, illness, disaffection or boredom. Nurturing plants, cooking garden produce as food, and eating that food were interconnected phases of growing and making in the garden which was also a setting for personal narratives. As plants grew, relationships were created and nourished; as food was made so people entered into productive interactions which seemed to me to be as deeply felt as they were therapeutic.

Participants learned to grow and cook food; acts of basic provisioning. Food is essential, and growing it gave people a very tangible experience of control in the garden environment and over key aspects of their lives. When coupled with the preparation and cooking of that food, the process was rendered as a social, and sometimes emotional, activity. Participants seemed to learn and to internalize gardening as a cyclical activity, following the seasons of each year. Through gardening, time could be experienced as cyclical rather than linear, encouraging participants to see living forms in new ways and perhaps even transforming their sense of their own personal histories. Thus processes of growing plants, human growth and self-realization were symbiotic in the garden, which developed as an intensely social and therapeutic enterprise.

**References**

Bhatti, M. 2006. 'When I'm in the garden I can create my own paradise': Homes and gardens in later life. *Sociological Review*, 54 (2), 318–41..

Blezard, E. 2007. *Mr Basil in the Garden of Eden.* Unpublished MA dissertation. University of Edinburgh.

Campkin, B. and R. Cox (eds) 2007. *Dirt: New Geographies of Cleanliness and Contamination.* London: I.B.Tauris.

Carsten, J. 1995. The substance of kinship and the heat of the hearth: feeding, personhood and relatedness among Malays in Pulau Langkawi. *American Ethnologist*, 22(2), 223–41.

Conrad, P. 2005. The shifting engines of medicalization. *Journal of Health and Social Behavior*, 46(1), 3–14.

Conrad, P. 2007. *The Medicalization of Society: On the Transformation of Human Conditions into Treatable Disorders.* Baltimore, MD: Johns Hopkins University Press.

Cordain, L. et al. 2005. Origins and evolution of the Western diet: health implications for the 21st century. *American Journal of Clinical Nutrition*, 81(2), 341–54.

Crouch, D. and Ward, C. 1988. *The Allotment: Its Landscape and Culture.* London: Faber and Faber.

Csordas, T. 1994. *Embodiment and Experience*: *The Existential Ground of Culture and Self.* Cambridge: Cambridge University Press.

Douglas, M. 1966. *Purity and Danger.* London: Routledge and Kegan Paul.

Gell, A. 1992. *The Anthropology of Time: Cultural Constructions of Temporal Maps and Images.* Oxford: Berg.

Gonzales, M.T. et al. 2010. Therapeutic horticulture in clinical depression: a prospective study of active components. *Journal of Advanced Nursing*, 66(9), 2002–13.

Ingold, T. 1993. The temporality of the landscape. *World Archaeology*, 25(2), 152–74.

Jepson, A. 2006. Gardens and the nature of rootedness in Cyprus, in *Divided Cyprus: Modernity, History and an Island in Conflict*, edited by Y. Papadakis, N. Peristianis and G. Welz. Bloomington: Indiana University Press, 158–75.

Kaplan, S. 1995. The restorative benefits of nature: toward an integrative framework. *Journal of Environmental Psychology*, 15(2), 169–82.

Lock, M. and V-K. Nguyen 2010. *An Anthropology of Biomedicine.* Chichester: Wiley-Blackwell.

Markee, K. M. and Janick, J. 1979. A bibliography for horticultural therapy (1970–1978; comparison of literature search techniques in an interdisciplinary field. *Horticultural Science*, 14(6), 692–97.

Marmot, M. and R. Wilkinson (eds) 2005. *Social Determinants of Health.* Oxford: Oxford University Press.

Milligan, C., A. Bingley, and A. Gatrell 2003. *Cultivating Health: A Study of Health and Mental Well-being Amongst Older People in Northern England.* Lancaster: Institute for Health Research, Lancaster University.

Neuberger, K.R. 1995. Pedagogics and horticultural therapy: the favourite task of Mr. Huber, digging up potatoes. *Acta Horticulturae*, 391, 241–51.

Parr, H. 2007. Mental health, nature work, and social inclusion. *Environment and Planning D: Society and Space*, 25(3), 537–61.

Relf, D. 1981. Dynamics of horticultural therapy, in *Social and Therapeutic Horticulture: Evidence and Messages from Research*, edited by J. Sempik, J. Aldridge, and S. Becker. Loughborough: Thrive and Centre for Child and Family Research: Loughborough University.

Scottish Government. 2008a. *Planning and Open Space.* Planning Advice Note (PAN) 65. Edinburgh: Scottish Government.

Scottish Government. 2008b. *Good Places, Better Health: A New Approach to Environment and Health in Scotland.* Edinburgh: Scottish Government.

Scottish Government. 2008c. *Healthy Eating, Active Living: An Action Plan to Improve Diet, Increase Physical Activity and Tackle Obesity 2008–2011.* Edinburgh: Scottish Government.

Scottish Government. 2008d. *Equally Well: Report of the Ministerial Task Force on Health Inequalities.* Edinburgh: Scottish Government.

Scottish Government. 2008e. *Choosing the Right Ingredients: The Future For Food in Scotland.* Discussion Paper. Edinburgh: Scottish Government

Scottish Government. 2009. *Recipe for Success – Scotland's National Food and Drink Policy.* Edinburgh: Scottish Government.

Scottish Government. 2011. *Grow Your Own Working Group: Report for Scotland's National Food and Drink Policy.* Edinburgh: Scottish Government.

Sempik, J., Aldridge, J. and Becker, S. 2003. *Social and Therapeutic Horticulture: Evidence and Messages from Research.* Loughborough. Thrive and Centre for Child and Family Research: Loughborough University.

Skultans, V. 2007. *Empathy and Healing: Essays in Medical and Narrative Anthropology.* Oxford: Berghahn.

Thaler, R.H. and C.R. Sunstein 2009. *Nudge: Improving Decisions about Health, Wealth and Happiness.* London: Penguin.

Thin, N. 2011. Socially responsible cheermongery: on the sociocultural contexts and levels of social happiness policies, in *Positive Psychology as Social Change*, edited by R. Biswas-Diener. Heidelberg. New York, London: Springer, 33–49.

# Chapter 9
# Making Plants and Growing Baskets

Stephanie Bunn

**Introduction**

Basketry is often seen as an unremarkable, rather homely craft, and its role in social life has been given little more than brief attention. But one only has to consider the practical uses for which basket-weaving has been employed in Britain – agricultural baskets, factory skips, fish traps, load carriers, ship fenders, wattle walls and fences, babies' rattles, hats, bee skeps – to appreciate that this rather mundane woven artefact has been an enduring historical feature, enmeshed in the social and cultural fabric, from home to farm, from herring fishery to textile mill and from town to city dwelling, until the very recent past.

In regard to making and growing, it might be supposed that baskets lie clearly in the domain of making. Indeed the boundary between growing plants and making baskets appears 'clear cut'. Arguably, 'cutting' marks the division between plant and artefact in basket-making, for when the plants used for basketry are cut, it seems that they are conceptually transformed from plant to material and begin their journey towards a 'finished object'. Implicit in this argument is the notion that plants grow of their own volition, in domains quite distinct from that of humans, and that once cut, the plant is now 'dead', ceasing to grow through its own efforts. What future 'growing' the plant may do, it is assumed, is henceforth managed through the nurturing agency of human hands, which control the transformation of material into artefact through the act of making. This assumption is underpinned by the idea that making takes place in a uniquely human domain, quite distinct from the domains of plants and from processes of growing.

To a degree, both these views on growing and making reflect the division often presupposed between nature and culture, and related implicit parallels in other domains, as Strathern (1980: 91) has demonstrated with regard to gender in Mount Hagen. A further assumption is that what is natural (i.e. growing plants) has no intention, whereas what is cultural (i.e. making) is the result of human intent. In the case of making baskets, however, botanical factors are also at play, since some basketry materials such as willow are not immediately 'dead' once cut, but continue to be vital and – unless allowed to dry out – can take root again if replanted.

I would therefore like, firstly, to explore the quite 'fuzzy' boundaries between these domains of growing and making. After all, humans grow plants – they nurture them and bring them to fruition – so that the growth of plants is not at all distinct from human activity. Conversely we might also ask whether plants reciprocate and, through people's engagement with them, participate in growing or making people and artefacts. Secondly, it is not only the practical, skilful aspects of the transformation from plant material to artefact that concern me in this chapter. While the process of making and the act of engagement are my starting points, there are further aspects of the interactions between maker and material that contribute to the rich texture of people's relationship with plants in crafts such as basketry. While Sigaut (1994: 424–38) argues that one cannot see techniques, only people doing things, I would also suggest that technique alone does not reveal the entire process of engagement between people and material in craft work.

In this chapter I explore these other aspects of making that might be construed as forms of growing, addressing the realms of the social and of reflective thought as well as the practical and technical. Specifically, I wish to examine the relationship between growing and making baskets, focusing on the generation of different kinds of learning from cooperation, intergenerational relations and knowledge production to oral and social history, along with the practice of skill itself. I do so with reference to basket work in contemporary England and Scotland.

Much has been written by anthropologists and artists about the engagement between mind and body in making (Ingold 2000, Marchand 2011, Bunn 1992, 2000). Their focus tends to be on the embodied act, rather than on what comes before or after, or on what kinds of thought, intellectual development or action emerge beyond the immediate coming together of maker and material. Yet there are aspects of skilled practices such as in basketry which provoke thought, enquiry and future action in the practitioner, and, whether these can be described as embodied or not, it is this aspect of making and how it might be linked to practice over time which interests me in this chapter.

I intend to examine these concerns by drawing on the recent practice of 'willow sculpture' alongside ways of making baskets regarded as 'traditional' by current makers. Thus I explore different kinds of learning that basket-weaving provokes, drawing on the work of a variety of researchers, from anthropologists and historians to basket-makers and willow sculptors. In the process, I hope to show how baskets, and the plants used in their making, are both grown and made, both cultivated and culture.

**The Basket**

The English term 'basket' conflates the *technique*, basketry, with the *artefact*, basket, which in common usage is a form of woven container (Figure 9.1). But basketry techniques may be used to make many non-containers, as archaeologist Willeke Wendrich notes. In her view, baskets can be defined in relation to *materials*, as

**Figure 9.1** Traveller's frame basket, Highland Folk Museum, Kingussie, 2012. Photo: Stephanie Bunn

a class of artefacts made out of vegetable fibres of limited length or with a shape which is specific to the raw material. Basketry thus defined comprises: baskets, bags and mats; brushes and brooms; hurdles, wattle-and-daub constructions; sandals; hats, and belts. (Wendrich 1991: 4)

Roy Ellen contributes a third dimension, including the semi-rigid *structural* properties of baskets in his definition: 'A container created by weaving semi-rigid vegetable fibres' (2009: 248).

From these definitions two distinctive features of baskets can be identified. The first is the way baskets develop their semi-rigid structure from the tension created in the material through the maker's weaving technique. Without human skill and engagement with the plant material there would be a pile of unstructured, loose sticks or fibres. The effort involved puts strength where none was there before, and the tension which emerges through engagement between maker and materials produces a lightweight self-contained structure, strong enough to hold heavy loads, flexible enough even to act as the base for a hot air balloon.

Tim Ingold describes such making processes as 'the gradual unfolding of that field of forces set up through the active and sensuous engagement of practitioner and material' (2000: 342). In a sense, however, the emerging basket does not simply 'unfold', or flow, since the strength of the artefact is also an outcome of the *resistance* produced between maker and material, and the ways this is resolved through their meeting and exchange. Working with willow can be a battle at times. The willow flicks back, hurting eyes, even breaking teeth, and hands can kink or snap willow stems. Thus, while the willow worker has to find a kind of attunement with the material, the product is often the outcome of a kind of sublime wrestling match or tempestuous dance between two partners, using deft techniques of manipulation and strong thumbs, in an engagement with sinuous, whippy, and stubborn yet fragile stems, rather than the kind of smooth process that the term 'unfold' evokes.

The second distinctive attribute of baskets is their irreproducibility by machine. Otis Mason, author of *The Origins of Invention* (1895), first noted this of baskets. In the act of making the basket-maker is at the same moment making the form and performing the technique of weaving or interlocking the fibres. This dual action effectively bypasses the need for a weaving loom, since in most cases, the maker is developing, building up, even growing their own frame or 'loom' while weaving the artefact. This 'frame', in the process, becomes part of the structure. The complexity of creating form in the act of weaving deters the mechanization of the process. Thus, while most clay, wood, metal, glass and textile manufacturing processes have been modified to suit machine production during the past two centuries, it has not been possible for a machine to create the form of a basket and weave it at the same time. Mechanized replacements for baskets, therefore, have usually not attempted to emulate the making process. Instead the cardboard box, metal shopping trolley, plastic crate and plastic bag have been developed as alternatives to baskets.

## Interweaving Practice and Theory in Basketry

My initial interest in basketry stemmed from a concern to profile an understudied skill. But it also takes an auto-ethnographic perspective, in that as well as working as an anthropologist, I have worked with basketry, making woven fences, small dwellings and structures since the mid-1980s. My interests in this subject are also inspired by recent involvement with a group of Scottish basket-makers, the Scottish Basketmakers' Circle (SBC), who are very concerned to maintain local basketry skills, create new ones and thoroughly learn about the subject in order to ensure that traditional techniques, skills and associated knowledge endure. It is through both these involvements that I have come to understand that basket-weaving has much to teach us about practical skill, and that it also inspires further reflective learning and knowledge production, which is in itself a kind of human 'growth' that is intimately related to processes of making.

Perhaps it is not surprising that basketry skill can extend beyond the act of making a basket. As Ellen (2009) points out, the knowledge required to produce a basket extends across multiple domains. Thus, basket-work may comprise regional plant knowledge and management, a diversity of technical skills, as well as knowledge of basket forms. But these quite concrete concerns with the practical making of baskets are further complemented, among basket-makers I have worked with, by the role of basketry in promoting reflection upon the skill, the material used and the history of basketry. This reflection is further promoted among basket-makers through autodidactic research and the development of local knowledge. Exploring these concerns reveals valuable insights into the dynamic between learning through practical activity and learning which places more emphasis on intellectual development, although these two modes are interrelated.

In this vein, academic writings about basketry have often been of as much interest to basket-makers as to fellow scholars, while basket-makers over the past century have often been inspired by their practice to conduct their own self-motivated research into the subject. Thus while Mason (1895), when curator at the Smithsonian Institution, placed basketry at the heart of his review of cultural and technological evolution, George Wharton James, founder of the American Basket Fraternity, also conducted extensive research into indigenous American basket-work for both his ethnographic publications (James 1903) and his 'how-to' basket-making books. In the UK, early basketry research developed mostly in the basketry community. Thomas Okey of the Ancient and Worshipful Company of Basket-Makers (later, professor of Italian at the University of Cambridge) wrote the first 'how-to' book of British basketry (Okey 1915), while H.H. Bobart, also of the Worshipful Company, produced an historical study, *Basketwork Through the Ages* (Bobart 1936), showing how basketry had long been an integral part of social life. Aside from revealing the interwoven nature of academic and practitioners' basketry concerns, this pattern of research suggests that 'how-to' books themselves are means to reflect upon and communicate practice, and are thus neither as insignificant nor as separate from ethnographic or historical research as scholars have tended to assume. The pattern continues today with significant recent research into the social history of British and European basketry conducted by Mary Butcher, President of the Basket-Makers' Association.

Research interest in basketry declined during the first half of the twentieth century in parallel with reduced production following the technological developments of the industrial and petro-chemical revolutions, especially after the Second World War. In the UK, basket works closed across the country, as cardboard boxes and plastic bags were introduced (Manthorpe 2009: 19). Yet basketry continued, promoted through evening classes, occupational therapy and the 'hobby', although these were often interpreted as 'trivial' manifestations of its use and value. However, again in parallel with this, developments in American art and design school practices in the mid-twentieth century drew basketry into the arena of 'art', as 'constructed textiles' were made into installations and art pieces in themselves, without the necessity of function. Ed Rossbach of the University of California was a pioneer of this new approach. His *New Basketry* (Rossbach 1976) featured extraordinary and often bizarre forms. Such developments enabled people to explore basketry materials and techniques in new and creative ways, despite its apparent obsolescence.

## The Growth of Willow Sculpture

A defining moment in the growth of interest in basketry-as-art in Britain was the *New Forms in Willow* symposium at Ness Botanical Gardens, Cheshire, in 1991. This event comprised an interdisciplinary conference and a series of practical workshops in 'willow crafts, fibre and sculpture' convened by arts impresarios, Projects Environment. Over 200 people from across the world attended, including basket-makers, sculptors, willow growers, botanists, and representatives of the Long Ashton National Willow Collection (where many diverse specimens of the species are gathered), as well as academics from a range of university departments.

This event shifted attention away from basket-as-artefact, to refocus it on basket-as-material – in this case, willow. As mentioned above, a special feature of willow is its retention of vitality when cut and the capacity of a cut stem to re-grow when put into the soil. Following *New Forms in Willow*, the flourishing interest in 'willow sculpture', especially 'living willow sculpture', was fed by this vital property of willow which enables it to both be woven into a structure and grown at the same time. Shortly after this event, I was appointed Willow Worker in Residence at Ness Botanical Gardens in South Wirral, and so witnessed some of the outcomes of this symposium, while developing my own practice as a willow sculptor and conducting research in the National Willow Collection, housed there, alongside the botanists and other experts.

The developments that followed *New Forms in Willow* capitalized on willow's dual status as both plant and material, and what inspired practitioners was its potential for a new kind of sculpture in contrast to traditional basketry techniques which held less initial interest. This was a truly multisensory engagement. Willow is a material which can be worked still green, freshly cut, experienced through the hands, and, when working on a large scale, through the whole body. Because of its growth potential and use in outdoor sculpture, it also generally involves working outside, often directly into the ground, enabling the connection between artist, material and environment to be directly experienced.

## Willow: Plant and Material

What makes willow of great value to basket-makers is its potential for growth in several senses. Unlike most shrub-type plants, willow is not branchy, and if cut back each year, new shoots will grow as straight stems, which means it weaves neatly. At the same time, its vitality is such that if all the stems on a stool (willow trunk) are cut back in winter, they will grow back to the same length the following year, so it can be grown as a crop and harvested annually. Some willow stems grow 10 or 12 feet in one year. Willow is also flexible when cut, and does not easily snap or break, allowing it to be woven. But the stems can also be dried for future use, and later soaked, whereupon they will become flexible again, and once woven will dry semi-rigid. Thus willow can be cut, stored and later used, and while initially flexible, the combined effects of the tension introduced by weaving and the slowly hardening stems produces artefacts of great strength.

Two additional growth-linked properties of willow are of particular value to willow sculptors. First, willow of one-, two- and three-years' growth has different tensile properties. While willow of one year is flexible for the entire length of its stem and can be bent to create a perfect curve, two-year willow will be much more rigid on that part which has been growing for two years. Sculptors can use this to great effect in their work. Second, willow's potential to strike roots and re-grow make it particularly exciting to many willow sculptors. Artists can construct sculptural forms from willow stems set into the ground which will then take root and grow, putting out leaves and new growth year on year, growing beyond the artist's initial sculpture in a way that can never be entirely controlled, even if the sculpture is annually maintained. Working in this way the artist is effectively planting growing woven forms, or even small groves of trees in patterns, as seen in the work of Ben Platt Mills in Suffolk, Jim Buchanan at the Earth Centre in Doncaster and Swiss architect, Marcel Kalberer. Material and artefacts become plants again, so that making is not a one-way conversion from plant to artefact. A living willow sculpture thus incorporates processes of both making and growing.

**Willow Sculpture as Practice**

In contrast to the close attention given to materials subsequent to *New Forms in Willow*, the initial resistance to using traditional basketry strokes among many willow sculptors was also significant, since it allowed them a kind of 'intuitive space' in which to develop their work. Rather than following through a set of familiar strokes, they could make imaginative leaps to find solutions to problems in new and innovative ways, often tying together their material with string, wire, or even sticky tape. As they developed, however, some willow sculptors incorporated more formal techniques as part of their artistic vocabulary, attending basketry workshops to learn these, but by then they had usually developed a more unconstrained form of practice. To many basket-makers, this initial rejection of classical technique seemed to be a travesty. It was, they said, 'like trying to re-invent the wheel'.

In my view, the rejection of established formal technique led to an intimate focusing on materials, allowing makers to explore willow's potential, unfettered by conventional practice. Makers are confronted with the varying flexibility of different varieties of willow, their unique, soporific scent and vivid fresh colours. This closely honed focus on the material, along with working outdoors in spring when willow is at its most vital (when the sap is rising and it is most prone to striking new growth), often results in artists' work that suggests resonance with other aspects of the environment. For instance, artists might draw upon willow's curving, flexible, sinuous qualities to create flowing, moving, dynamic forms, suggesting parallels between the willow and features of the environment such as nests, shelters, spirals, pods, running animals, birds, or even wind, rather than

**Figure 9.2** *Na Hale 'Eo Waiawi*, 2003, by Patrick Dougherty. Strawberry Guava and Rose Apple saplings, total area 20 ft long × 30 ft wide × 30 ft high. The Contemporary Art Museum, Honolulu, HI. Photo credit: Paul Kodama

aiming for realistic depictions. This is seen in Patrick Dougherty's dynamic pieces, and in Laura Ellen Bacon's recent work. For all these reasons, willow sculpture has been categorized as 'art' rather than 'craft' (Figure 9.2).

However, more formal basket-makers, with their extensive practice of basket strokes and basket forms, did not always take so easily to willow sculpture. Many basket-makers' attempts at sculpture produced much more naturalistic forms, where the material was used to represent likenesses rather than to evoke a quality or movement, and the results often appeared static. There were notable exceptions. David Drew's beautifully crafted baskets transcend any boundary between art and craft, while Lee Dalby made the transition from large-scale, powerful frame basketry to sculpture, exploring Japanese forms of construction with bamboo (Butcher and Hamilton 2007). But many makers tended to stay on one side or the other of what they might have seen as an art-craft divide (see Buszek 2011).

## Willow-generated Learning

While developing sculptural practices from a material perspective inspired new ways of working, it also inspired new learning beyond the immediate act of making. This learning extended in several directions, not just into the many properties of willow which make it so suited to basketry, but towards its other attributes in associated domains of practice, including techniques for growing it and subtle knowledge of specific varieties. With the fall in basket production during the twentieth century, the number of willow beds had declined (Manthorpe 2009), except in a small area of the Somerset Levels, and it was only through the work of the National Willow Collection at Long Ashton that the range of British willow varieties was retained. In the 1990s, during my time at Ness Gardens, it seemed that through the growth of willow sculpture the British decline in willow growing had been reversed. This was encouraged, in my view, by willow's capacity to generate a response in practitioners: engagement with willow during this period certainly influenced willow sculptors. This is not the same as suggesting that willow has 'agency', which implies a quality attributed to willow by humans (Gell 1998). It is, rather, to emphasize that 'engagement' with willow was a compelling interaction, which required a kind of 'listening' to the material and a response. Through engagement, the perceived sensory qualities and potential of willow inspired people to embark on its cultivation and to further examine its properties. At Ness Botanical Gardens, with its duplicate National Willow Collection, I witnessed a steady stream of people collecting cuttings to establish new beds. Some were growing willow for their own use, others aimed to grow beds to supply basket-makers and willow sculptors, yet others for biomass or sewage filtration. This process resulted in the further cultivation of knowledge with regard to this plant and its uses.

Long-standing willow workers' knowledge of specific willows was discussed and emulated. Practitioners such as Molly Rathbone, who had explored the Ness beds for years, found themselves in great demand. Interest might focus upon the most refined features of a specific variety. Did this one grow best on light or heavy soil? How did it change colour when dry? What happened when it dried slowly? Was it easy or hard on the hands? There was a great premium to be had from the few varieties of willow which would dry a 'true' black. The purple bloom on *Salix daphnoides* was highly valued because it dried bluey-mauve. Catkins were also valued for living willow sculpture, such as the fine small ones on *Salix purpurea* and the large fluffy ones on *Salix caprea*. *Melanostachys* had unique black catkins and was much sought after. The newly developed biomass willows, such as Bowles Hybrid, ideal for willow sculpture because of being so long and flexible, had their merits examined and, in Bowles' case, ultimately rejected because of its propensity for canker and squidgy black aphids. Here Ness's interdisciplinary position was of value, since willow workers could also ask the knowledgeable resident botanist Hugh MacAllister for his views (Figure 9.3).

**Figure 9.3** Willow in a variety of colours and tones, from shades of black to red and yellow, 2010. Photo: Stephanie Bunn

But interest also extended to non-basketry domains. These included willow's ecological and environmental value due to its capacity for absorption and nitrate filtration (important for use in small-scale sewage filtrations systems) and its capacity to cleanse poisoned ground (Goat Willow can take up heavy metals in water). The future potential of willow for biomass fuel supply, due to its capacity for rapid renewed growth, was also investigated (Watling and Raven 1992, Rosillo-Calle et al. 2007, Aronsson and Pertuu 1994, Grant, Moodie and Weedon 1996, Punshon 1996). Some willow workers were drawn to review past knowledge of willow, revaluating this in the light of contemporary findings, touching on such issues as its use as an analgesic in pain relief and healing (willow is a basic ingredient of aspirin), in making cricket bats, in wattle and daub, for promoting root growth in other plants and even in folklore and literature.

Thus, refocusing on willow-as-material led to a new practice of effectively growing 'baskets' through sculpture which, in turn, grew people through practical engagement, generating the motivation to develop associated domains of willow knowledge, and encouraging old and new understandings to be recombined and developed over time. It also inspired people to grow willow. Through making practices that placed materials at the centre of attention, willow became a significant 'source' of inspiration to learn, a purposeful generative system, as Küchler describes (1999) it, and a core knowledge domain in Ellen's (2009) terms. In the process, artists were freed up to explore new ways of working and new domains of knowledge. This was a signal moment for 'basketry culture', when basket-work was revaluated in many ways which cut across disciplinary boundaries such as those between botany, plantsmanship, ecology and history. It was also a signal moment for willow, and interest in it has continued to grow ever since.

**Back to the Basket-maker**

In contrast to practices that focus on willow as material, most basket-makers I have worked with in Scotland over the past five years have been motivated by an interest in the hand-made, in skills and techniques, and in regional baskets *per se*. Materials are also an important aspect, but not usually predominantly so. In the main, people want to learn how to make specific baskets and the different strokes involved. For woven (as opposed to coiled or plaited) baskets, strokes include randing, pairing, waling and twining. All these strokes involve similar moves, adapted in relation to variables such as the number of strands used and the number of stakes the strands cross in front of or behind. This work is done through actions similar to those detailed in Anne Butler Morrell's (2007) description of embroidery stitches. Along with understanding how to work with the tension in the material, there is also a focus on the rhythm and pattern of the weave. Basket-makers frequently use phrases such as 'in-front-of-two, behind-one', or 'tip-to-tip, butt-to-butt'. These spoken formulae vocalize the moves while at the same time enacting them. This ongoing, integrated dynamic between embodied practice and verbal articulation, as Greg Downey (2010: 528) suggests (in relation to capoeira), facilitates recall, bringing practical moves in and out of conscious understanding, aiding embodied learning. This is also the case with regard to basket-making. Each stroke, or crossing of stakes and strands in different ways, creates a different form of tension, useful for different aspects of the basket, whether for setting in the uprights to the base, for in-filling, or for borders or handles. Coiled and plaited basketry techniques likewise have their own variations of moves and rhythms.

A maker's first basket is usually a simple, round form, and as they become proficient, they may be motivated to learn more complex forms such as rectangular baskets or creels. Having become established 25 years ago, early members of the SBC learned some of their skills from previous generations of basket-makers, observing and copying them as they worked. But they also learned through classes, with 'how-to' books, and by making replicas and repairing damaged baskets for museums. They disseminated these skills and techniques through workshops, encouraging new generations of practitioners.

Most of the group I am acquainted with are women, along with a few men, who have taken up basketry through creative choice since the mid-1980s. This contrasts with the previous generation of predominantly male practitioners in Scotland, and the UK in general, who took up the craft through necessity, either for trade or to provide equipment for their own domestic needs, as crofters did until recently. Interestingly, however, recent research on the motivations to work in basketry in Scotland does suggest that for many trade basket-makers there was also a strong element of enjoyment and personal choice. However, the group continues to form a community of practitioners, whether they make baskets for recreation, to teach basketry, to sell, or to create 'high-end craft' in which makers develop their own individual styles. In contrast to willow sculptors, who tend to work alone as artists, these members meet whenever possible in local or regional groups, and stay in touch through newsletters, Facebook, Skype and SBC activities.

They are motivated mainly by their enjoyment of the hand-made; their practice generates pleasure through the very process of skilfully using bodily technique and of engaging with the materials to create well-made, crafted products. This engagement can inspire commitment, aspiration to improve, a sense of complete absorption, even joy while practising. The practitioner enters into a sensuous relationship with materials through bodily practice. Such pleasure in making is similar to what Pallasmaa calls a 'condition of haptic immersion', where the hand moves almost independently in a dynamic relationship between hand, eye and mind (2009: 72–82). This immersion is, of course, not always attained. If the practice does not suit the maker, it can be frustrating, boring and difficult. There are thus emotional and creative as well as social dimensions at work in these practices.

This motivation to 'do craft', maintain skilfulness, or make things, despite its reduced 'use-value', has continued in Europe and North America over the past century, and reflects changing ways of thinking about and doing craft generally, following the mechanization of production. The SBC was not the first group concerned with the continuation of Scottish basketry and other crafts. Pioneers from previous generations include renowned collector and curator of the Highland Folk Museum, Isobel Grant (Grant 2007), and birdwatchers and basketry collectors for the National Museum of Scotland, Leonore Rintoul and Evelyn Baxter, who established basketry classes for the Scottish Women's Institute in the 1930s. However, making baskets and learning technique is fundamental for the SBC, and while hand making may no longer be essential for the production of goods, it exemplifies an approach to work which continues to be valued.

Further manifestations of such concern with artisanship in general are evident in exhibitions such as the recent *Power of Making* at the Victoria and Albert Museum (2011) and Grayson Perry's *The Tomb of the Unknown Craftsman* (2011–12) at the British Museum, both in London. The growth of craft activism or 'craftivism', where the hand made can act as a form of political resistance, even of environmentalism, is a further manifestation of commitment to contemporary 'hand-work' (Greer 2011).

**Basket-generated Learning**

The SBC was established at a critical time, during the 1980s, when the need for local baskets was fast receding and Scottish vernacular baskets had almost ceased to be produced. Around this time some members also began to explore local basketry's ancestral connections, documenting local practices, or learning about the variety and locations of local materials – which are highly prized and often kept secret. They also collected archival information about the social history of basketry from regional museums. Some interviewed and made video recordings of practitioners, including several celebrated as the last person to have known or made particular forms of basket for their livelihoods. Some collected oral histories. Occasionally supported by local funding bodies, makers have researched and published their findings in newsletters and booklets, located archival photographs, and collected together a library of resource materials.

For many Scottish basket-makers, enjoyment of the past and a concern for continuity into the future has been a core factor in learning basketry. Makers are often drawn to make forms they consider traditional, such as Shetland *kishies* or Highland creels. In the case of *kishies*, people travelled to Shetland to learn under Lowrie Copeland – the last person who still made *kishies* for his crofting livelihood – and his pupil, now a great expert, Ewen Balfour. Sadly, Copeland recently passed away, but those who had the privilege to meet him were usually invited into his home and, even when elderly and frail, he would talk about the difficulties of making *simmens* (the twine used for binding *kishies*) and each visitor was given a wooden needle, which he had hand-made, for sewing the straw coils (Figure 9.4).

**Figure 9.4** Shetland *kishie* made in a workshop led by Ewen Balfour, 2007. Photo: Stephanie Bunn

For some basket-makers, learning to make traditional baskets such as *kishies* or creels has provided a focus for learning about their social and historical context. Until very recently, almost all aspects of local life, from bringing in the peats, to growing potatoes, to curling and grouse shooting, needed baskets. The range of baskets required by the fishing industry was extensive, and baskets even formed nationally prescribed measures for fish, for example the herring quarter *cran*. Learning to make these entailed the development of technique, and learning about local materials, such as Black Oat straw, *bent* (marram grass), *dockens* (docks) and *floss* (indigenous rush) used in Orkney and Shetland basketry. It also entailed learning about the life-style of those who used them, such as East Coast fisher-lassies or travellers, and visiting museums to see original baskets.

Thus baskets themselves have formed the main 'source' of inspiration and motivation to learn in this context. The interest in learning generated by baskets has grown out of the practical engagement involved in making. It extends to the social history of baskets and places importance on learning from someone for whom basket-related skills have been particularly meaningful. Here, in Ellen's (2009) terms, it is the basket which acts as the overarching domain of knowledge, or, in Küchler's terms, a generative source of 'purposeful coordination' (1999: 155). In making baskets, people feel themselves part of an interwoven community about which they want to know more. As they weave themselves into this community, their interest engages with and extends into past and future generations of makers and researchers. Thus, knowledge grows through making baskets: makers gather and cultivate information which generates an understanding of the practice's place in society, and in so doing they gain insights into their own community dynamic.

**Patterns of Growing, Making and Learning**

The above discussion suggests that learning plays an important role in the relationship between growing and making, with regard to baskets. I have discussed two kinds of engagement, one with materials, and one with artefacts and the skills required to make them. In both cases, the practical skills required to work with materials or to make artefacts are just the beginning of a process of becoming a skilful practitioner. Each kind of engagement generates its own form of learning across different domains beyond the immediate making of an artefact. Thus making in this context is a generator, a dynamic for growing knowledge, which further generates making, and so on.

Furthermore, the kind of making which takes place appears to bear a relation to the kind of growth in learning that emerges. Thus willow sculpture, with its focus on material rather than technique, encourages a focus on the plant, its properties, its capacities and its role in community and local lore. Here, the source of 'purposeful coordination' is willow itself. In contrast, the basket-weaving that I have explored in Scotland focuses more on regional basket forms and techniques, along with greater emphasis on learning about historical and community aspects of the practice.

With regard to knotting and looping bags in the Pacific, Küchler (1999) suggests that specific forms of practical engagement maybe entwined with different kinds of social practice and social organization. What seems to be the case with basket-weaving and willow sculpture is that the latter, by prioritizing closer engagement with materials and a more individually-centred and inventive practice, focuses more on relations with the environment, personal creativity and knowledge generation. Basket-makers, on the other hand, are more concerned with learning basket-forms and weaving strokes within a community of practitioners, and with basketry's place in the wider community of basket-makers and users.

The significance of these different kinds of knowledge, emerging from but moving beyond the act of making, can perhaps be elucidated by examining the temporal aspects of knowledge generation involved in both making and growing. Following D'Arcy Wentworth Thompson's work *On Growth and Form*, Ingold has argued that the morphology of an organic structure such as a shell, or of an artefact such as a basket, is not determined by a preconceived plan in either growing or making *per se* (Thompson 1961 [1917]: 178–9, Ingold 2000: 342–5). Both organisms and artefacts develop in a 'field of forces' which 'cuts across the interface between the object … and an environment', as the entity emerges, whether through ontogenetic development or skilled activity (Ingold 2000: 345). Thus, Ingold argues that growing and making are both autopoietic processes entailing 'self-transformation over time of the system of relations within which an organism or artefact comes into being' (2000: 345). In the case of both shell and basket, the resulting form over time is a spiral, since in each case the growth is from one end only. This is visibly evident in the way that a basket is built up from a central point at the base, seen in Perigord baskets, and also in most round-based woven and coiled baskets. This temporal aspect to basketry formation results in similar forms to those of growing organisms and plants, such as spiral snail shells, sunflower seeds, pine cones and many others (Thompson 1961, Ingold 2000), providing visible evidence of the morphological relationship between growing and making (Figure 9.5).

But how does the learning and knowledge generation that I discussed earlier fit within this dynamic? The importance of learning through practice and apprenticeship has been highlighted in many recent anthropological studies of skill (see Coy 1989, Lave 1990, Rogoff 2003, Sigaut 1994, Marchand 2010). For the purposes of this chapter, however, the insights of educational psychologist Jerome Bruner are most relevant (Bruner 1960, see Downey 2010: 528). A follower of Lev Vygotsky, Bruner proposed that several prerequisites are necessary for developing learning or skill. These are: understanding the common principles of a task; intuition; revisiting and building on a baseline of knowledge; and finally, *interest and the will to learn*. The pattern of developing basketry skills within and beyond immediate practice would, in Bruner's (1960) terms, result in a spiral of learning through time, as the practitioner grows in knowledge and skill, building upon and revisiting past knowledge and, above all, continually developing knowledge through her or his enjoyment of practice and will to learn. Learners thus follow a spiral trajectory, exploring and developing skills and ideas.

**Figure 9.5**     **Spiral base of woven basket, 2012. Photo: Stephanie Bunn**

At certain points they come full circle, and yet, due to the temporal and cumulative nature of learning, they invariably find they have moved ahead of where they were the last time around.

    I would argue, then, that in conjunction with the morphological and temporal laws manifest in making and growing artefacts, the dynamic at the heart of the generation of forms such as baskets, and their regeneration, is learning and the pleasure that lies in such work. Engagement leads to learning which generates further action, beyond the immediate act of basketry, thus producing further knowledge. This learning takes place across a lifetime, and between generations, as we have seen above, through each cohort's drawing on the work of their foremakers. This learning process incorporates pleasure through skilful making, through engagement with material, and through the emergence and development of new learning. The process also entails the ongoing application of that learning and its communication, building upon the skills of the past with the aim of sustaining them in the future. This is not cultural transmission, concerned only with the replication of past forms. Rather, it is a process whereby practices and the forms to which they give rise are continually generated and regenerated. What lies at the heart of this process is engagement, enjoyment of skill, and learning, a cultivation of body and mind, bringing plants and humans into dynamic relationships that both make plants and grow baskets.

# References

Aronsson, P. and K. Pertuu. 1994. *Proceedings of the Conference: Willow Vegetation Filters for Municipal Wastewaters and Sludges: A Biological Purification System*. Swedish University of Agricultural Sciences Report 50.
Bobart, H.H.1936. *Basketwork Through the Ages*. London: Oxford University Press.
Bruner, J. 1960. *The Process of Education*. Cambridge, Mass.: Harvard University Press.
Bunn, S. 1992. *The Kyrgyz Tent*. MA thesis, University of Manchester.
Bunn, S.J. 1999. The importance of materials. *The Journal of Museum Ethnography*, 11, 15–29.
Bunn, S.J. 2000. *The House of Meaning: Tents and Tent Dwelling Among Kyrgyz Pastoralists*. PhD thesis, University of Manchester.
Buszek, M.E. (ed.) 2011. *Extra/Ordinary: Craft and Contemporary Art*. Durham, NC: Duke University Press.
Butcher, M. and L. Hamilton 2007. *East Meets West: Basketry from Japan and Britain*. Glasgow: Collins Gallery.
Butler Morrell, A. 2007. *The Migration of Stitches and the Practice of Stitch as Movement*. Ahmedabad: Mehta Foundation.
Coy, N. 1989. *Apprenticeship: From Theory to Method and Back Again*. New York: SUNY Press.
Downey, G. 2010. 'Practice without theory': a neuroanthropological perspective on embodied learning. *Journal of the Royal Anthropological Institute*, S22-S40.
Ellen, R. 2009. A modular approach to understanding the transmission of technical knowledge: Nuaulu basket-making from Seram, eastern Indonesia. *Journal of Material Culture*, 14(2), 243–77.
Gell, A. 1998. *Art and Agency: An Anthropological Theory*. Oxford: Clarendon.
Gell, A. 1999. Vogel's net: traps as artworks and artworks as traps, in *The Art of Anthropology*, edited by E. Hirsch. London: Athlone, 187–214.
Grant, I. 2007. *The Making of Am Fasgach: An Account of the Origins of the Highland Folk Museum by its Founder*. Edinburgh: National Museums of Scotland.
Grant, N., M. Moodie and C. Weedon 1996. *Sewage Solutions: Answering the Call of Nature*. Powys: Centre for Alternative Technology.
Greer, B. 2011. Craftivist history, in *Extra/Ordinary: Craft and Contemporary Art*, edited by M.A. Buszek. Durham, NC. Duke University Press, 175–83.

Harrod, T. 2000. For love and not for money: reviving peasant art in Britain, 1880–1930, in *The Lost Arts of Europe: The Haslemere Collection of European Peasant Art*, edited by D. Crowley and L. Taylor. Haslemere: Haslemere Educational Museum.

Ingold, T. 2000. *The Perception of the Environment*. London: Routledge.

Ingold, T. and E. Hallam 2007. Creativity and cultural improvisation: an Introduction, in *Creativity and Cultural Improvisation*, edited by E. Hallam and T. Ingold. Oxford: Berg, 1–24.

James, G.W. 1903. *Indian Basketry*. New York: Henry Malkan.

Küchler, S. 1999. Binding the Pacific: between loops and knots. *Oceania*, 69(3), 145–56.

Lave, J. 1990. The culture of acquisition and the practice of understanding, in *Cultural Psychology: Essays on Comparative Human Development*, edited by J.W. Stigler, R.A. Schweder and G. Herdt. Cambridge: Cambridge University Press, 309–28.

Manthorpe, C. 2009. *Fifty Years on the Plank*, edited by M. Butcher. The Basketmakers' Association.

Marchand, T. 2010. Making knowledge: explorations of the indissoluble relation between minds, bodies and environment. *Journal of the Royal Anthropological Institute*, S1-S21.

Mason, O.T. 1895. *The Origins of Invention*. London: Walter Scott.

Mason, O.T. 1904. Aboriginal American basketry: studies in a textile art without machinery. *Annual Report of the Smithsonian Institution for the Year Ending June 30, 1902, Report of the U.S. National Museum*, Part II. Washington, DC: Government Printing Office, 171–548.

Okey, T. 1915. *An Introduction to the Art of Basket-making*. London: Pitman.

Pallasmaa, J. 2009. *The Thinking Hand: Existential and Embodied Wisdom in Architecture*. Chichester: Wiley.

Perry, G. 2010. Let the artisans craft our future. *Resurgence*, 263, 53.

Punshon, T. 1996. *Heavy Metal Resistance in Salix*. PhD thesis, Liverpool John Moores University.

Pye, D. 1968. *The Nature and the Art of Workmanship*. Cambridge: Cambridge University Press.

Rogoff, B. 2003. *The Cultural Nature of Human Development*. Oxford: Oxford University Press.

Rosillo-Calle, F. et al. 2007. *The Biomass Assessment Handbook*. London: Earthscan.

Rossbach, E. 1976. *The New Basketry*. New York: Van Nostrand Reinhold.

Sigaut, F. 1994. Technology, in *Companion Encyclopedia of Anthropology: Humanity, Culture and Social Life*, edited by T. Ingold. London: Routledge, 420–59.

Strathern, M. 1980. No nature, no culture: the Hagen case, in *Nature, Culture and Gender*, edited by M. Strathern and C. MacCormack. Cambridge: Cambridge University Press, 174–222.

Thompson, D.W. 1961 [1971]. *On Growth and Form*, abridged edition, edited by J.T. Bonner. Cambridge: Cambridge University Press.

Watling, R. and J.A. Raven (eds) 1992. *Willow Symposium: Proceedings of the Royal Society of Edinburgh 1992 (for 1991)*, 98. Edinburgh: The Royal Society of Edinburgh.

Wendrich, W. 1991. *Who Is Afraid of Basketry? A Guide to Recording Basketry and Cordage for Archaeologists and Ethnographers.* Leiden: Leiden University, Centre for Non-Western Studies.

## Chapter 10
# Skill and Aging: Perspectives from Three Generations of English Woodworkers

Trevor H.J. Marchand

**Introduction**

In 2005, I embarked on a two-year, full-time training programme in fine woodwork at the historic Building Crafts College in Stratford, East London. Direct participation in a community of learners and practitioners formed an integral part of a longer anthropological study of skill acquisition, practice and professional identity among contemporary English furniture makers. Based on that fieldwork, this chapter explores the growth, development and deterioration of craft skill over a lifespan from the perspectives offered by three generations of woodworkers.

A carpenter's dedication and skilled know-how may extend well beyond the working life of the individual craftsperson. This chapter begins and ends with George, a 90-year old woodworker whose memories of apprenticeship and practice draw my starting point back to the 1930s in southeast England, and whose acts of generosity have made training possible for future generations in the trade. The accounts in between from carpenters Jack and James investigate in turn the early woodworking education of a young man and the professional practice of an established, middle-aged designer–maker whose initial role as apprentice has, with passing years, turned to mentor.

Woodworking presents a constant challenge and mastering the craft demands a persistent willingness to learn and develop. A woodworker's skill is measured by his or her ability to respond creatively, solve problems and incorporate new information into working processes. Design and making, therefore, are skills that grow in response to, and in relation with, the total working environment of tools, machinery, materials, fellow carpenters and clients. This theme remains central throughout my investigation. Design and making, as interrelated skills, evolve in unforeseen ways, producing unique solutions to problems that gradually come to be associated with individual 'style'. But skill-based knowledge does not merely grow and develop. Like the organic properties of the timber they work, the skill of woodworkers, too, is susceptible to deterioration and decline. The final section of the chapter returns to George in order to explore the impact of aging, injury and illness on tool-wielding practices, and the re-skilling strategies devised by those determined to remain active in their cherished trade. In relation to this, I reference literature from the neurosciences that examines transformation in the nervous system as the body grows, practises and ages. Anthropologists have long challenged Cartesianism and entrenched divisions between the 'exterior person' and the 'interior self', and have suggested that self and identity are constantly in the making. The neurosciences literature lends further support to this claim by illustrating how our brains and nervous systems, too, are ever-changing. Engagement with such interdisciplinary research deepens our understanding of ageing and transformation, and in so doing informs discussions of what is entailed in processes of growth and making.

In this chapter, I weave theory and analysis into the ethnography. The woodworkers I trained with and interviewed reflected carefully on their own processes, choices and personal development as craftspeople, and they articulated their thinking on these matters as elegantly as they wielded their tools. I therefore include detailed quotations from their accounts alongside my own explanations, through which I bring narrative order to the events we discussed and the things that I learned from them.

**George: A Woodworker's Training in Decades Past**

> There was a great deal of unemployment in the 1930s, so you did what you could. I left school, at 14 of course, which you had to do in those days. And a year later my sister married a carpenter whose father had a workshop in Croydon, so I went there. He had quite a good place, though the machinery was old-fashioned and wouldn't be allowed today. My first job every morning was to start up the gas engine which drove a series of shafts with pulleys that came down to each machine. The fly-wheel on the machine was bigger than I was and had a great big handle. Legally speaking, I wasn't allowed to work machinery until I'd gone past 16. That was a law. In fact, once a year the government would send an inspector around. It was always a big laugh because the inspector would come to see if you were physically fit. They'd ask 'Are you deaf, dumb, daft or dippy?' 'Yes Sir we are', we'd say. 'That's alright then, you're fit!' We didn't know much then about health and safety, or what not.

I visited George Pysden at his home in leafy Woldingham, Surrey, on 22 January 2008. George, aged 90, was a widower and ably looked after himself. He graciously offered me a cup of tea on arrival before taking me on a tour of the spacious reception rooms to view examples of the furniture he made during his long career as a woodworker. The cabinets and tables were classical in form, proportion and detail, and their highly-polished surfaces displayed intricate geometries of precious inlaid woods – a skilled art for which he was renowned. We proceeded to the conservatory where we sat together chatting for much of that sunny afternoon, overlooking a lawn that sloped steeply away from the house down to a small garage-cum-workshop along the main road. He told me about his life and work.

> When I was a young boy, people didn't look at computers and what not. They had hobbies. I got pleasure from making things. I bought an old treadle-lathe for making candle-sticks and we did a bit of woodwork at school. From an early age, without saying 'Yes this is what I'd like to do', I knew instinctively that I was going to do it.

Wood, perhaps more than any other material, holds widespread allure for those wanting to make or build useful objects. Historian and woodworker Harvey Green observes that 'ordinary people assume that they know or can readily discover how to work with wood, whereas working with metals and plastic is mysterious, dangerous and requires tools that are too expensive and too large for most people to acquire or use' (2006: xx–xxi). Wood and woodworking also appeal to the senses: different varieties of timber possess distinct colour, odour, density, grain and figure, and every plank responds differently to the teeth of a saw or the blade of a plane. Notably, the processes of working with hand tools and giving shape and form to a plank of timber also serve to *re-form* the maker (Ingold 2006, Marchand 2008). Focused practice and repetition gradually bring about new configurations in perceptual awareness (Grasseni 2009, Rice 2010), physiology and neural circuitry (Downey 2010, Johnston 2009, Landi and Rossini 2010, Marchand 2012, Rees 2010, Xu et al. 2009), as well as changes to one's emotional state, disposition and sense of self (Damasio 1994). A history of past hobbies, sport and play regularly form the backdrop to the more intensive training that, in effect, *grows* the body and mind of the learner into a full-fledged craftsperson. I asked George to tell me more about a woodworker's training in the past.

> In the days before I was born, if your dad wanted you to be a woodworker, you would be 'articled'. And it probably cost your dad about £25, which was a lot of money then. But then that firm was obliged by law to train the boy until the age of 21. Articling was gradually phased out because there wasn't much affluence in the 1920s and 30s. There were expensive colleges that those at my end of the spectrum had no hope of attending. It was all pie in the sky.

George came from a working-class background and his father was a train driver for Southern Railway. 'If you wanted to be a woodworker you had to get a job with a woodworking firm. And if you were really keen, you'd attend night school, which was much more affordable at about £1 a term'.

According to George, there was no standardized form of learning when he was a lad.

> You worked with the governor and he told you what to do and you had to do it. Otherwise you might get a thick ear. It was like that in those days. You learned your job the hard way. We did everything by hand: we bought the timber in ready-planed; we set it out by hand, and cut and mortised-and-tenoned it by hand. To start off with, I was given a cutting list and it was my job to find the

right sizes of timber. We never threw the small pieces away. We had a place where all the short ends were stacked up. I measured them up to see what we could get out of them, and then I stood next to my governor while he set it out for the cuts. As I progressed, my governor put me on more advanced work. After all, he couldn't do everything, and that's why he employed me – to do the work. An apprentice has to be taught, of course, but then they have to learn it themselves.

After six years of service during the Second World War, George found civilian work and soon married, put a deposit on a house and started his own business, moonlighting as a carpenter in his spare time. The volume of commissions grew steadily, and by the start of the 1950s he set up a workshop in Croydon. Six months later George took on his first apprentice, Fred, a young man in his mid-20s. Originally, Fred had served an apprenticeship to a bookbinder, but after two years of national service his sights were fixed on woodworking and he approached George for employment and training. George gradually purchased second-hand machinery – scarcely available after the war – and he and Fred accepted any commissions that came their way. 'I took on work to earn money because, after all, you've got to pay the bills', George recounted. 'But every so often I got something that was really fascinating to make. And as I got more interested in [finer woodwork], I gradually changed over to making furniture, like the pieces you've seen here', gesturing with a backhand toward the interior rooms behind us. George soon outgrew his premises and so purchased a bomb site on the opposite side of the road where he erected a brand new workshop. He moved yet again to a larger piece of land which he profitably developed over the years to include his own large workspace and a multi-storey commercial unit which he rented.

Fred stayed four years at George's workshop before embarking on his own business, but he continued to pay regular social calls to his former mentor. Over the course of his career, George estimated that he trained nearly 10 people on the tools. 'It's a trade where young people come and go. Some, like Fred, stayed a long time before going off to promote their own lives, while others were gone after just a few months' he told me. 'You've got young people who come in thinking they want to be a woodworker: "I'll work with my hands! It'll be easy". They perhaps do it for 18 months, two years; then they're off wanting to do something else'. I asked him what sorts of qualities he looked for in a trainee. 'Woodwork is a trade where you've got to think. Really think. There's nothing automatic. I say to the youngsters who come to me: "Any fool can get a big hammer and smash things up. It don't require brains. But can you take a hammer and make something worthwhile?"' George continued: 'You've got to want to produce something and to be able to say "I made that". You've got to create and have pride'. If a young person knocked at his door today, George would recommend that 'they find a small workshop that does varied work, and start there'. A small workshop doing bespoke joinery and furniture offers trainees the best opportunity to 'learn it themselves'.

## Jack: Learning the Basics

An emphasis on small-scale individual work is retained at the Building Crafts College where the day is spent at the bench, not in the classroom. Jack was among the youngest members of the fine woodworking cohort, arriving straight from secondary school and supported by a grant from the Carpenters' Company that founded the college in 1893. He was a tall and lanky 16-year old boy with bright brown eyes, a sprinkle of freckles on his pale nose and cheeks, and a faint shadow of downy hair over his upper lip. Jack's family lived in Aldersbrook, an Edwardian housing estate in northeast London, and his older sisters and parents were engaged in artistic occupations. Jack readily acknowledged that growing up in a creative household motivated his career choice, but he also conceded that he was better at making 'practical things' than doing art and design. He was first introduced to carpentry in year seven at school and was immediately drawn to working with his hands. 'I also tried metalwork and electronics, but I kept burning my fingers in electronics and things moved too slowly in metalwork'. While fidgeting with his collection of fraying festival wristbands, Jack told me:

> Kids who went to my primary school just moved onto the secondary school. That's what people from my estate do. My school friends are all jealous that I've jumped ship and I'm out there doing something I enjoy. They're just stuck in school doing something they hate. But it's quite pleasing to know that I'm doing something to get where I want to be. (Figure 10.1)

**Figure 10.1  Jack at the Building Crafts College, 2005. Photo: T. Marchand**

In the beginning, however, the full days at college dragged on for what seemed an eternity to Jack. By mid-afternoon he was counting down the minutes, and he routinely had his tools stored away and his work area swept long before official leaving time. The first-year joinery instructor, Con, would gently but firmly reprimand Jack and delegate small tasks to keep his mind and hands occupied until 4:30 p.m. Punctual timekeeping, along with accurate diary keeping and general tidiness of working areas were rigidly reinforced. By his own admission, Jack was impatient and careless, preferring to be active with his hands and tools and less concerned with the end result. Indeed, impatience was one of his defining characteristics, in large part due to the exuberance of youth but also owing to a certain intensity of spirit. 'I would like this carpentry thing better if things were quicker', he told me. 'If I get it wrong, I'll just start again and catch up. It doesn't bother me'. But he also had an impressive capacity for critical reflection on his own actions and decisions, as well as on the broader social dynamics in the workshop and his position within the community of trainees. 'I get annoyed with myself when I make a mistake. I start working faster and the mistakes build up, and I try to cover them up'.

Jack executed his early projects with haste and a degree of recklessness, so, accordingly, Con tailored the project specifications to alleviate the time pressure and channel Jack's energies into improving basic hand skills and heightening his level of concentration. In the first year we worked nearly exclusively with softwood, and more specifically with pleasantly aromatic 'redwood' pine (*Pinus sylvestris*), also popularly known as Scots pine. The resinous nature of redwood, compounded with dead or encased knots, can pose certain challenges to the carpenter, but for the most part the timber is easily worked with hand tools and can be polished to a good finish. For these reasons, it is ideally suited to learning and practising rudimentary hand tool manoeuvres, and for executing design prototypes.

Our very first task was to take apart and reassemble a bench plane and to sharpen its cutting iron on a diamond stone. The importance of sharpening and maintaining tools was underscored together with the necessities of safe practice and protective attire. Producing a simple, basic halving joint using a tenon saw and chisel was the starting point for a repertoire of more intricate wood joints that enabled us to make in turn a modest frame, a casement window, a panel door, a dovetail-jointed tool cabinet and a staircase. Producing joinery with precise measurements, square cuts, tight joints, and well-finished surfaces was a prerequisite for progressing to fine furniture at the end of the year. But achieving this posed a serious challenge to Jack and others, and the reasoning behind such high standards would not be fully comprehended until we began working with hardwood timber and assembling our first pieces of furniture. After marking out the dovetail joints for his redwood tool cabinet, Jack asked Con what kind of chisel he should use to chop them out. 'Good question Jack', the instructor replied and then walked away. 'I didn't have a clue what to do', Jack confessed. 'Just had to make a decision and go with it. So I followed my instinct of what's best'. Con's Socratic method of instruction encouraged trainees to make use of available workshop resources creatively to improvise solutions. These included the tools to hand, a small library of reference material and, importantly,

Figure 10.2  Jack machining a piece of timber, 2006. Photo: T. Marchand

one's community of fellow practitioners, offering a diversity of perspectives and approaches to any set problem (Figure 10.2).

Jack struggled with carpentry manuals and photocopied hand-outs – indeed, the abstract nature of book learning had driven him from school to handwork in the first place. He insisted that demonstrations worked best for him, but then qualified the claim: 'Sometimes it goes on for too long. I need to be shown quickly'. Periodically, Jack abandoned his workstation to pay social visits. He pulled up a stool at a neighbour's bench, made himself comfortable and struck up casual conversation while watching them work, or generously offered to lend a hand. 'I pick up things that way', he told me. Jack also kept a regular eye on his age-mate Billy who worked at the adjoining bench.

> With Billy, I'm generally ahead of him in the projects so I get to see a different way of how I might have done things. But sometimes he doesn't have a clue what he's doing, so I just show him. I've picked it up from Con or Toby, so I teach Billy.

Jack recognized explicitly that instructing others, either verbally or through demonstration, and sometimes merely with straightforward encouragement, formed an integral part of his own learning processes. When he eventually completed his tool cabinet, he did so with a tremendous sense of satisfaction: 'When I'm doing something nice, and I do it well, I just get a happy feeling from it. Forty-eight dovetails! I feel like I've achieved something. And that's the main reason I came here'.

When I sat down with Jack at the end of the first year, we reflected together on the past months and spoke at length about his future goals and aspirations. 'I've learnt a lot', he said.

> Considering what I learned from five years at school and what I've learned here … It's done what I wanted it to do. I've learned to think about what I'm doing and how I should do it … and about how I come to a decision. I know now that I need to come up with an action plan for how I'm going to make something – otherwise I get muddled up in what I should do.

I asked what know-how he was hoping to leave with by the end of the second year: 'With the knowledge that I can make things. I want to have the confidence to see something and say "I can make that", and just know that not many people can do the stuff I'm able to do', he replied with a beaming smile. 'What are you hoping to do with your life when you finish here?' I probed. 'I know I don't want to go into full-time work at 18 or 19 [years old], making doors and windows for the rest of my life'. He conceded that he would probably need additional training to gain the necessary design skills to become a furniture maker. Jack paused to reflect, and then continued:

> By 21-ish, after a BA in furniture making, I could have those qualifications and a better idea about what I can do. It'll give me that little bit more to be first in the

queue for a nicer job, a bit more money and, best of all, the freedom to do what I want to do. It'll be a good investment.

Like all the fine woodworkers I met during my study, and since, Jack was seeking a sense of control over his future working life and satisfaction from the quality and kind of things he would produce (Marchand 2007). By growing and diversifying his skill set he was strategically mapping out an 'action plan' to reach these goals.

**James: From Apprentice to Mentor**

I met with bespoke furniture maker James Verner at his workshop in the tranquil village of Hawkchurch, Devon, where we discussed his personal experiences of apprenticeship and training. James's first exposure to the world of furniture making was on a visit to Parnham House, Dorset, where John Makepeace had set up the renowned School for Craftsmen in Wood in 1977. But, like most middle-class British children, his parents and school teachers never intimated the possibility of going to college to learn woodworking. After completing joint honours in psychology and art history at the University of St Andrews, James found itinerant work making steeplechase fences at racecourses around England and Ireland, doing what he described as his 'finest work with a chainsaw' (Figure 10.3).

**Figure 10.3** James Verner at his workshop in Devon, 2008. Photo: T. Marchand

At 25, James decided to get serious about woodworking and to become a furniture maker. He proffered free labour in return for an apprenticeship and, following a long string of polite refusals, he was taken on by Nick Smith whose workshop specialized in furniture restoration but also accepted occasional commissions for new pieces. 'When there weren't things being made, I was dismantling and restoring the most wonderful bits of furniture which is a great way to learn how to build new ones', James told me. He described his training with Nick as 'entirely informal', a model he would later adopt for training his own apprentices. The first task Nick assigned him was to plane a plank square, cut it in half, and join the two pieces at a right angle with three dovetails; and then repeat the exercise with more refined lapped dovetails. 'I found it satisfying', James reminisced. 'I was good at it, and faster than others [in the workshop], so very soon I was moved onto making things'. In his view, Nick's workshop provided a 'superb learning environment' where trainees were 'able to learn without undue pressure'. 'He gave us enough rope to hang ourselves but not enough to ruin the whole piece'. The workshop also instilled traditional values, both in design and craftsmanship, and it took time for James to realize that perhaps 'there were alternative ways more appropriate to furniture making in the twenty-first century'. James's own contemporary designs combine sleek, modern elegance with traditional joinery, and he employs a mixture of hand tools, machinery and jigs to produce them.

Since opening his own workshop in 1996, James has trained more than a dozen young men and women. He feels a certain responsibility to pass on the skills, but more importantly he enjoys teaching and, through teaching, learning: 'I love what I do and I enjoy sharing it with others by providing a good, interesting workplace where people can develop and grow'. That ethos becomes part of the furniture that his team produces. According to James, 'a beautifully crafted object cannot be forged in a crucible of misunderstanding, pressure or unpleasant working conditions. It has to grow out of a space of understanding, communication and resources. The more you put around its base, the better it's going to be. Without becoming too mystical', he continued, 'I do believe that objects embody the energies that are put into their making'. James's personal satisfaction comes from the 'immersion and focus' he experiences at the bench. For him, woodworking 'is a mixture between writing and yoga. There's a little bit of ballet, movement, smell, touch, sound – the whole thing. When you're actually working, every sense is focused on what you're doing'. Regardless of one's level of expertise, woodworking is a process of constant learning and discovery. For James, that process ought to be 'like going for a walk. You enjoy the process, you enjoy the journey, but it's not a forced march'.

Like his former mentor, James strives to make the process of learning, discovery and personal development available to his employees. 'Historically', he mused, 'apprenticeships were so much more than just learning the trade. They were really about learning how to make the transition from youth to adulthood'. This transition is achieved mainly through learning to think for oneself, and, by doing so, nurturing self-respect. He offered a recent example of self-directed learning, pointing to a young man busily assembling a cabinet component at a bench across the workshop:

> I was talking to Warren just this morning. He needed to join one piece of wood to another, so I started going into great detail about a jig that might be made for the job. But in the end I said to him, 'You're actually the person doing the task, so it's up to you to work out a way to do it'.

Like all experienced woodworkers, James recognized that making mistakes is an essential part of learning and growing, but, equally, exploration and experimentation need to be kept in check with the real financial costs of error and lost time. He didn't need to watch to determine whether his carpenters were getting it right; rather he only had to listen to their tools and materials: 'If something sounds harmonious, the work is flowing. If it doesn't, I need to go over and have a chat' (Figure 10.4).

**Figure 10.4   James mentoring a trainee, 2008. Photo: T. Marchand**

Over the years, James became acutely aware of the time needed to help someone develop their skills, and increasingly cautious about taking on school-leavers who possessed no prior training or experience. 'To have someone turn up and take away your time from bench or business is really limiting', he explained.

'In bespoke furniture, the biggest factor in the cost of the piece is the time spent at the workbench. Materials are about 10 per cent of the total, the rest is all labour. So any limitations on time are going to affect the bottom line'. When hiring new trainees, James claimed he could gauge an applicant's aptitude by what they could tell him about timber and, more significantly, by the way they moved. 'A woodworker needs to have an awareness of what they're doing in an environment. A natural gesticulator, for instance, would be dangerous around machinery and a hazard around a piece of furniture that's had hundreds of hours put into it'. Elaborating on the importance of good proprioceptive and kinaesthetic awareness, he added, 'In a way, it's a form of intelligence – to know where one's body is in space and to be aware of one's surroundings'. Social competence and enthusiasm were other essential attributes that James looked for in an applicant. He needed to be confident that the individual would integrate with the team and be sympathetic to the kind of furniture he designed: 'They must convey that they're passionate – frankly, they're going to have to be passionate because they're getting paid bugger all'. So far as technical competence was concerned, James was certain that he could teach almost anybody to cut timbers, but that wasn't his ambition: 'I want to help people become exceptional woodworkers'. When trainees reached that stage of development, however, they typically moved on to set up their own business. James took a philosophical perspective on that cyclical loss of in-house expertise and of the resources put into training: 'As long as I get my pound of flesh, that's okay. After all, life's about a great deal more than money'. He derived greater pleasure, he told me, from observing the growth in an apprentice's skillset and in their sensitivity to the medium. 'And maybe' he added, 'they grow in other ways as well: as people'.

**George: Final Years**

In November, two months before our meeting, George Pysden humbly received the Master Craft Certificate in Joinery at Carpenters' Hall.[1] He shared his thoughts about achieving mastery in the trade. 'When I make a piece of furniture now', George told me animatedly, 'even before I cut a plank of timber, I know what I'm going to do. I can see every part of it in my mind. That ability has developed over the last 15, 20 years'. He nodded in the direction of a delicate inlaid table where a tray of fresh tea and biscuits sat waiting, and continued: 'I could make that without a drawing as long as I've got some measurements for the height, width and centre. I've got it so engrained. I can see every joint I'm going to make'. George conceded to making sketches on paper to which he could revert during the process because, he added almost apologetically, 'you can't remember everything'.

---

1   The Master Craft Certificate scheme is sponsored by the Worshipful Companies of Carpenters and of Joiners and Ceilers, the City & Guilds London Institute and the Institute of Carpenters, and provides independent recognition of the holder's superior mastery of their craft beyond NVQ Level 3.

But, again he insisted, 'I can see every bit of that in my mind before I start it'. George's 'seeing in his mind' involves more than merely an ability to visualize the overall design: as a minimum, it is the multifaceted ability to conceptualize the joints connecting the legs to the table top, the width of the rails, and the pattern of the inlay; to imaginatively compare and contrast varieties of timber, and select pieces appropriate to the task; to think viscerally about the process of physically making and assembling the table, and to calculate the costs of labour and materials. If he were making the table for a client, knowledge of that individual's personal taste, needs and budget would also enter the equation. The long accretion of entwined experiences – practical, conceptual, sensory and social – endows craftspeople with a skill for 'envisioning' a new project as a whole and in its complexity. Indeed, it is the ability to imaginatively anticipate and simultaneously plan for the design, the making and the business of craft that qualifies a 'Master' (Figure 10.5).

Growth and development into mastery are equally marked by an ability to respond effectively to the unexpected and to improvise creatively in face of the unforeseen. For the woodworker, the material nature and performance of their tools changes over time, and the character of the timber they saw, chisel or plane differs not only between varieties, but within the same variety and even within a single plank. In handwork, the orchestration of grasp, stance and posture, and of applied pressure, motion and direction, is in constant need of often subtle calibration (Marchand 2012). New projects and designs introduce novel problems demanding novel solutions, typically arrived at by recombining and reconfiguring the resources and technologies to hand. But an ability to respond and improvise is critical not only to daily mastery with tools and materials; it is critical, too, when slow, and occasionally sudden, physical, mental and sensorial transformations are experienced by the ageing or injured woodworker. In order to persist in one's trade and execute the necessary tasks, the body-mind must compensate for loss by reconfiguring its muscular, neurological and sensory resources, often achieved in coordination with a reorganization of the working environment in which they are immersed – a subject I return to shortly.

Like a craftsperson's skills, the wooden furniture they make transforms, deteriorates and perishes over its lifetime. In recounting a story about a client's cherry-wood table warped by the radiators in their dining room, George exclaimed, 'Since the War, more expensive furniture has been ruined by central heating!' A tree dies when felled, but its timber continues to absorb and exude moisture with changing atmospheric conditions, causing swelling, shrinkage, splitting, cupping or bending. The colour and durability of timber are also susceptible to a host of factors including heat, light, rot and insect infestation. Many of these reactions and alterations can be minimized or delayed through appropriate selection of timber for the purpose and location; by using veneers in place of solid hardwoods; by applying polish, wax or lacquer, or through restorative intervention which may include the use of fungicides or chemical preservatives, or grafting new wood onto perished components. Some defects and forms of deterioration, however, are desirable to woodworkers and clients. Burrs, burls and abnormal growths may yield timber with prized character, used frequently for turning bowls or handles,

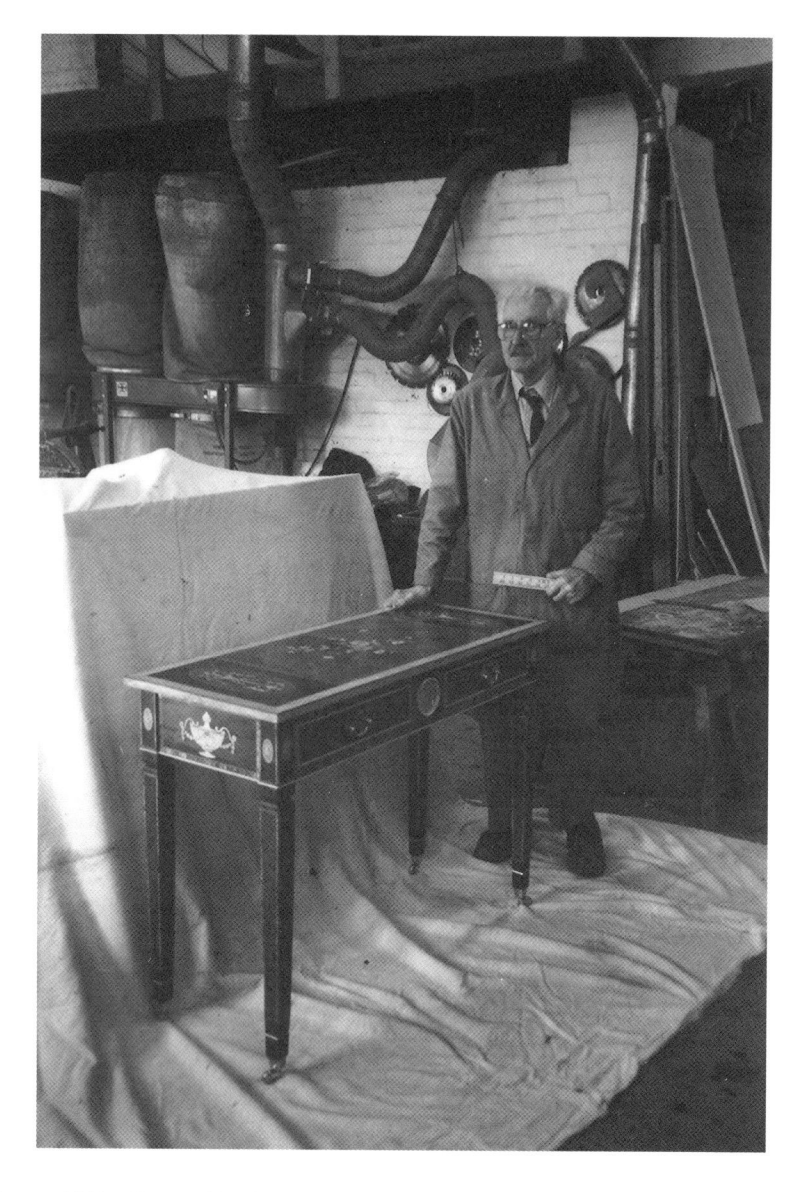

**Figure 10.5  George Pysden, Master Craftsman, 2007. Photo: Geoffrey Alan Pysden, cousin of the master woodworker**

or for producing costly, exotic veneers. Diseased wood, too, might present unique figures that can be accentuated under the sharp iron of the smoothing plane. The squiggly traces of long-departed woodworm; a deepening or mellowing hue of the timber; the crackle of old lacquer, and even a discernible history of wear and tear, contribute to the cherished patina of antique furniture and family heirlooms. In such cases, ageing and deterioration are positively conceptualized, valued and accommodated within a set of narratives that restore purpose and usefulness to the furniture, and salvage it from the trash heap or the fireplace.

Through restoring old furniture, George, like James Verner, had learned a great deal about the behaviour of timber and about earlier woodworking techniques which, in turn, informed his own design and making. During an interview published in *The Independent* newspaper (Lacey and Yiasoumi 1998), he explained that 'the basics have stayed much the same' in furniture making though 'there's been a great improvement in the tools and machinery'. And, he added humorously, 'everything's electric now and I wish I was too'. In 1998, aged 81 and after 65 years in the trade, George reported that he still worked every day in his Croydon carpentry shop from 7:30 a.m. to 2:30 p.m. (ibid.). His pace steadily declined, however, over the following decade, and notably so after the death of his wife Joan in 2000. With no children, he was alone in the house. His last trainee, Bob, a middle-aged man who had lately taken up the trade, visited George regularly and lent a hand with small woodworking tasks. George no longer had the physical strength to move large planks or to operate heavy machinery, and the fingers of his once strong, large hands were bent and their joints swollen. With age, his eyesight deteriorated and he now wore thick-lensed glasses, but his hearing was surprisingly good despite working for so many decades with the thunderous noise of heavy machines.

A life of woodworking exercises, disciplines, shapes and, eventually, strains the body. Ageing carpenters frequently suffer from arthritic joints and worn cartilage, and these afflictions are typically compounded by more general kinds of deterioration including diminished muscular strength, decreased flexibility and dexterity, and a gradual loss of bone mass. The perceptual senses of sight, hearing, smell and touch, all of which play important roles in the processes and pleasures of woodworking, become impaired at varying rates with old age, and in various combinations. Accidents and injury over the span of a woodworker's career may also result in chronic pain, loss of sight or hearing, or missing digits. But ageing and injury are not simply stories of fragility and decay (Degnen 2007). Loss can entail the generation of new coping mechanisms, the growth of alternative ways of sensing and processing environmental stimuli, or the development of novel methods and embodied strategies for performing tasks and achieving goals. I use the term 'embodied', here, to include the brain and nervous system, as well as viscera, muscle tissues and sensory organs.

Until recently, it was believed that the brain and nervous system were fully formed by the time of early adulthood, resulting in a brain that is organized into fixed, function-specific regions (Amunts et al. 1997, Landi and Rossini 2010, Rees 2010). Although neuroscientists and cognitive scientists generally acknowledged the functional plasticity of the adult brain in response, for instance, to the acquisition of new motor skills, they did not believe that repeated practice could result in structural changes to the central nervous system. Thus the possibility of structural plasticity was effectively denied. During the past 15 years, however, studies employing advanced imaging techniques, including magnetic resonance imaging (MRI), demonstrate that the adult brain does indeed undergo activity-dependent structural change (Maguire et al. 2000, Draganski et al. 2004).

Most significantly in relation to my account of George Pysden, it is now accepted that brain plasticity continues throughout one's lifetime and into old age (Boyke et al. 2008). Indeed, plasticity – defined as 'the brain's continuous embryogenetic potential to induce new nervous tissue, and thereby to change its form' (Rees 2010: 151) – is deemed to be an inherent property which enables our brains to react to both internal and external stimuli at a structural level (Landi and Rossini 2010). Our brains, like our sense of self, are therefore in a state of ongoing and dynamic change in relation with our total environments and physical bodies. Neurological studies conducted within the past five years suggest that the potential for reorganization within the primary sensorimotor areas of the ageing brain not only allows for the acquisition of new skills, but also serves as a compensatory mechanism, making possible the formation of alternative neural circuits for achieving a particular goal when the original synaptic arrangements break down or deteriorate. As George's eyesight weakened and the dexterity and strength in his fingers, hands and the rest of his body declined, the pace of his work slowed and the scale of projects decreased. But he did not stop woodworking. He found other carpentry jobs to do and his brain–body organized alternative ways of realizing them.

At the close of my interview with George, having learned about his long and successful career, I asked him what he still hoped to achieve as a carpenter and furniture maker. 'Well, I actually wish I could go back to work again', he replied somewhat regretfully.

> I retired in 2000. That's eight years ago now, and I was already quite old then. As people left me, I didn't hire anyone else and gradually I was left on my own. In any case, I've kept my workshop and that's full of machinery, of course. Planers, a spindle moulder, a massive belt sander, a vertical sander, a lathe which I fiddle around with ... But I suppose what I'd love to do – but at my age I'm not going to spend the money – I would love to have what they call a 'copy lathe' so I could make a 'barley twist'.[2]

In the past, the ability to manufacture this decorative feature by hand was the mark of a highly accomplished turner or carver, and a comprehensive apprenticeship once included turning and carving alongside joinery, cabinetmaking and shop fitting. George was still determined to learn new skills and further master his craft.

Two months after my pleasant visit to Woldingham, I received an email from the Carpenters' Hall informing me that George Pysden had died peacefully at his home on Easter Monday, aged 90. Just two weeks previously, he reportedly

---

2  A 'barley twist' is a double-helix spiral shape composing chair or table legs.

attended lunch at the Hall and was in good form. The full-page obituary published in the *Carpenters' Company Broadsheet* (2008, 38: 4) announced that 'In an act of typical generosity, George willed 75 per cent of his estate to the Company's college ... for young people wishing to enter or study the trade'. It was later revealed that an impressive sum of three-quarters of a million pounds had been willed to the Charitable Trust in annual support of two Pysden Scholars embarking on the fine woodwork programme at the Building Crafts College (*Carpenters' Company Broadsheet*, 2009, 40: 12). George's legacy in his beloved trade was secured.

**Conclusion**

In this chapter I have investigated the growth and deterioration of skill through personal accounts offered by three woodworkers. Although Jack, James and George were at different stages of life and career, their individual motivations coalesced around a desire to further their learning and enskilment, and to progressively attain mastery in their chosen trade. All three embarked upon a carpentry career by joining communities of practice that afforded access to workshops, mentors and role models. The luxury of time for experimenting with tools and materials, making mistakes and solving problems within a supportive environment was deemed critical for evolving the combination of motor ability and sensory awareness that squarely defines a woodworker's skill.

Jack, James and George also listed the requisite personal qualities of patience, disciplined focus and, importantly, self-respect. As James explained, self-respect breeds the confidence to confront new challenges and improvise solutions, thereby growing one's skill set and fuelling the transformation from trainee to mentor. Young Jack improved his own practice, as he noted, by regularly exhibiting the procedures for workshop exercises to a fellow trainee. James and George, with greater experience, have successfully scaffolded and guided the skill learning of aspiring furniture makers of all ages. In doing so, and by founding their own workshops, both men gained a fuller, more complex mastery of not only the craft of fine furniture making but also the operational and business dimensions of the trade.

Remaining financially afloat as a furniture maker is a steady challenge, calling for constant update of one's full gamut of trade skills. In time, and with perseverance, James and George established solid clientele bases, and George steadily won status among his peers and eventually earned institutional recognition from the Carpenters' Livery Company. By this point, however, the deterioration and decline in his motor skills, physical strength, endurance and sensory acuity had become more apparent and increasingly hampered his woodworking abilities. As I have shown, George nevertheless continued to set new goals and his determination to carry on working resulted in novel reconfigurations of his muscular, neurological and sensory resources in order to execute tasks, alongside modifications in his workshop setting and his carpentry methods.

The ethnography and theory introduced in this chapter demonstrate that the growth and the deterioration of skill are not mutually exclusive processes, but rather the development of one skill may result in the simultaneous decline of others, and, significantly, vice versa. As young individuals, like Jack, hone their skill within a particular field of practice, constraints on time and resources force them to neglect or abandon other activities causing associated potentials to stagnate and existing skills to regress. Jack's promise as a talented footballer, along with his academic schooling, were relegated to the sidelines as he immersed himself more deeply in his vocational training at the Building Crafts College and focused his efforts on acquiring carpentry skills. In James's case, as demand rose for his furniture creations, he expanded his workforce and invested in machinery. Consequently, a greater proportion of his time was now spent managing the business operations and less 'on the tools'. The skilled use of hand tools demands a regular regime of practice, without which dexterity declines and the 'feeling' for efficient and rhythmic movements at the bench recedes.

In the event of injury or illness, or through the processes of ageing, muscular, neurological and sensory abilities are impaired or deteriorate at varying rates, affecting the woodworker's skilled operations. In response, alternative pathways, methods and means for realizing tasks may grow and develop, resulting in new skills. Following from this observation, it is important to underline that realizing a given task can be achieved in a variety of different ways, each enrolling a distinct array of physical, cognitive and sensory resources; and the way that individuals continue to accomplish that task over their lifetime is likely to change in response to changes in the resources available. The anthropology of craftwork therefore needs to account more carefully for the diversity of resources that are drawn together in producing a personal skill-set, and to better record, analyze and theorize the ways that such configurations change with time and according to events and circumstances.

**Acknowledgements**

I am grateful for the generous support from the ESRC for my research and training with woodworkers (RES-000–27–0159), and to Parvathi Raman, Julie Tancell and John Heywood for their feedback and comments on earlier drafts. I thank my fellow trainees and woodwork instructors at the Building Crafts College for sharing their love of the craft, and the furniture makers I interviewed for their time and generosity. This chapter is dedicated to the memory of George Pysden, a true gentleman and craftsman.

# References

Amunts, K. et al. 1997. Motor cortex and hand motor skills: structural compliance in the human brain. *Human Brain Mapping*, 5(3), 206–15.

Boyke, J. et al. 2008. Training-induced brain structure changes in the elderly. *The Journal of Neuroscience*, 28(28), 7031–5.

Damasio, A. 1994. *Descarte's Error: Emotion, Reason and the Human Brain*. New York: Putnam's.

Degnen, C. 2007. Back to the future: temporality, narrative and the aging self, in *Creativity and Cultural Improvisation*, edited by E. Hallam and T. Ingold. Oxford: Berg, 223–35.

Downey, G. 2010. Practice without theory: a neuroanthropological perspective on embodied learning. *Journal of the Royal Anthropological Institute*, S22-S40.

Draganski, B. et al. 2004. Neuroplasticity: changes in grey matter induced by training. *Nature*, 427, 311–12.

Grasseni, C. 2009. *Developing Skill, Developing Vision: Practices of Locality at the Foot of the Alps*. Oxford: Berghahn.

Green, H. 2006. *Wood: Craft, Culture, History*. London: Penguin.

Ingold, T. 2006. Walking the plank: meditations on a process of skill, in *Defining Technological Literacy: Towards an Epistemological Framework*, edited by J.R. Dakers. New York: Palgrave Macmillan, 65–80.

Johnston, M. 2009. Plasticity in the developing brain: implications for re-habilitation. *Developmental Disabilities Research Reviews*, 15(2), 94–101.

Lacey, H. and Yiasoumi, V. 1998. Away in a manger in frosty. *The Independent*, 20 December, 1998.

Landi, D. and P.M. Rossini 2010. Cerebral restorative plasticity from normal ageing to brain disease: a 'never ending story'. *Restorative Neurology and Neuroscience*, 28(3), 349–66.

Maguire, E.A. et al. 2000. Navigation-related structural change in the hippocampi of taxi drivers. *Proceedings of the National Academy of Sciences of the United States of America*, 97(8), 4398–4403.

Marchand, T.H.J. 2007. Vocational migrants and a tradition of longing. *Traditional Dwellings and Settlements Review*, 19(1), 23–40.

Marchand, T.H.J. 2008. Muscles, morals and mind: craft apprenticeship and the formation of person. *British Journal of Educational Studies*, 56(3), 245–71.

Marchand, T.H.J. 2012. Knowledge in hand: explorations of brain, hand, tool, in *SAGE Handbook of Social Anthropology*, edited by R. Fardon et al. London: Sage, 260–69.

Rees, T. 2010. Being neurologically human today: life and science and adult cerebral plasticity (an ethical analysis), *American Ethnologist*, 37(1), 150–66.

Rice, T. 2010. Learning to listen: auscultation and the transmission of auditory knowledge. *Journal of the Royal Anthropological Institute*, S41-S61.

Xu, T. et al. 2009. Rapid formation and selective stabilization of synapses for enduring motor memories, *Nature*, 462, 915–20.

# Chapter 11
# Movement in Making: An Apprenticeship with Glass and Fire

Frances Liardet

**Introduction**

While the verb 'to grow' may take an object, as in 'she is growing marigolds', it does not have to. 'She is growing' is grammatically complete and describes a process of development. However, the phrase 'she is making' is incomplete. *What* is she making? The uncompromising transitivity of the verb 'to make' demands a grammatical object in order to be meaningful, and it is to the object in life that attention is often drawn with reference to the notion of making. As Ingold (2000b: 346) points out, 'The notion of making … defines an activity purely in terms of its capacity to yield a certain object'. But making is, like growing, a developmental process, a transformation and a becoming. The question is: of what kind, and how exactly does this take place? Some theorize making as a process of coming to belong: makers, as they learn, participate increasingly in a community of practice (Lave and Wenger 1991). Others engage with the tradition of Merleau-Ponty (1962) and Bourdieu (1977, 1990, 2000) to discuss making as coming to know or understand (Keller and Keller 1996, O'Connor 2007, Harris 2007, Marchand 2010, Portisch 2010). I propose to look specifically at making as *moving*; more precisely, the experience of moving dextrously with tools and materials.

I will begin with a brief description of core-formed glass working, the subject of my craft apprenticeship, before reviewing the two common approaches outlined above – that is, making as a kind of belonging, and making as a kind of knowing. After illustrating some of the difficulties that can arise when these approaches are applied to skilled making, I turn to the related concepts of dexterity and kinaesthesia, and use them to discuss skilled making in terms of moving and of experience. I will then show how, by developing related concepts to analyze an apprenticeship in ancient glass working, I was able to gain an insight into the power of skilled making to generate meaning. Making, when viewed through time, can be seen as the contingent, dynamic interaction between makers and made things, as a process which amounts to a kind of growth.

**Figure 11.1**  A core-formed alabastron made by the author. Photo: Frances Liardet, 2009

**Making Core-formed Glass Vessels**

Core-forming is an archaic glass-working tradition dating from the sixteenth century to the first century BCE, when it was superseded by the tradition of glassblowing (Grose 1989). It involves forming glass around an internal clay mould, or core, which is scraped out later. The clay is mixed with straw, chaff or other plant material (Bimson and Werner 1969) which burns out on firing, leaving the core riddled with interstices. This allows the core to crush slightly as the glass contracts upon cooling. A solid, uncrushable core produces a cracked vessel. Core-formed vessels have been made in many shapes but one of the most popular was the alabastron, a tall bottle-shaped vessel (Figure 11.1).

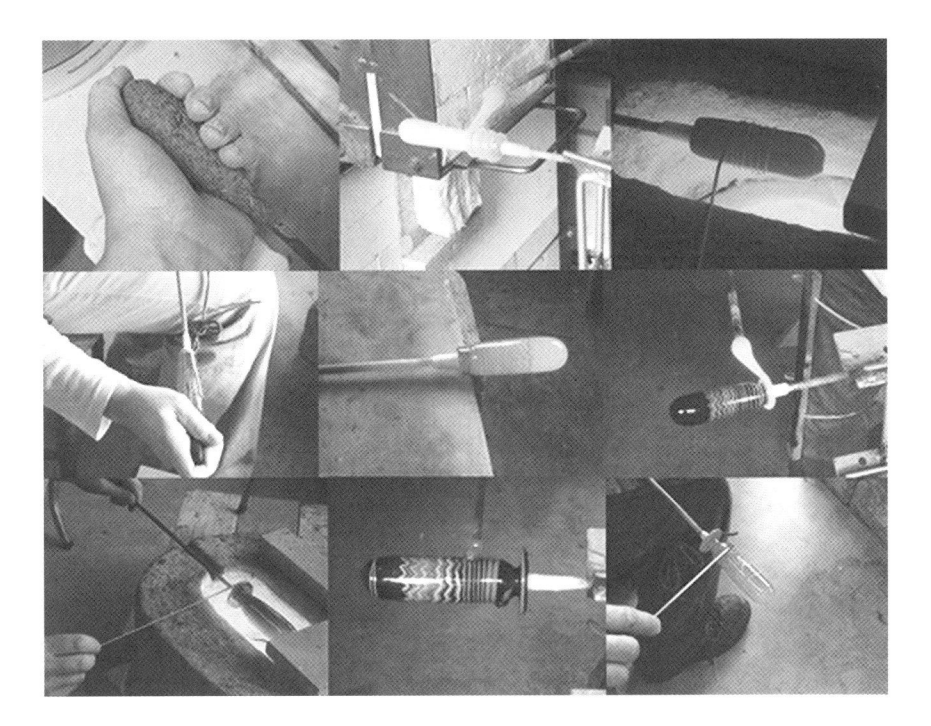

**Figure 11.2** **The order of procedures for the making of core-formed alabastra. Photos: Frances Liardet, 2008**

The sequence of work steps involved in making a core-formed vessel can be seen in Figure 11.2. These steps include: making the core, covering it with body glass, and adding decorative coloured glass to the body (Figure 11.2, top row); making patterns in the coloured glass, shaping the neck, and fashioning the rim (Figure 11.2, middle row); and decorating the rim, adding the handles, and shaping them (Figure 11.2, bottom row). It is possible that the handles of the original vessels were made before the rims, but this is unlikely, since handles can easily be damaged while the rim is being repeatedly heated and shaped; as relatively thin extrusions, they can also easily become too cool and consequently snap off.

I undertook my core-forming apprenticeship with the archaeological glass researchers and craftsmen Mark Taylor and David Hill of Andover in Hampshire, England. Taylor and Hill are skilled in ancient glass composition, tool manufacture and adaptation, ancient furnace manufacture, and archaic glass-working techniques. To make vessels we focused on Mediterranean Group I, a chronological group of core-formed vessels dating from c.525 BCE to c.400 BCE and probably made on Rhodes (Grose 1989, Harden 1981). A substantial collection of these vessels is held at the British Museum. From within this group, I chose a set of alabastra with a particular combination of body shape and decorative motif known as Class IB

(Grose 1989). This type of vessel has an upwardly tapering body between 8 and 14 cm tall with a rounded base, two ring handles, and a flat rim. It is made in cobalt blue translucent glass and decorated in turquoise and yellow opaque glass in the pattern of spiralling turns and zig-zags (Figure 11.1). The varying levels of consistency among these vessels made them ideal for exploring skilled making.

**Making and Belonging: Part of a Community**

My apprenticeship in core-forming can be analyzed as an instance of legitimate peripheral participation (Lave and Wenger 1991). Learning, according to this perspective, is a process of increasing participation in a community of practice. I first visited Taylor and Hill's Roman furnace reconstruction project[1] at their workshop space near Andover in 2005, three years before my apprenticeship. I began observing Mark Taylor and noting his gestures as he made blown vessels of Roman forms. (In this earlier project I was focused on glass*blowing* rather than core-forming.) I then returned in 2006 as a doctoral student for a second session to film Taylor and Hill's craft work. This time, because I was already known to them and because of the strong professional relationship between Taylor and Hill and my supervisor Ian Freestone, I was able to become involved in significant events: the initial lighting of the furnaces, stoking the furnaces, and recording furnace temperatures. Night stoking in turn earned me lessons in glass craft work, where I gained experience in gathering and blowing glass of a standardized Roman composition at a low furnace built of daub. I became familiar with a basic set of tools for glass working, including tweezers, rods and irons – some of which I would later use for core-forming – and with the radiation from glass heated to 1000°C. By this time I was also identifying different contexts of making, which I called novice work, familiar tradition, and expert experimentation (Liardet 2009). So when I visited Taylor and Hill in 2007 and showcased original core-formed vessels on film and in photographs, in order to interest them in teaching me this archaic technique (it was entirely up to them whether they became involved or not), I was not simply a doctoral researcher but someone who had already begun to be a glass worker, and my engagement with the tools and materials merely continued what was an ongoing process.

However, the analytical perspective of legitimate peripheral participation addresses learning in general and does not focus on making *per se*. Lave and Wenger's studies put the practice of apprentice tailors on a par with those of trainee naval quartermasters and newly recovering alcoholics – all, equally, as instances of increasing social participation (Lave and Wenger 1991) despite the fact that only the tailors were learning to make things. The advantage of analyzing making in terms of legitimate peripheral participation is that it encourages us to

---

[1] The Furnace Project 2005 and 2006: see www.romanglassmakers.co.uk. Accessed September 2008.

place making within the world in which it is situated. Yet while this acknowledges the sociality of making, it is not sensitive to the processes involved in particular kinds of participation; it does not help us to explain how exactly people come to be skilful makers in specific fields of making activity.

## Making and Knowing: The Problem of Body/Mind Distinctions

I now turn to the second of the approaches mentioned above: theorizing skilled making in terms of coming to know or understand. Merleau-Ponty (1962) cites the example of a brain-damaged man who, while able to grasp his nose to swat a mosquito, was unable simply to point to his nose in order to indicate its location. Merleau-Ponty proposes two ways in which we 'know' the location of our bodies in space: one skilful, unreflective and task-oriented; the second cognitive, reflective and declarative (Merleau-Ponty 1962: 103). 'We are brought to the recognition of ... something which is an anticipation of, or arrival at, the objective and is ensured by the body itself as a motor power, a "motor project" ... a "motor intentionality"' (Merleau-Ponty 1962: 110). The repeated performance of motor-intentional actions results in *habit*. Bourdieu's concept of *habitus* adds a social-historical dimension to this notion of habit (Foster 2005: 95). Bourdieu uses the term 'bodily intentionality' to emphasize that the locus of intentionality, knowledge, and understanding, is the body. As Bourdieu explains, 'There are a great many things we understand only with our bodies, at a subconscious level, without having the words to say them' (Bourdieu 1988: 160). Knowing how to type is neither a conditioned reflex nor a declarative knowledge of individual key positions: it is 'knowledge in the hands, which is forthcoming only when bodily effort is made, and cannot be formulated in detachment from that effort' (Merleau-Ponty 1962: 144). But as Merleau-Ponty and Bourdieu argue against incorporeal intellectualism (Foster 2005, Carman 1999), so they both necessarily distinguish 'the body' and 'the mind'. This investment in the mind-opposed body explains why the tacit nature of knowledge is so often emphasized. From this perspective an intentionality grounded in the body cannot be accessed, articulated or conveyed by the faculties of the conscious mind and must perforce be unreflective. Bodily understanding is attained by mimesis, without any conscious imitation (Bourdieu 1990: 73), in a 'silent and practical communication, from body to body' (Wacquant 2004: 113).

Within this analytical framework, the main insight into making would be that it is of a bodily nature: tacit, motor-intentional, and inaccessible to the conscious mind. This in itself is problematic as many craft practices appear to be at once reflective *and* rooted in the body. For example, communities of lace-makers see the lace they make as 'a result of ... [their] physical activity, of which calculations, decisions, and assessments ... [are] an integral part' (Makovicky 2010: 86–7). Likewise, Kazakh carpet makers teach explicit lessons about craft practice through encouraging learners' 'sensory-somatic engagement' with their materials

(Portisch 2010: 76). A trainee glassblower moves in and out of conscious engagement with problematic procedures as necessary, 'making an implicit technique explicit, improving and re-aligning that technique with its intended purpose, and allowing the revised technique to again recede into unconsciousness' (O'Connor 2007: 130).

However, even among those who rightly assert that explicit teaching is an integral part of bodily learning, there is still a tendency to structure the discussion of craft learning around the polarized terms of the 'conscious' and 'unconscious' and their respective synonyms. Even when an alternative model of non-discrete 'levels of awareness' is proposed (Noble and Watkins 2003), the continuum still stretches between unconscious and fully conscious states. It is illuminating to enquire into how makers come to know and understand their craft, but the elaboration of this highly-developed set of terms relating to knowledge, understanding and consciousness has tended to be at the expense of other important aspects of making, specifically that of moving.

## Making and Moving: Dexterity and Kinaesthesia

Kinesiology studies have traditionally contextualized the moving human body in terms of body, task and environment (see for example Newell 1986, Brenière and Bril 1988, Bril and Gouasdoué 2009). Parlebas (1999) goes further and substitutes the idea of an intended and culturally embedded 'action' for the comparatively impoverished notion of 'movement'. Warnier, for his part, proposes that there are 'three dimensions of human activity tightly interwoven: perception, motricity, emotion' (Warnier 2001: 13). But to say that things are tightly interwoven is not the same as explaining why they are interwoven, or in what way. It is necessary to explore the relationship between the first two elements, 'perception' and 'motricity', before considering the role of emotion.

The neuroscientist and kinesiologist Nikolai Bernstein provides the basis for an answer in his explanation of controlled movement. Because our muscles are so elastic and our joints so enormously mobile, the brain, when starting to move a particular muscle, cannot predict exactly how the limb will move (Bernstein 1996: 180). The brain depends on perceptions, the feedback from the sensory organs, to 'continuously and watchfully check the movement … and harness the movement with the corresponding corrections' (Bernstein 1996: 180). Because the movement can only be controlled through sensory corrections, repeating the same movement will entail slightly different motor impulses from the brain to the muscles (Bernstein 1996: 180). For example, describing his experience of learning to play jazz piano, Sudnow tells of how he groped again and again for a chord, each time having to reconfigure his fingers as if for the first attempt, but eventually found his hand beginning to prepare for the chord as he reached for it (Sudnow 1978: 9). Because the reach to the chord was never precisely the same each time due to micro-alterations in body position, Sudnow exercised for subtle and precise compensating micro-alterations in hand shape and grip. Bernstein calls this 'manoeuvrability'; similarly, learning craft gestures entails the development of manoeuvrability for various tasks. Bernstein's work dissolves the body-mind dichotomy that has continued to plague discussions of embodied practice, by demonstrating that Merleau-Ponty's 'knowledge in the hands' can be more precisely described as the coordination of body systems, including the nerves and muscles of the fingers, by the brain. It is because movement is constantly corrected that skill can be described as a form of 'attunement' (Ingold 2000a: 353, 2006: 74) or 'continual adjustment' (Mark Taylor, personal communication).

The necessarily temporal dimension of learning to move is best encapsulated by the concept not of kinesis, or of movement *per se*, but of kinaesthesia, the experience of movement (Sheets-Johnstone 2009). The concept of kinaesthesia compels us to consider the experience of makers as they move in the here and now, as well as their experience of years of moving in particular ways. Bernstein defines dexterity (which, he argues, increases with age) as 'an accumulation of life experiences in the field of movements and actions' (Bernstein 1996: 19). Kinaesthesia is mentioned in craft studies as part of an array of other elements involved in reasoning and conscious action (see for example Keller and Keller 1996, Portisch 2010). But the central importance of kinaesthesia to craft work can best be conveyed by *defining* craft work as the experience of coming to move dextrously with tools and materials.

This brings us to the third strand of the braid, what Warnier refers to as 'emotion'. It is through movement as experience that feelings arise, along with values and social meanings. But how exactly does this happen? How are meanings and values generated out of the experience of moving? This is the subject of the next section, in which I examine aspects of craft learning in my glass working apprenticeship with a view to more precisely locating the production of meaning within making.

**Making and Meaning: A Feeling of 'Rightness'**

Figure 11.3 sets out the terms which can be used to analyze making as the exercise of dexterity and kinaesthesia: to document the experience of coming to move dextrously with tools and materials. The diagram, necessarily schematic and two-dimensional, comprises three main elements: experience of tools, materials, artefacts and work steps; the sensory activities of feeling, listening and watching; and the interplay between gestures, tools and materials. In this section I will draw on my glass-working apprenticeship to explain and illustrate the interaction between these elements, which are seamlessly interrelated in practice. I will begin with kinds of experience and sensory activities before moving to the central element of 'gesture–tool–material', in order to show how the performance of gestures with tools and materials not only creates experience and skill in sensory activities, but also generates meaning and value.

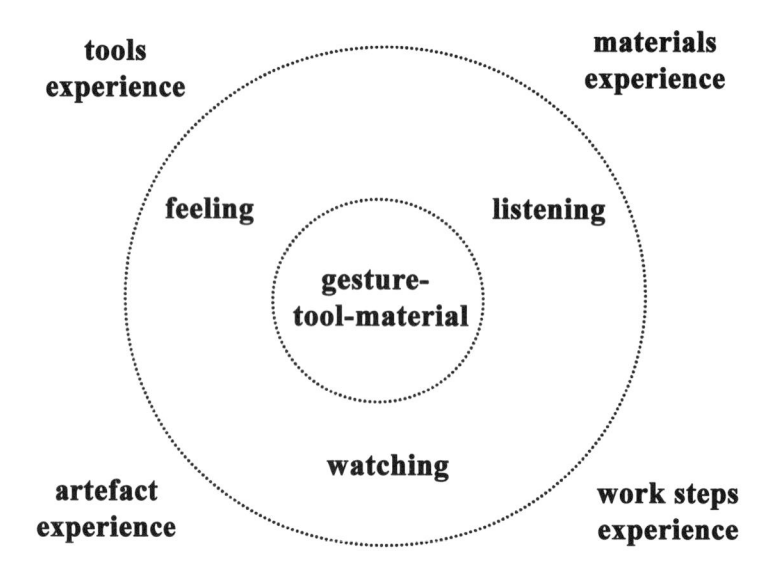

**Figure 11.3** Aspects of the experience of becoming dexterous with tools and materials. Diagram: Frances Liardet, 2009

*Experience*

I refer to 'experience' here to describe a worker's relationship with tools, materials and work steps, as well as the way in which a worker's growing relationship with these things is cumulative, open to revision, and acquired through craft work. This is illustrated by my experience of yellow decorative glass. Core-formed alabastra are decorated by trailing threads of melted coloured glass onto the sides of the vessel and around the edge of the rim (Figure 11.2, top right and bottom left). The decorative glass is softened in the heat and touched to the vessel, which is then rotated so that the glass is drawn onto it just as a thread is wound onto a spool. This is known as 'trailing'.

During my work with Mark Taylor the decorative glass was prepared in two forms: rods, and cones. Rods were pulled quickly out of a large and extremely hot lump of glass, twisted off, and allowed to cool. Cones were formed by allowing the large lump of decorative glass to cool before breaking it into chips which were then attached to a metal rod, softened in the furnace heat, and rolled into a conical shape about the size of a brazil nut. I began my apprenticeship using glass rods prepared by my teacher, but a change in the composition of our yellow glass made it impossible to use rods: the prolonged high temperatures necessary for rod making made the new yellow glass turn pale cream. Because of this we turned to the relatively low-temperature method of preparing cones.

However, for day after day, as Mark Taylor's cones flowed in regular spirals of uniform thickness onto the vessel just as if they were made of toffee, mine lengthened reluctantly only to stiffen into unwieldy ropes, dragging the body glass away from the vessel wall and forcing me to plunge the vessel deep into the furnace, melt off the recalcitrant cone, and start again. What was the problem? My experience of yellow glass up to this point was that it melted quickly. It had seemed to take no more than 20 seconds to soften the rods enough to be wound on to the vessel. Since Mark Taylor had made the rods for me I had not done any preparation and had simply heated the end of the rod and then wound it. But thick squat cones were a different matter. I had been told to heat the cone thoroughly, but in my simple interpretation of 'thoroughly' I had not grasped how long this would actually take, even though I could see Mark Taylor reheating extensively. Until I had performed the gestures myself, dipping the cone in the heat, rolling it on the slab, and repeating this perhaps five or six times, the process would not work properly. The necessary sense of rhythm which informs work and daily life (Lefebvre 2004) had to be acquired kinaesthetically, and it was through this that I increased my experience of decorative glass via work steps, tools, materials and the resulting artefacts.

*Sensory Activities*

Feeling, listening and watching are modes of active engagement with the task of glass working (Figure 11.3). Looking has to be learned: 'skill is required for perception as for speech' (Pye 1978: 116); it is a matter of the 'education of attention' (Gibson 1979: 254) or of 'skilled vision' (Grasseni 2009: 213). This was apparent when preparing the cores of glass vessels. We made cores by applying a mixture of clay and organic matter – chaff, straw or dung – to a metal rod and shaping it into an internal mould for the vessel (Figure 11.2, top left). Applying the core mixture involves many cupping, squeezing, dabbing, stroking, rubbing and rolling gestures, some gauged by eye and others by feel.

While Mark Taylor made the mixture of clay and chaff stick to the metal rod, my attempts resulted in lumps of mixture sliding off the smooth metal of the rod as fast as I plastered them on. A video clip of myself working on the fifth day of my apprenticeship shows me standing at a counter, roughly and rapidly rolling cores across a slab as if I actually wanted the core mixture to slide off the metal rod, which it did with great regularity. The camera angle makes it seem as though I am looking down my nose at the cores, and indeed not once do I stoop to more fully examine my work.

Eventually I began to watch my teacher closely. The gesture for applying the first layer of core mixture to the rod, I discovered, was a gentle squeezing action which worked the mixture *upwards* from the bottom of the rod to form a thin but coherent coating. I had been starting at the *top* of the area to be covered and squeezing the material down to the end of the rod with open-fingered, clutching grabs. I also observed the lightness of touch needed, especially in my teacher's response to loose fragments of mixture. Whereas I, faced with disintegration, would tear the entire layer off and start again, Mark Taylor patiently smoothed the fragment back into place. As I in turn altered my fingerings and grips, I came to understand that I needed to be watchful in every detail. Dexterity with tool and material both produced and entailed skill in watching. Furthermore, these elements augmented my experience of the behaviour of materials. A core mixture which might have been judged unusable proved, with the right handling and skilled attention, to be workable.

*Gesture–Tool–Material*

While Ingold describes the synergy of *practitioner*, tool and material (Ingold 2006: 70), I refer to 'gesture-tool-material' to emphasise movement. In this scheme, the 'practitioner', as craft-working person, can be understood to encompass all the interrelated elements in Figure 11.3.

In order to cover the core with glass to create the walls of the vessel, I was instructed by my teacher to gather glass onto the end of the core – by placing the end of the core in the pot of melted glass and twisting it before taking it out again – and then pull it over the core with the blade of a knife (Figure 11.4, top). My initial pulls with the knife blade were unfamiliar, wildly variable, and done with conscious effort. But with time I acquired the necessary manoeuvrability to do it smoothly. The most important thing about this newly dextrous action, the gesture of pulling, was the almost instantaneous attachment of value to it. The moment that it physically felt 'right', that is to say, comfortable and easy, able to be reliably reproduced without concentration, it also became 'right' as in 'the correct way to cover the core'. A second kind of 'rightness' had therefore emerged: this was an ethical rightness, guiding what I *should* do, which appeared to be contingent on and inseparable from the first, physical, kind of 'right' concerned with *how it felt* to do the work. Dexterity, or a growing capacity for manoeuvrability in a particular gesture, thus produced a physically generated ethical sense of correctness. I refer to this as kinaesthetic rightness.

This was emphasized by the changes which followed as I worked with the glass. Knife work was fast but produced thin patches in the glass. But the 'rightness' I felt when using the knife also encouraged me to minimize this problem. I attributed my thin patches to clumsy knife work and remained fully engaged in refining the necessary gestures, remarking on the ninth day of my apprenticeship that 'I've got used to this knife' (a springy blade designed for cutting grapefruit) and anticipating the conquest of thin patches over the following weeks. I rejoiced in the growing sense of physical and ethical 'rightness' as I practised a gesture which, along with those for the remaining procedures for core-formed vessel making, constituted my entire glass-working experience. However Mark Taylor saw that the behaviour of the glass was becoming an intractable issue. Because he possessed a repertoire of alternative skills which might eliminate the problematic thin patches, he was able to instigate a new core-covering technique using gestures similar to those used for decorating glass: winding the glass for the body onto the core from top to bottom (Figure 11.2, centre top and Figure 11.4, bottom) and then rolling the thick spirals of body glass on a stone block so that they became flattened.

*Movement in Making: An Apprenticeship with Glass and Fire* 213

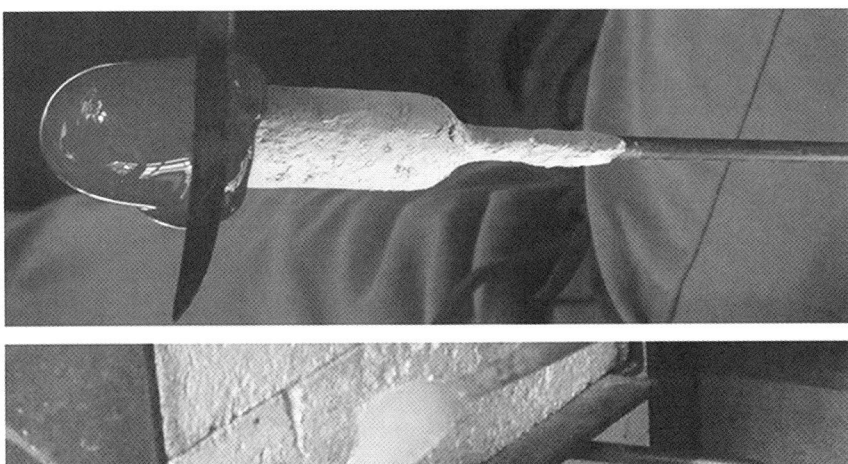

**Figure 11.4  Top: core covering, knife technique. Bottom: core covering, trailing technique. Photos: Frances Liardet, 2008**

This shift in technique negated almost everything I had learned about making core-formed vessel walls. The old knife technique involved taking a core, heating it, and then gathering glass straight onto the base of the core before tugging it up the sides. But the new trailed-glass technique entailed the following operations: taking a long, heavy metal rod, known as an iron, to the furnace; propping the iron in a yoke and trapping the tip in the furnace door to heat it; checking to see whether the tip of the iron had become the desired cherry red (if not, the glass wouldn't stick); heating my core in the furnace; taking the gathering iron in my right hand; propping the metal rod bearing the core in the yoke; opening the furnace door; cooling the gathering iron if the tip had become brighter red or orange; dipping the gathering iron into the pot of melted glass inside the furnace and turning it until an egg-sized blob of glass adhered to the tip; lifting the iron out of the furnace and placing the tip above the core; rotating the core so that the hot glass trailed from the gathering iron onto the core and wound around it; casting off the gather (i.e. pulling the gathering iron away to separate the glass trail from the core); putting the used iron in the bucket; and closing the gathering furnace door. This was even before any rolling and flattening had been done.

Just as kinaesthetic rightness arose from performing the gestures of knife work, so it was involved in reacting to this change in technique. My relationship of apprenticeship with Mark Taylor had been constructed around knife work, and the fact that he had checked my work and adjusted my gestures to an agreed norm had reinforced what I had thought was his approval of the old technique. But when we changed technique I was at a loss. My routine had been destroyed and I was exposed to skills in which my teacher was an expert but of which I had no previous experience. I was challenged by the preparatory steps involved and demoralized by the considerable increase in the time it took to cover the core. I found myself laboriously trailing thick masses of fast-cooling, unworkable glass onto my cores, feeling as stiff and tentative as on my first day of glass working. I eventually learned the new gestures, but continued, when I felt it necessary, to give the glass a helping hand with a knife blade because it felt so right to do it, even though that gesture was now regarded in the workshop as a 'bad habit'.

This transition showed me that the meaning and value that I attached to the knife stemmed from my own experience of making craft gestures, rather than from any collectively-held social norm. For my value judgement went against, and not with, the prevailing social grain – here represented by my teacher's view that the new method was the correct way to cover the core. Craft teachers often have to work hard to eradicate what they view as bad habits in their learners, because to the learners these bad habits can feel so right, however much they conflict with the current collective idea of how tasks should be carried out.

**Growing Makers and Artefacts**

It is suggested above that making, as it has been described here, is a kind of growth. But what does it have in common with 'organic' processes of growing and reproduction? The model provided by the classical Darwinian synthesis implies a quite different notion of making: one where skills and artefacts are replicated in makers and by makers, through a process known as cultural transmission. In biology, however, the idea that the genotype is the sole architect of heritable change in an organism has been challenged by an alternative model which proposes that an organism's development is the result of an array of heritable factors (Oyama et al. 2001, Griffiths and Gray 2001, Jablonka and Lamb 2005) and comes about through the 'reconstruction of a system of resources' (Griffiths and Gray 2001: 196). Along similar lines, the notion that cultural behaviour can best be analyzed in terms of discrete transmissible units is increasingly questioned (Ingold 2000a, Bloch 2005). This questioning moves interpretations of the way in which both making and growing happen, from a focus on replication and transmission, to one which highlights emergence, reconstruction, and relations.

The latter interpretation, to which I also subscribe, informs the scheme of interacting elements I have used to describe making (Figure 11.3). 'Artefact experience' refers to the craft-worker's growing kinaesthetic awareness of the emerging artefact's features. This experience, as noted earlier, is cumulative and open to revision over time. Furthermore, this applies not only to artefacts but also to pictures, designs and other representations of artefacts, whether completed or in the making. For instance, to aid my work on the handles of glass vessels, I placed a photograph of a core-formed alabastron at eye-level when I was seated at the glass working furnace. At first the picture seemed useless: whenever I looked away from it, I could not visualize the handles at all. The alabastron in my mind's eye effectively had no handles. Only when I had become dextrous enough to achieve a semblance of a handle in glass did the handles in the picture begin to appear clearly in my mind's eye. This is what is meant by 'mental imaging' (Keller and Keller 1996) in craft. However the image has no existence independently from the work; instead of generating work, it is *generated by* it. Moreover, because my artefactual experience was kinaesthetic, the relationship between the alabastron we desired to make and the alabastron we were actually making was constantly changing. My teacher and I became aware of a spiral of dexterity involving artefact experience, tool and gesture: as we worked on the necks of the vessels, we came to value a symmetrical and clean cut profile to the neck. This attribution of value made us search for 'better' – that is, shorter and narrower – pincers which we could use to shape the necks more finely. With these new pincers in my hand, I squeezed less hard, held my hand closer to the orange-hot vessel, and brought my eye-line to a more perfectly perpendicular point above the neck, the better to shape it symmetrically. Now I scrutinized my vessel necks, and those of the original vessels I had examined in the British Museum, more minutely. In seeing profiles and tool marks I had not noticed before, I was only now beginning to see the vessels as my teacher Mark Taylor saw them. This kinaesthetically generated increase in skill in looking shows how neither artefacts nor their representations are immutable: their appearance shifts as their viewer's skill develops.

In this context the notions of replication and reproduction, which are often applied to artefacts and to organisms respectively, require critical examination. With regard to glass vessels, extremely similar artefacts, with a high degree of consistency, come about as a result not of identical gestures repeated over and again, as if 'run off' from a template, but of micro-alterations in body position and movement arising from the physical manoeuvrability which is so crucial to skill (Ingold 2000a). In addition, the added dimensions of communality and time make it difficult to talk exclusively in terms of a single, unchanging maker. In studies of ancient technology, it is too often assumed that work processes were undertaken by a single individual (Dobres 2000). Dobres points out that there are no grounds for this assumption: the further one departs from a context-free notion of technology, the easier it is to consider a default position of communality. Abandoning the 'lone worker' paradigm enables students of ancient technology to consider a group of core-formed vessel-makers sharing tools and materials not as an exceptional situation but as entirely unexceptionable. The term 'working group' is proposed here, in preference to 'workshop', because it more closely defines the relationship between maker and artefact (in that a workshop may contain one or more working groups).

The working group would consist of people who are continually gaining experience in sequences of work steps, who have become, or are becoming, dextrous with particular gestures, tools and materials – a process helped by their wider technical and material experience. Working groups are composed of individuals who have become accustomed to each other's proximity, and whose respective gestures, working tempos, and habits are in tune – for example, when it comes to the preferred placement of prepared cones of decorative glass on the edge of the furnace.

Rarely would all members of a working group join it at exactly the same moment. The members of such a group, essentially and not exceptionally, possess varying levels of skill. The most basic driver of turnover is death – the departure of the old, experienced and highly dextrous. Newcomers would therefore be brought into the group to form their skills in the context of its collective values. A working group, therefore, is a changing entity with multiple interrelated constituents, undergoing continual renewal. It is constituted by a 'field of relations' (Ingold 2000a: 353) between people, materials, tools and fire, out of which artefacts emerge.

**Conclusion**

Although analysis of legitimate peripheral participation illuminates the sociality of learning, a more fine-grained approach is necessary to discuss skilled practices of making. As I have shown, there are difficulties with the concepts of bodily intentionality and associated assumptions regarding the relationship of explicit and implicit teaching and learning. However, analysis of dexterity and kinaesthesia, with reference to glass working, allows making to be reframed as the experience of coming to move dextrously with tools and materials. The process begins with moving – in this case, with grasping a tool and wielding it in relation to materials. The interplay between gesture, tool and material generates dexterity as well as the feeling of 'rightness' which gives rise to craft values. Makers and their artefacts are mutually creative: the relations between them enable both to grow, or to develop. A maker is not, therefore, a clearly-bounded single person, or even one bounded set of identically-skilled people. Rather, processes of making emerge through a multiplicity of interacting elements. The process described here entailed the accretion of experience with materials, tools, work steps and artefacts, skilled watching, listening and feeling, and dextrous movement. This process produces meanings and values, is physically and ethically transformative, and is thoroughly social.

**Acknowledgements**

I wish to thank Mark Taylor and David Hill for their expertise, patience and support during the Core-Forming Project. I am indebted to Professor Ian Freestone for his insights into ancient glass and his supervisory contribution to my PhD thesis.

# References

Bernstein, N.A. 1967. *The Coordination and Regulation of Movements*. New York: Pergamon.

Bernstein, N.A. 1996 [1950]. *On Dexterity and Its Development*. Mahwah, NJ: Lawrence Erlbaum.

Bimson, M. and A.E. Werner 1969. Two problems in ancient glass: opacifiers and Egyptian core material, in *Annales du 4e Congrès de l'Association Internationale pour l'Histoire du Verre* 4. Liège: Centre de publications de l'A.I.H.V, 262–6.

Bloch, H. 2005. *Cultural Transmission*. Oxford: Berg.

Bourdieu, P. 1977. *Outline of a Theory of Practice*. Cambridge: Cambridge University Press.

Bourdieu, P. 1984. *Distinctions. A Social Critique of the Judgment of Taste*. Harvard: Harvard University Press.

Bourdieu, P. 1988. Program for a sociology of sport. *Sociology of Sport Journal*, 5(2), 153–61.

Bourdieu, P. 1990. *The Logic of Practice*. Cambridge: Polity.

Bourdieu, P. 2000. *Pascalian Meditations*. Stanford, CA: Stanford University Press.

Brenière, Y. and B. Bril 1988. Pourquoi les enfants marchent en tombant alors que les adultes tombent en marchant? *C. R. Académie des Sciences Paris*, 307, 617–622.

Bril, B. and R. Gouasdoué 2009. Du mouvement sans sens ou du sens sans mouvement: rôle des finalités et des contextes dans l'étude de comportements moteurs. *Intellectica*, 51(1), 273–293.

Carman, T. 1999. The body in Husserl and Merleau-Ponty, *Philosophical Topics*, 27(2), 205–26.

Dakers, J. (ed.) 2006. *Defining Technological Literacy*. New York: Palgrave MacMillan.

Dobres, M.A. 2000. *Technology and Social Agency*. Oxford: Blackwell.

Foster, R. 2005. Pierre Bourdieu's critique of scholarly reason. *Philosophy and Social Criticism*, 31(1), 88–107.

Gibson, J.J. 1979. *The Ecological Approach to Visual Perception*. London: Houghton Mifflin.

Grasseni, C. (ed.) 2009. *Skilled Visions: Between Apprenticeship and Standards*. New York and Oxford: Berghahn.

Grasseni, C. 2009. Good looking: learning to be a cattle breeder, in *Skilled Visions: Between Apprenticeship and Standards,* edited by C. Grasseni. New York and Oxford: Berghahn, 47–66.

Graves-Brown, P. (ed.) 2000. *Matter, Materiality and Modern Culture*. London: Routledge.

Griffiths, P.E. and R.D. Gray 2001. Darwinism and developmental systems, in *Cycles of Contingency: Developmental Systems and Evolution*, by S. Oyama, P.E. Griffiths, and R.D. Gray. Cambridge, MA: MIT Press, 195–218.

Grose, D.F. 1989. *Early Ancient Glass. The Toledo Museum of Art*. New York: Hudson Hills Press.

Harden, D.B. 1981. *Catalogue of Greek and Roman Glass in the British Museum. Volume 1*. London: British Museum Press.

Harris, M. (ed.) 2007. *Ways of Knowing*. New York and Oxford: Berghahn Books.

Ingold, T. 2000a. *The Perception of the Environment. Essays on Livelihood, Dwelling and Skill*. London: Routledge.

Ingold, T. 2000b. Making culture and weaving the world, in *Matter, Materiality and Modern Culture*, edited by P. Graves-Brown. London: Routledge, 55–69.

Ingold, T. 2001. From the transmission of representations to the education of attention, in *The Debated Mind: Evolutionary Psychology versus Ethnography*, edited by H. Whitehouse. Oxford: Berg, 113–53.

Ingold, T. 2006. Walking the plank, in *Defining Technological Literacy*, edited by J. Dakers. New York: Palgrave MacMillan, 65–80.

Jablonka, E. and M. Lamb 2005. *Evolution in Four Dimensions*. Cambridge, MA.: MIT Press.

Keller, J.D. and C.M. Keller 1996. *Cognition and Tool Use: The Blacksmith at Work*. Cambridge: Cambridge University Press.

Lave, J. and E. Wenger 1991. *Situated Learning. Legitimate Peripheral Participation*. Cambridge: University of Cambridge Press.

Lefebvre, H. 2004. *Rhythmanalysis. Space, Time and Everyday Life*. New York and London: Continuum.

Liardet, F. 2009. Learning by hand: artefact consistency and craft tradition, in *Annales du 17e Congrès de l'Association Internationale pour l'Histoire du Verre*. Antwerp: Aspéditions, 184–88.

Makovicky, N. 2010. 'Something to talk about': notation and knowledge-making among Central Slovak lace-makers. *Journal of the Royal Anthropological Institute*, S80–S99.

Marchand, T.H.J. 2010. Making knowledge: explorations of the indissoluble relation between minds, bodies, and environment. *Journal of the Royal Anthropological Institute*, S1–S21.

Mauss, M. 1979. *Sociology and Psychology*. London: Routledge and Kegan Paul.

Merleau-Ponty, M. 1962. *Phenomenology of Perception*. London: Routledge and Kegan Paul.

Newell, K.M. 1986. Constraints on the development of coordination, in *Motor skills acquisition*, edited by M.G. Wade and H.T.A. Withing. Dortrech: Martinus Nijhoff, 341–60.

Noble, G. and M. Watkins 2003. So, how did Bourdieu learn to play tennis? Habitus, consciousness and habituation. *Cultural Studies*, 17(3–4), 520–38.

O'Connor, E. 2007. Embodied knowledge in glassblowing: the experience of meaning and the struggle towards proficiency. *Sociological Review*, 55(s1), 126–41.

Oyama, S., P.E. Griffiths and R.D. Gray 2001. Introduction: what is developmental systems theory?, in *Cycles of Contingency: Developmental Systems and Evolution*,

edited by S. Oyama, P.E. Griffiths and R.D. Gray. Cambridge, MA: MIT Press, 1–11.
Oyama, S., P.E. Griffiths and R.D. Gray (eds) 2001. *Cycles of Contingency: Developmental Systems and Evolution.* Cambridge, MA: MIT Press.
Parlebas, P. 1999. *Jeux, sports et sociétés. Lexique de praxéologie motrice.* Paris: INSEP.
Portisch, A.O. 2010. The craft of skilful learning: Kazakh women's everyday craft practices in western Mongolia. *Journal of the Royal Anthropological Institute*, S62–S79.
Pye, D. 1978. *The Nature and Art of Design.* London: Barrie and Jenkins.
Sheets-Johnstone, M. 2009. *The Corporeal Turn.* Exeter: Imprint Academic.
Sudnow, D. 1978. *Ways of the Hand: The Organisation of Improvised Conduct.* London: Routledge and Kegan Paul.
Wacquant, L. 2004. *Body and Soul: Notebooks of an Apprentice Boxer.* Oxford: Oxford University Press.
Wade, M.G. and H.T.A. Withing (eds) 1986. *Motor Skills Acquisition.* Dortrech: Martinus Nijhoff.
Warnier, J.-P. 2001. A praxeological approach to subjectivation in a material world. *Journal of Material Culture*, 6(1), 5–24.

# Chapter 12

# Growing Granite: The Recombinant Geologies of Sludge

David A. Paton and Caitlin DeSilvey

This slow flowage makes one conscious of the turbidity of thinking. Slump, debris slides, avalanches all take place within the cracking limits of the brain. The entire body is pulled into the cerebral sediment, where particles and fragments make themselves known as solid consciousness. (Smithson 1968: 100)

## Following the Sludge

*There's a granite slab ready on the saw bed, everything is set, all the measurements are punched in, the slab has been codified. I press the button. The diamond-tipped saw blade kicks in, and I pull the lever for the water to flow. Up to speed, 1450 rpm ... auto – and off it goes, toing and froing, down through the slab, 4 mm at a time. As the blade cuts down through the granite, water flows continuously as a lubricant over all surfaces. Water spins off the blade and runs down over the granite slab and the saw bed. The water, in motion, has tiny particles of granite suspended within it. The saw cuts multiply the slab's surface area, and all the cast off micro-blocks of granite drift outwards, seeking new connections. As the momentum of the particle-infused fluid slows in contact with the concrete floor, on its transit from the building, the particles bind and a residue of sludge begins to build up. If the floor has not been washed down with the hose after a day of sawing, sludge forms in layers ranging from pale grey to cream, slate grey to brown, a temporary sedimentary accumulation, a palimpsest of granite idiosyncrasies that is then peeled back as the jet of water makes contact. The sludge has thixotropic properties – the substance cracks under sudden foot pressure, resisting the moment of refluidity until it gives in and is swept away in the watery flow.*

This chapter examines the processes of material growth and transformation implicated in the working of stone. We begin in motion, with the movement of a saw through stone, and the movement of water over both. The chapter works through one of the authors' – David's – lived experience as a sculptor, sawman, mason and researcher at Trenoweth dimension granite quarry, near Penryn, Cornwall. Through extracts based on David's fieldnotes from 2010–11 (shown throughout in italics) we follow the flow of material through the quarry's spatial and temporal contexts, with a particular focus on how sludge's movement weaves together embodied geographical knowledge and durational geological processes. Sludge – minute particles of ancient mineral cast off as watery waste – allows us to explore a world-in-formation, to 'follow the multiple trails of growth and transformation' that converge in this material narrative (Ingold 2007: 9).

*The flow of silty water emerges from the back of the little saw shed, and encounters a sprawling buddleia, a tree whose dusty branches drop their leaves into the water course, setting up mini dams. This buddleia is destined for the chop. Just past the buddleia, the little saw outflow joins the sludge stream from the big saw (£50,000 well spent, as Tim the quarry owner would say), and the two water courses merge before plunging down a foliated rock face. Over a murky waterfall, the sludge stream negotiates and overflows a series of corroded steel drums before its course disappears underground and re-emerges in a small delta-like accumulation. The watery transit continues down the inside edge of the quarry-face access road, passing by half-submerged and tired old forklifts and pallets, wild plant growth and the unseen machinations of insect and mammal activity, navigating all manner of rusty quarrying artefacts and cast-offs.* (Figure 12.1)

**Figure 12.1** *'The sludge stream negotiates and overflows a series of corroded steel drums …'* **Photo: David A. Paton**

Granite sludge concentrates in the quarry at different densities and at different locations. Sometimes the water to granite ratio is heavily in favour of the water, and the substance moves quickly; at other nodes, concentrations of sludge build up over decades. The sludge is at once sad and epic: it is the residual trace of the industrialized dismantling of the granite batholith, the by-product of the transformation of granite from matter to functional material. Tim Edensor, in his investigation of the processual activity of building stone, comments on the presumed durability of stone as 'matter emblematic of obduracy, with a hardness, weightiness and apparent immutability epitomized by the phrases "hard as rock" [and] "stony-faced"' (Edensor 2011: 40). He goes on, however, to point out that 'unpredictable processes of change' mean that the rate of decay and relative stability is always variable: 'Its destiny depends upon the changing and particular agencies of particular contexts' (ibid.). Sludge is the product of an accelerated degradation of the granite, where the rock is shunted from its geological slumber into the life cycles of quarrymen and machines. The process of erosion by water and abrasion, which usually occurs over extended time-scales, is mechanized and intensified in order to meet the demands of the local building trade.

> *As the flow slows and levels out at the bottom of the quarry, it filters off through rocky embankments into the quarry's water sump* [or drainage reservoir] *where, at the far end, a sludge beach has formed, and milky murky waters form littoral-like markings on its shoreline. There is a small pump house hidden in the undergrowth, and blue plastic pipes carry water up from the sump pond back to the top of the quarry, to the saws, for another go around. Half submerged in the middle of the sump are granite boulders, their peaks bleached white with dried out sludge – resembling Anish Kapoor's early stone and pigment sculptures with their brave simplicity. The water in the pool is partly sieved of its granite particles by the vegetation that it passes through, but on the other side near the gathering piles of granite off-cuts I can still see the trace of suspended granite. Time is the collector here, and the sump pond is definitely not clear water. It might be that some particles have been in transit for at least a decade, and some for 100 years or more, in other motions around the shifting spatial context of the quarry.* (Figure 12.2)

The making of a granite headstone or an ashlar block is not a linear performance; it branches and twists, takes odd paths and loops back on itself. By analyzing the animated life of sludge (in which the production of the desired, discrete granite object is a significant interval), we highlight how specific materials function as components within much larger growing entities. Sludge is more than waste; it is a thing in the making, and the study of it reveals how human making intersects with geophysical making (and growing) in unpredictable ways. While human making effects change through manipulation and applied labour, geophysical making works through accretion, erosion, pressure and time. By giving attention and value to the movement of sludge we are able to track how granite – a material archetype of stony durability – circulates as a dispersed, expansive element within complex lifeworlds. Trenoweth Quarry emerges as a mobile and mutable environment, where the restless process of landscape comes into sharp focus, and where 'even the most inert objects are [revealed to be] made up of the spin of microscopic particles that will eventually split, decay and transform' (Yusoff and Gabrys 2006: 447). Trenoweth's granite – its processing and by-products, and the lives that are woven through it – asserts a persistently transient agency not independently attributable to either material or persons in isolation. Rather, granite becomes a kind of cosmological drifter, generating creative and emotive convergences between persons and matter.

In the rest of this chapter we experiment with the idea that sludge has the potential to form a recombinant geology out of layers sedimented in the sump pond at the bottom of the quarry pit – a geology collaboratively emplaced by people and machines. The concept of recombinant geology extends from work in ecology that has focused on the emergence of novel plant and animal populations in sites with a legacy of intensive human use, where ecological processes absorb the chemical and mineral residues of the industrial past with often unpredictable results (Barker 2000). Others have extended the concept of recombinant ecology to describe 'ecological cofabrications', in which a unique 'politics of conviviality' accommodates both human and non-human agency (Hinchliffe et al. 2005). A recombinant geology, as we imagine it, works a parallel cofabrication with primarily mineral and geological substance.

In the quarry sump pond, deltas and beaches of sludge gather up and make visible the convergence of cultural process and synthetic geomorphology; they are an emergent landscape feature formed out of the workings of mechanical abrasion, fluid dynamics, gravity and granular deposition. Granite becomes enrolled in a socio-economic process (driven by the demand for durable material) that then allows the residue of production to reconnect with geological timescales. The sludge slips between natural and cultural registers, in its transit and eventual (but temporary) settlement. Other such landscapes where recombinant geologies are evident include beaches 'nourished' with stone-processing waste products, such as the 'marble beaches' of Tuscany (Nordstrom et al. 2008) or the beaches at Carlyon Bay, Cornwall, enhanced with 'stent' waste rock from the nearby china clay industry. The recombinant geology that we explore in the rest of this chapter takes its inspiration from a preserved footprint pressed into the coastal mud of the Irish Sea around 4,000 years ago. By placing our own footprint in the Trenoweth sludge, we imagine some of the tactilities and properties of granite sludge that might resonate 4,000 years into the future of the emplaced sediments. This exploration of granite's evolution unfolds through an experimental narrative that uses the granite's past to try to understand its potential future, working through a research method that understands *story* as an active tool for analysis and understanding (Price 2010). The anticipatory history (DeSilvey, Naylor and Sackett 2011) that emerges folds the future of an emergent landscape feature into the past and present co-productions of Trenoweth Quarry.

## In the Quarry

*As my relationship with the quarry deepens it becomes apparent how materials can act as conduits and conductors for the messiness of lived experience. Sludge is a specific kind of matter, a waste; it is an altered form of granite, expressive and mobile. Granite does other things too. My identity is partly produced through my encounters with the granite, and I in turn produce the granite as a knowable and workable substance. Tim, Ernie and Peter, and the other workers at the quarry, also have formative, reciprocal relationships with the granite. Apart from Tim, who owns the quarry, Ernie is the longest-standing worker at Trenoweth. Ernie is 63 years old and has worked granite for most of his adult life. He is able to mason the hardest of granites with a precision and speed unrivalled in the quarry. He lives in Bodmin and commutes most days, proud of the speeds he can get out of his old Volkswagen van. Ethnographic practice positions the researcher in a blurred region, a self-imposed other-life, which runs alongside everyday life but has its own specific agendas to feed. It can be awkward, overbearing. Life necessities drive the research; while research (and the decision to study for a PhD) drives the necessities of life. My job as a sawman and mason helps to pay my mortgage and is also fundamental to my research. The sharp realities of life become entwined with the granite, too; they too flow with the sludge, down through the quarry, round and round, becoming silted up in the delta and settled out in the sump pond.*

**Figure 12.2** *'Near the gathering piles of off-cuts ... I can still see the trace of suspended granite ... '* **Photo: David A. Paton**

Granite is valued as a building stone for its properties of hardness, durability and flexural strength, and for its relatively uniform structure (Hunt 2005), but the character and composition of granite can vary widely. Trenoweth Quarry processes several different types of granite, and the masons often re-work salvaged stone to serve new functions. The local granite, the granite that forms the sheer walls rising from the base of the quarry at the sump pit, is 'Buckle and Twist'. It is a bluey-grey, very hard, fine-grained stone, and, as the name suggests, it can be a bit tricky to work. Local masons gave the stone this name because the grain flow frequently shifts direction, much like a contorting grain in a piece of oak. To work the stone cleanly a sinuous path has to be followed through the material, navigating the history of its formation and deformation in the Cornubian batholith 300 million years ago. Trenoweth's Buckle and Twist lies within the Carnmenellis 'boss', a sub-section of the batholith that has provided building stone for structures such as Waterloo Bridge and the Eddystone Lighthouse (Stanier 1999).

People employed at Trenoweth Quarry have their own vernacular lexicon that situates the personality of each type of granite within a hierarchy according to its salient properties and its relative ease of working. Buckle and Twist, for example, may not necessarily cleave well all the way across a plain on 'grain way'; it may lean into 'tough way', making it necessary for a bit more force to be delivered to the pitch tool, the heavy duty chisel used in the initial rough shaping of a block of granite. The language of granite working (as with the language that attends other stone trades) is derived from generations of familiarity, as well as frustration, with the material properties of the stone (Leitch 2007). The first granite workings in the region were concentrated around the surface stones, often called 'moorstones'. Boulders and granite outcrops of the exposed uplands were transformed into an impressive array of functional objects – tin moulds, cheese and cider presses, millstones, troughs, gateposts (Stanier 2000). Many of these objects were crafted in situ. As the industry advanced, masons developed tools to cut pits or grooves into the surface of the rock; they would then drive metal wedges in to split the material along the desired plane.

An applied, idiosyncratic language emerged from the flesh-metal-stone nexus; this language carries through into the current era of automation and diamond-tipped saws. The name Buckle and Twist still speaks deeply of the relationship between bodies and materials, and signals an ongoing process of growing through a condensed history of human-matter making – growing knowledge, growing relations and growing material potentialities. The name speaks of the density of a relationship between human, place and material over time; it speaks of *process*. Unlike the word 'stone', which fixes a generic identity on the material, and is useful primarily as a crude shortcut for ease of communication, a name like Buckle and Twist implies a lived material knowledge. The name suggests that a richer and more dynamic set of relations are at play here, which redirects 'our attention from the materiality of objects to the properties of materials' (Ingold 2007: 12). This is granite not as inert substance but as worked matter, generated through recurring encounters between person and stone.

A similar expression of relational geology was outlined by Ithell Colquhoun in her book *The Living Stones*:

> The life of a region depends ultimately on its geological substratum, for this sets up a chain-reaction which passes, determining their character, in turn through its streams and wells, its vegetation and the animal-life that feeds on this and finally through the type of human being attracted to live there. (Colquoun 1957: 46)

Shades of environmental determinism notwithstanding, Colquhoun's writing develops a rich evocation of a person who dwells intensely with a physical landscape. Her use of the phrase 'attracted to live there' suggests a mutual space for intersubjective relations to develop, that is, if one is willing to grant sentience to the landscape itself. The personal and the geological are intertwined and active across time.

Several hundred miles from the quarry in Cornwall, on the Sefton coast north of Liverpool, there is evidence of another entangling of the human, the geological and, indeed, the non-human animal. Over the past few decades, accelerated erosion on the exposed coastline near Formby has peeled away layers of marine sediments to expose traces of lives lived on the muddy foreshore close to 4,000 years ago. As the waves scour through successive layers of laminated strata, footprints appear: human footprints, but also the prints of red and roe deer, auroch and crane. Research carried out on the Formby formations indicates a wide range of activity occurring on the Holocene mud flats – women collecting shellfish, men tracking deer and wild cattle, and many children, collecting but also mudlarking, dancing about for the joy of feeling mud between their toes (Huddart et al. 1999, Roberts et al. 1996). Imaginative reconstructions are given sustenance when such human-matter relations are laid bare and when the enfolding of lives into the processes of matter formation becomes visible. If we can allow the accustomed boundary between 'then' and 'now' to waver, we become witnesses to geological time shimmering on the upturned hand of a woman picking razor shells from the mud, her footprints pooling with silty water behind her.

What might this seemingly distant and unrelated story tell us about the granite sludge at Trenoweth Quarry? At the edge of the quarry sump pond sludge is being 'grown', layer by layer, as the muddy sediments grew at Formby – though at Trenoweth the growing is a by-product of the process of sawing up granite for memorials and new buildings. The sludge is also growing in terms of the relations that it attracts. There is the granite, sat in its 'bed'. There are humans extracting it and processing it, shaping it into parts of buildings and sculptures, headstones and hearths. Around this process there are people talking, and weaving their worlds together. One of many products of these doings – sludge – is a new deposit of sediment in formation, a future landscape under construction. We offer a speculative story to help the reader imagine how this future might unfold.

Through the passage of geological time, the sludge deposit at the bottom of the quarry could solidify into a coarse sediment, with rough grains of quartz held in a matrix of finer decaying mica and plagioclase feldspar. Assuming this relic of the landscape's industrial past doesn't get washed out to sea, it will gradually get buried under other layers of material, and with steadily increasing pressure it may re-crystallize into a more durable sandstone, laced with traces of steel and iron from the quarry's abandoned infrastructure as the 'tools of technology became a part of the Earth's geology' (Smithson 1968: 104). If this sandstone formation happens to get caught up in a major (if extremely slow motion) collision – the subduction of the North Atlantic seabed under the North American continent, for example – the long-buried sludge would be subjected to intense pressure and heat. These forces would realign platy minerals in the sandstone to give it a cleavage, and cause the sedimentary beds to fold and buckle, eventually forming gneiss, on their way to becoming granite again. It is more likely, however, that the sludge will adopt clay-like properties in its afterlife, and 'some clays, if kept at a constant moisture content, regain a portion of their original strength after remoulding, with time' (Skempton and Northey 1952). A comparable recuperation of 'original strength' would be more complicated for our granite sludge, implausible but not impossible.

What if we were to attempt to leave a footprint in the sludge, an intervention available for some future uncovering? A Trenoweth footprint might form part of a new bio-geological feature that, like the Formby footprints, expresses the interface of human action with the properties of matter. Artist Rona Lee, in manipulating a block of clay, notes how 'the visible traces of my handprints upon these lumps of clay conjure an infantile desire to know the world by sensation rather than observation' (2010: 217). These moments reveal our emplacement in a material stream, seeking some form of geological conversation that suggests we are engaged with matter on a sensual level, without the hierarchical constraint implied by subject-object distinctions. This might lead us towards an understanding of matter based on mutual relation and relevance. Matter, as emotive as the weather (Ingold 2011), as mundane as house dust, as bright as a thought, stimulates a person's senses, prompting that person in the world into a more fluid and openly responsive mode. Who is to say that as the Neolithic people crossed the mudflats they were not relishing the sensation of soft, cool sludge between their toes?

**Footprint**

*I arrive at the quarry around 1.30 p.m., having just come from Trewidden Garden near Penzance, where I was completing the finishing touches on a granite and bronze sculpture commission for the Bolitho family. It had taken four years to complete. The granite section of the sculpture was roughed out at Trenoweth, and it was after working on the sculpture at the quarry for three months that I embarked on the research project. Now, I walk into the 'crib hut' to have a cup of tea and a chat before heading down to the sludge beach to dip my toes in, and take some photos.*

*The conversation moves to Tim's schedule and to the fact that he's running out of time to get some granite sawn for Ernie the mason to work on at home. The pieces that have already been sawn have so many cracks they are not worth using. I sense I could be useful this afternoon, and I offer to work on the saws –*

*possibly compromising the clarity with which I am able to consider the issue of growing and recombinant geologies. Tim says how grateful he would be if I could just clear the saw of the faulty slab, and run off a few post supports. He asks if it'll be okay to do this for him, as he knows I am there to take photographs; 'I'll sort you out', he says, meaning he'll pay me for the extra work, but I am not bothered, he does enough favours for me. So I get to work on clearing the saw bed and loading on the new slab for the post supports. Half an hour later I am done, the saw is doing its thing, and I go down to the bottom of the quarry to search around for a route to the beach. This is not going to be easy.*

*While I am scrambling around, doubts emerge about whether I put in the right measurements on the saw. I go back up to the top of the quarry to the saw shed, and check that all is well. All is well. Back down the quarry and more rummaging through dense bramble and buddleia cover. I am coming to the conclusion that I may need a dinghy to get to the beach. I ponder my dual roles at the quarry as sawman and researcher, where a reciprocating sensuality generates deeper knowledge. Working through the two merged roles, trying to work out how best to think and write the sludge. I know I have to go back up and turn the saw table round 90° to finish the blocks off, so I can't really get too involved in finding a route and following it through. I have almost given up anyway.*

*At the top of the quarry again, I set the saw going on its final run and then go back down, rather despondently. Then I spot a gap in the buddleia, where a short climb over piled up boulders seems to provide access. Other routes are too risky, presenting the threat of rock slides. My chosen route still has the potential for a calamity, but to a lesser degree. Camera in bag, I descend, over mossy rocks and under tree branches, towards the water's edge. Moving over the partly submerged rocks I begin to think about those people ranging across these mud flats 4,000 years ago. In what sense is my activity related to theirs?*

*Focus. Don't fall in. Don't dislodge a big rock. Get to the destination, do your thing and get out of there. Well, there might be similarities. But really I am aiming to make a footprint, that is my goal. They were most probably not aiming to make footprints, not thinking about how geological processes might bring it about that the marks in the mud would still be around in several thousand years. I consider the physical action of pressing my foot into soft matter – whatever my motivation, a mark is made, and it will have a life of its own. Anyway, the beach. I get there.*

*I stand on the beach in my steel-toe-capped boots.*

*There is a thin layer of leaves on the surface of the skirt of sludge that fans out into the sump pond. I move my boot up and down and the sludge ripples; it is fluid. I press down harder and it is resilient, resistant. It seems to have strange quicksand-like properties. My boot is quickly submerged and I know my time on this embankment will be necessarily short. I take off my boot and sock, press my bare foot into the sludge with its leaf and moss covering, and try to make my mark. There, a clear footprint.*

*I take the photos ...* (Figures 12.3, 12.4)

**Figure 12.3** '*I … press my bare foot into the sludge … and try to make my mark…*' **Photo: David A. Paton**

**Figure 12.4** '*The edges of the print gradually close in, erasing the surface trace …*' **Photo: David A. Paton**

*The edges of the print gradually close in, erasing the surface trace. I look around. I am very nearly at the bottom of the quarry and it seems different from here. I see how the rock face is arranged in layers. Then there are the recent deposits of granite infill dumped into the sump and levelled off, forming a new storage yard for high quality rough block. This infill is taking up some of Tim's sump capacity that is pumped up and used to lubricate the saws; if too much sludge continues to settle in the sump then eventually there will be no room for the water. This has resulted in the need for sludge 'settling tanks' to be built further up the line, to stop the sludge from finding its way down to the bottom of the quarry.*

*Then there are the benches of Buckle and Twist waiting to be blasted.*

*The 7,000 tonnes.*

*The sheered faces where granite has been and gone, and the corvids move through stolen space.*

*Up to the raggedy gorse outline that meets the jet stream-ing in from Culdrose.*

*Maybe the Formby gatherers didn't concern themselves with the sensuality of the mud; maybe they just had to get the job done.*

*I retrace my route back over the boulders, and pull myself up through the branches and back up onto the road. Chuffed, I am. Task complete. Back in one piece with camera un-dunked. At first I thought of all the plants growing up and between the rocks as obstructions, but I now think they stabilize the slopes and make it safer. No one spotted me with a bare foot submerged in the sludge either, as I would likely fall prey to some of Ernie's notable ability to ridicule.*

*I go back up to sort out the saw.*

*I put the sawn blocks on a pallet ready to be loaded into Ernie's van, wash the saw and put the waste in the bin that goes to fill more of the sump. I see Ernie. He's not feeling great and so we walk back to the crib hut and he has a cup of tea and a few pain killers; he'll carry on working nonetheless. I load the blocks into Ernie's van by hand, and head home.*

**Growing Pains**

The simple act of pressing a bare foot into sludge helps us understand the relational properties of matter. Just as Bender, Hamilton and Tilley (2007) used archaeo-sculptural practices to explore the Neolithic site at Leskernick, seeking to rematerialize past sensualities within a lived present, David's footprint articulates a desire to enter into a conversation with the decades of material manipulation that have taken place at Trenoweth. He sought to react with sensual porosity to the shifting modalities of granite, and to see the quarry in a different light. Although separated by millennia and intention, both David's footprints and the Formby footprints highlight the reciprocity and receptivity of human relations with matter. Physical and emotional immersion in place opens up the possibility of a universal, shared sentience. From this unifying position, new knowledge is grown (not merely established) about the evolution of human-material relations. The Formby footprints appear to us as the outcome of a series of geophysical processes, and are relevant here because they indicate how traces of physical human presence have led to a greater understanding of the cyclic accretion and erosion of that stretch of land over the past several millennia (Knight 2005). Through the optic of Formby we can understand the Trenoweth sludge in a more expansive and fundamental way; engaging with a geological dimension, the sludge is no longer merely a human product. The footprints indicate an entangling of geophysical process with human biographies, a potent recombinant geology.

There are other parallels between the Formby footprints and the Trenoweth footprints. The same life necessities persist across millennia: David as a sculptor and researcher provides sustenance for his family, as did the beach hunters' shellfish gathering at Formby. Granted, David's footprint in the sludge at Trenoweth was an intentional outcome – he aimed, and nearly failed, to reach the beach and submerge his foot. But this action produced a deeper understanding of the properties of sludge, of what happens to granite in certain conditions, and what it feels like to inhabit this part of the quarry.

Engagement with matter carries with it life threatening dangers – at Trenoweth, the potential to be sucked down in quicksand or crushed by falling rock. Yet humans have always risked their lives during endeavours to improve livelihoods. The Formby footprints demonstrate a set of material relations that played out in a potentially dangerous environment, driven by the day-to-day requirements of sustenance. The mud absorbs a human life in action, drawing us into the pragmatics of existence, across time. The process of learning to navigate the physical world may involve pain, healing, and regeneration. The title of this section, 'growing pains', refers to the slow, sometimes awkward and strained gathering of material knowledge. Materials, while hard and resistant on first encounter, become familiar and develop richly embedded relations over time. For example, for the novice, using a hammer and chisel to work a stone surface can be a painful and frustrating experience; yet gradually, the ease with which actions are performed increases and the degree of fatigue and injury lessens with the increasing skill generated through practice. With growing familiarity matter takes on sentient properties, which are filtered through a perception of reciprocal knowing – both knowing the stone and the stone's seeming to know its worker in return (Paton, 2013). Sustained engagements with a material prompt new understandings.

To make a footprint in the sludge at the bottom of a quarry is to reach out multi-dimensionally and materially across millennia, to speak to the bodies and machines that ground away the great Cornubian batholith. The footprints at Formby and David's footprint at Trenoweth Quarry are not isolated events; they both bring into focus the movement of emotive bodies trying to understand their role in the world. David's attempt to place a foot in the sludge led to new knowledge of the quarry, and allowed the material to instigate sensualized perceptions of place (Ingold 2011). As Lee (2010) asserts in her discussion of how her multidisciplinary arts practice engaged with deep sea geo-scientific mapping, we attain new relationships with the unfamiliar by entering into sometimes uncomfortable mutual exchanges. Referring to Bennett's (2010) notion of vibrant matter, Tolia-Kelly articulates the monadic material cosmology made up of 'vital materialisms' in which humans and non-humans are 'not dividable, separate or separable, but integrated, co-constituted, co-dependent' (Tolia-Kelly 2013: 154). Material relationships need time to develop, in a reciprocating sensual exchange of properties that feed and influence each other.

Trenoweth's waste material, sludge, offers insights into granite's other passages through time and space. With our exploration of sludge's journey, we witness how a fuller understanding of the myriad objects that move through our lives must include an appreciation of the residual matter produced through their making. The processing of any material usually produces some form of waste, a point that has preoccupied sculptors as varied as Constantin Brancusi, Phyllida Barlow, Robert Smithson, Rachel Whiteread, and Eduardo Chilida. Yet waste can communicate significant aspects of the creative process and disclose essential information about a material's properties. Most made things produce a shadow product, the overlooked other to the finished product. Both of these products have a life journey of equal significance, an awareness that challenges the negative connotations of the term 'waste'. A visit to a sculptor's studio or workshop offers a glimpse of the generative-destructive process often hidden in the finished product: examining discarded matter can reveal how material allows itself to be moulded and manipulated. The same holds true for the product that is sludge at the bottom of the quarry, even though the sculptor is the sawman and the artwork is often as simple as a granite sill or post.

Smithson's *Asphalt Rundown, Rome* (1969) – in which a sheet of asphalt cascades down an exposed earthen bank – expresses some of the poetic dialectic between humans and their waste production, as a material associated with industrial road-building performs a collaborative event with a scarred geological feature. In their discussion of Smithson's work, Yusoff and Gabrys describe 'how mind and matter map back onto one another, always transforming and working upon each other – chart[ing] an active relation with landscape' (2006: 448). Waste, as Smithson so eloquently articulates in his work (as quoted at the start of this chapter), has a distinctly anthropomorphic disposition – oozing, flowing, bulging, rotting, being subsumed. We thus come to understand a 'made' thing as emerging from a diverse substrate of materials and potentials. Smithson understood that the world of matter-in-process seeks out (but never secures) equilibrium, and that from degradation and wasting other forms always materialize. In his 'pulverisations' he mimicked processes of rock and mineral disintegration – oxidation, hydration, carbonization and solution – to 'begin to know the corroded moments, the carboniferous states of thought, the shrinkage of mental mud, in the geological chaos' (Smithson 1968: 107).

By witnessing (or encouraging) granite's properties of dispersion and mutability we call attention to the fact that while the number of potential material relations and transformations increases exponentially across time, the potential always also remains for reversion to geological matter. If we perform a 'deep mapping' (Biggs 2011) – a multi-sensual, multi-disciplinary and multi-durational investigation of place, people or objects – we see that all material narratives return to a geological source or influence. Within this kind of expansive frame of reference, granite's enrolment in cultural projects, such as headstone, sill, trough or cladding seems radically ephemeral, a brief stop on a much longer passage through time. Matter moves in and out of different registers of meaning – social and scientific, architectural and geological – and cultural artefacts are exposed as temporary arrangements of physical substance, only stabilized through a substantial investment of conceptual and physical labour (DeSilvey 2006, 2012).

Things 'made' are not irrevocably static. They continue to be made, or more specifically, they grow, according to the capacities and tendencies of long term encounters between people and material properties. Both making and growing register deep material exchanges between persons and matter. Where making and growing perhaps diverge is in the notion that making suggests focused working towards the realization of a pre-ordained human design, at which point the making is considered complete. Descriptions of a thing as 'made', at least in contemporary western contexts, tend to reduce that thing to an isolated and bounded form, assuming it to be a singular and circumscribed entity that performs in the world only in specific and delimited contexts. Growing, on the other hand, suggests a more-than-human process unfolding across multiple life-cycles, and implies that the made thing has potential applications beyond its originally intended function. As Sennett (2007) suggests of tools used in the wrong way or in a way for which they were not intended, such usages might well throw up a sudden advance in technology in directions previously unimagined. Thus our sludge has been given new meaning that allows it to function beyond notions of waste. The notion of growing can be used to undo the fixed designation of things, to acknowledge the porosity and mutability of bounded surface attributes. Through evidencing something as grown, the net of relational variability is cast much wider. Thus, our sludge can function as a recombinant geological feature, a creative springboard for human-matter investigations.

The design and intentionality embedded in a thing – for example, a granite headstone – is not simply imposed upon its material being. Rather, a thing is animated *through* the geo-temporal properties that people grapple with, in the construction of a lived-in environment. Human encounters with matter are porous and cyclic navigations. In this chapter, our investigation of sludge and its journey through the quarry, of the people it has become entangled with and of the textual speculations it has inspired, suggests that all of the countless products 'made' at Trenoweth in its 170-year history have also been 'grown', and continue to grow, whether they are built into a structure or silted up at the bottom of a stagnant pond. As Brian Massumi asks, 'from what does all individual awareness arise and return? Simply: matter. Brain-and-body matter: rumbling sea for the rainbow of experience' (Massumi 2002: 190).

## References

Barker, G. (ed.) 2000. *Ecological Recombination in Urban Areas: Implications for Nature Conservation*. Peterborough: English Nature/The Urban Forum.
Bender, B., S. Hamilton, and C. Tilley 2007. *Stone Worlds: Narrative and Reflexivity in Landscape Archaeology*. Walnut Creek, CA: Left Coast Press.
Bennett, J. 2010. *Vibrant Matter: A Political Ecology of Things*. Durham, NC: Duke University Press.
Biggs, I. 2011. The spaces of deep mapping: a partial account. *Journal of Arts and Communities*, 2(1), 5–25.
Colquhoun, I. 1957. *The Living Stones*. London: Peter Owen.
DeSilvey, C. 2006. Observed decay: telling stories with mutable things. *Journal of Material Culture*, 11(3), 313–38.
DeSilvey. C. 2012. Making sense of transience: an anticipatory history. *Cultural Geographies*, 19(1), 30–53.
DeSilvey, C., S. Naylor, and C. Sackett 2011. *Anticipatory History*. Axminster: Uniformbooks.
Edensor, T. 2011. Entangled agencies, material networks and repair in a building assemblage: the mutable stone of St Ann's Church, Manchester. *Transactions of the Institute of British Geographers,* 36(2), 238–52.
Hinchliffe S., M.B. Kearnes, M. Degen, and S. Whatmore 2005. Urban wild things: a cosmopolitical experiment. *Environment and Planning D: Society and Space*, 23(5), 643–58.
Huddart, D., Roberts, G. and Gonzalez, S. 1999. Holocene human and animal footprints and their relationships with coastal environmental change, Formby Point, NW England. *Quaternary International*, 55, 29–41.
Hunt, B. 2005. Building stones explained: granite. *Geology Today*, 21(3), 110–16.
Ingold, T. 2007. Materials against materiality. *Archaeological Dialogues*, 14(1), 1–16.
Ingold, T. 2011. *Being Alive: Essays on Movement, Knowledge and Description*. Abingdon, UK: Routledge.
Knight, J. 2005. Processes of soft-sediment clast formation in the intertidal zone. *Sedimentary Geology*, 181, 207–14.
Lee, R. 2010. Truthing the gap: imagining a relational geography of the uninhabitable. *Design*, 15(3), 217–230.
Leitch, A. 2007. Visualizing the mountain: the photographer as ethnographer in the marble quarries of Carrara. *Journal of Modern Italian Studies*, 12(4), 417–29.
Massumi, B. 2002. *Parables For The Virtual: Movement, Affect, Sensation*. Durham, NC: Duke University Press.
Nordstrom, K.F., E. Pranzini, N.L. Jackson, and M. Coli 2008. The marble beaches of Tuscany. *Geographical Review*, 98(2), 280–300.
Paton, D. 2013. The quarry as sculpture: the place of making. *Environment and Planning A*, 45(5), 1070-86.
Price, P.L. 2010. Cultural geography and the stories we tell ourselves. *Cultural Geographies*, 17(2), 203–10.

Roberts, G., S. Gonzalez, and D. Huddart 1996. Intertidal Holocene footprints and their archaeological significance. *Antiquity*, 70(269), 647–51.

Sennett, R. 2007. *The Craftsman.* London: Allen Lane.

Skempton, A.W. and R.D. Northey 1952. Sensitivity of clays. *Geotechnique*, 3(1), 40–51.

Smithson, R. 1968. A sedimentation of the mind: earth projects, in *Robert Smithson: Collected Writings*, edited by J. Flam. Berkeley, CA: University of California Press, 100–113.

Stanier, P. 1999. *South West Granite: A History of the Granite Industry in Cornwall and Devon.* St Austell: Cornish Hillside Publications.

Stanier, P. 2000. *Stone Quarry Landscapes: The Industrial Archaeology of Quarrying.* Stroud: Tempus.

Tolia-Kelly, D.P. 2013. The geographies of cultural geography iii: Material geographies, vibrant matters and risking surface geographies. *Progress in Human Geography*, 37(1), 153–60.

Yusoff, K., and J. Gabrys 2006. Cultural geographies in practice: Time lapses: Robert Smithson's mobile landscapes. *Cultural Geographies*, 13(3), 444–50.

# Index

abstraction, in pursuit of systematized knowledge 11–12
ageing 7, 9, 183, 195, 197–200
agency
    versus animacy 17
    human and non-human 16–17, 111
alabastra 204–6, 210, 215
Amberbach, Basilius (1533–91), jurist 57–9
anatomopoeia 65–8, 70, 76–80, 83
anthropology 14–15, 147
anthropomorphism 5, 115, 234
apprenticeship 19, 177, 206
    in caribou-skin processing 130, 134
    in glass-working 203, 205–6
    in metalworking 52
    in woodworking 183, 186, 191–4, 198, 209–14
    *see also* education; learning
art
    basketry as 167–8, 170
    bodies as 91–2, 104
    contemporary 15
    versus craft 170
    of the earth 56
    versus nature 9–10, 12, 52, 56–8
    *see also* artefacts
artefacts 1, 215, 235
    and bodies 92, 95–6, 98–9, 104, 109
    defined 6
    versus organisms 5–6, 15, 20, 73, 104, 128, 177
    as persons 96
    substance and form of 90
    *see also* art; making
autopoiesis 2, 177
awareness
    kinaesthetic 194, 214
    levels of 208

babies
    blood vessels cast 83–4
    making of (compared with making artefacts) 95–6
    versus pots 5
Bacon, Francis 6–7, 10
Barthes, Roland 79
Bartlett, Sydney, museum technician 74–5
basketry 1–2, 163–4, 166–7
    as art 167–8, 170
    *see also* baskets
baskets 164–6, 168; *see also* basketry
becoming 5, 121, 203
    versus being 4, 17
being, versus becoming 4, 17
Bernstein, Nikolai 208–9
bioengineering 15–16, 38–40, 41
biomedicine 15–16, 69, 150
bodies 19, 68
    as 'bundles of affects' 115
    and casts 73
    growing 5–6
    human 46–9
    living versus dead 69
    as loci of intentionality 207
    and minds 207, 209
    and pots 5, 108–13, 116, 121–2
    as seats of knowledge 118, 20
    'second' 76, 80, 83
    substance and form of 90
    supply of, for medical teaching 74–5
    as works of art 91–2, 104
    *see also* embodiment
*Bombyx mori*
    breeding of 38
    caterpillar of 2–3, 26–7
    cocoons of 31–4, 38
    *see also* silkworms
Bourdieu, Pierre 203, 207
Bruner, Jerome 177

Building Crafts College 187, 199–200
building, versus dwelling 4
Buzzard, Edward Farquhar, physician 69

carpentry, see woodwork
carving 92
    of *nuchukana* among Kuna people 92–5, 102
Cashinahua people, of Brazil 91–2, 95–7, 101, 115, 118
casting 19–20
    corrosion- 65–7, 70–76, 81, 83–4
    from life 45, 50–56, 57–8
    ritualized 74–7, 80
ceramics 20; see also pottery
*chaîne opératoire* 110
childbearing 100
    and craft 90
childrearing, and gardening 147–8
classification 11
clay 1–2, 224, 228
communities of practice 74, 82, 174, 176, 190, 203, 206
containers
    bodies as 109, 116
    cocoons as 33–4
    pots as 109–10, 116
    trees as 101–2
    uterus as 97
core forming, in glass work 204–6, 210–15
craft 46–7, 174
    anthropology of 200
    and childbearing 90
    and dexterity 209; see also dexterity; skill
    divine 6–7, 47–8
    Richard Sennett on 9
    see also skill
cultivation 20, 150–51
    of body and mind 179
    versus growing wild 153
culture
    versus nature 15, 163
    versus nurture 5

Damaris Ittukusuk Katdlutsiak 127–9, 131–5, 138–40, 142–4
decomposition 8, 76

design 20, 109, 121, 235
    amniotic 97–9
    and form 96–7
    and making 183, 195
dexterity 72, 203, 208–10, 212, 216
dissection, in pursuit of systematized knowledge 11–12
'do-it-yourself' (DIY) 72–4

earth 52, 56, 57–9, 148, 153; see also soil
education
    of attention 211
    medical 69–70, 73–4, 76
    see also apprenticeship; learning
embodiment 5, 197
    of knowledge 46, 66, 70, 96, 121, 150
    versus ontogenesis 17
    of skills 20, 66, 81, 120
    theories of 110–11
    see also bodies
emergence
    of form 112–13
    material 143–4, 234
    versus transmission 214
emotion 81–2, 185, 208–9, 224, 228, 232–3
    in basketry 174
    in gardening 157–8, 160
engagement
    with artefacts 176
    cognitive 18
    versus estrangement 144
    in gardening 151, 157
    and learning 178
    with materials 70, 164–6, 174–8, 233
    of mind and body 164
    multisensory 168
    with nature 59
    of people and animals 143
    with plants 164–5
    practical 171–2, 177
envisioning 195
ethnobotany 18
experience 203, 209–10, 214–15

fertility, women's 99–100, 102, 104
fibroin protein 39–41
finishing 1–2, 8
food 149, 154–6, 160

footprints 227–33
forestry 3
form 92, 104
    emergent 112–13
    versus substance 90, 108
Formby, coastal sediments at 227–8, 232–3
furniture-making 184, 186, 188, 191–2, 194–7, 199

gardening 17, 20, 151, 154, 157, 160
    and childrearing 147–8
generation 20, 104, 179
    of nature 55–6, 58
genes 7
geology, recombinant 224, 233, 235
gesture 46, 112, 128, 206, 209, 212, 214
glass working 204–6, 208–12, 216;
    *see also* core forming
goldsmiths 47, 50–52, 57, 59
granite 221–7, 234–5
Grey Turner, George, professor of surgery 68
growing
    of body and mind 185
    and decomposition 8
    defined 1, 3
    versus making 3–8, 12, 17, 45, 77, 90–91, 128, 163–4, 203, 214, 235
    *see also* growth
growth 109, 113–15, 12
    as material accumulation 2–3
    *see also* growing

habit 207
hair, caribou 133
haptic immersion 174
Heidegger, Martin 4–5
human–animal relations 12–19, 134, 141, 143–4
Hunterian Museum 68–71, 75, 82, 84
hunting 128, 134, 140–41
    and resettlement 142–3
    women's role in 135, 138
hylomorphism 108, 110, 113, 121

imaging, mental 215
imitation 10, 56, 58–9, 207
improvisation 72–4, 121–2, 188, 195

Ingold, Tim 90–91, 111, 114, 118, 121, 165, 177, 203, 212
intentionality 207, 235
Inuit, of the Canadian Arctic 127–9, 133–4, 137–8, 140, 142–4

Jamnitzer, Wenzel (1508–85), goldsmith 50–53, 56

Keith, Sir Arthur 68
kinaesthesia 194, 203, 208–9, 211–16;
    *see also* movement
kinesiology 208–9
kinship 66, 68, 74, 79, 83
    and bodily growth 115
    and memory 94–5
*kishies* (Shetland baskets) 175–6
knitting 5–6, 8
knowledge
    embodied 46, 66, 70, 96, 121, 150
    tacit versus explicit 207–8
    *see also* skill
Kuna people, of Panama 89–92, 94, 97–9, 102, 104, 119, 121

landscape 224, 227, 234
learning 20, 98, 133–4, 158–9, 167, 171–8, 185, 192–4, 208
    anatomical 66, 74, 79, 83
    in basketry 174–6
    from cooperation 164
    as legitimate peripheral participation 206, 216
    to sew 102, 130
    in woodwork 188–90, 192–4
    *see also* apprenticeship; education
Leibniz, Gottfried 59
Lévi-Strauss, Claude 7
listening 47, 171, 193, 209, 211, 216
lizards, and life-casting 45–6, 56–8

making
    as belonging 203, 206–7
    bodies 92
    and breaking 8
    as compulsion 6–7
    defined 1, 3
    and design 183, 195

engagement of mind and body in 164
furniture, *see* furniture-making
versus growing 3–8, 12, 17, 45, 77,
   90–91, 128, 163–4, 203, 214, 235
human versus geophysical 223
as knowing 59, 203
and learning 176, 178
pleasure in 174, 178
and unmaking 7–8
and using 18
manoeuvrability 209, 212
Mason, Otis 166–7
masonry, *see* stone-working
material culture, studies of 5, 16–18, 89,
   110–11
materiality 17, 110
materials, 19, 48–9, 119
for anatomical models 77–8
becoming dextrous with 209–10
library of 18
properties of 226, 233–4
resistance of 166, 233
smart 16
vitality of 78, 111, 118, 120, 168, 234
*see also* clay; granite; plastics; resin;
   willow; wood
measurements, in craft 46–7
mechanization 166
Merleau-Ponty, Maurice 203, 207
metalwork 47, 49, 52, 112
metamorphosis 19, 31, 33–4, 52
mimesis, *see* imitation
mittens 1–2, 5, 8, 127–35, 139, 141–4
models, anatomical 65–6, 69–70, 73,
   82–3
reconstitution of deceased persons as
   76, 79, 83
mortuary ritual 66
movement 20, 203, 208, 216; *see also*
   kinaesthesia
mulberry leaves, as food for silkworms 26,
   28–9, 34, 37–8
museums 12, 14–15, 18
medical 68–70, 72, 79; *see also*
   Hunterian Museum

names
   Inuktitut 138, 140

of materials 226
National Health Service (NHS) 69, 149,
   152, 158
natural history 12, 55
natural selection 7
nature
versus artefacts 9–10, 12, 52, 56–8
versus culture 15, 163
generativity of 55–6, 58
nest-building 7–8
neuroscience 183–4, 197–8
nurture 20
versus culture 5
versus nature 3
of plants 160, 163
of people 130–31, 149, 151, 153, 160
of silkworms 27, 41
and witchcraft 10

objects, as persons 89–91, 116
ontogenesis
anthropo- 5, 8
versus embodiment 17
ontologies 89, 97, 107, 111, 113, 120
'constructional' 91–2
organisms
versus artefacts 5–6, 15, 20, 73, 104,
   111, 128, 177
defined 6

Paley, William 7
Palissy, Bernard, potter 55–6
persons
as models 76, 79, 83
objects as 89–91, 116
reconstitution of, as artefacts 96
perspectivism, Amazonian 91, 109, 113,
   115–16, 118
pewterware 12–13
photography 14, 139
plasticity, neurological 197–8
plastics 78–9
*poiesis*, material 19, 66, 76
pots
and bodies 5, 108–13, 116, 121–2
La Candelaria 107–8, 110–14, 117–21
and wombs 97
*see also* pottery

pottery 1–2, 5, 119; *see also* ceramics; pots
pruning, of anatomical trees 79–82
Pysden, George, woodworker 184–6, 194–9

Quiccheberg, Samuel (1529–67), librarian 57–9

recipes 46–7, 49
reeling, of silk 30–31, 34–6, 41
reproduction, versus replication 215
resin, in corrosion-casting 72, 76–81, 83
rites of passage 2, 4

Scottish Basketmakers' Circle (SBC) 166, 173–4
Sennett, Richard 9, 235
senses
    in early modern craft workshops 47–8
    in glass-working 211
    in woodwork 185, 192, 197
Seremetakis, Nadia 66, 76
sericulture 25–8, 41
    in China 29–30, 37
    in Japan 30–31
    in North America 30
    *see also* silk
sewing 1–2, 20, 72, 98–100, 102, 127–9, 141, 144
    and storytelling 130
    *see also* stitching
silk 3, 19, 25–6, 39
    spider- 40
    *see also* sericulture
silkworms 3, 26–8; *see also Bombyx mori*
skill 121
    acquisition of 98, 119, 177, 183, 198–200; *see also* apprenticeship; learning
    as attunement 209
    of basketry, *see* basketry
    embodied 20, 66, 81, 120
    in looking 211, 215
    and ontological risk 119–20
    in woodworking 183, 199–200
    *see also* craft; dexterity; knowledge; technique
skin
    animal 2

caribou 127, 131–4, 141
    processing of 129–30, 132–3, 136–8, 141
    designs on 96–7, 99, 101
    garments 128, 133–4, 136, 141
    of snakes 56, 96–7, 99–101
    social 115
    and tree-bark 101
sludge 222–5, 227–9, 232–5
Smithson, Robert 221, 228, 234
snakes
    moulding from 54
    shed skin of 56, 96–7, 99–101
soil 37, 147–8, 153–4; *see also* earth
spirals 177–8
still life 14
stitching 127, 141; *see also* sewing
stone working 8, 221
    language of 226
storytelling 1, 224
    and sewing 130
    and gardening 157–8
Strathern, Marilyn 90, 115, 163
strokes (in basket-weaving) 173
substance, versus form 90

Taylor, Mark, glass researcher 205–6, 210–12, 214–15
technique 164, 169, 213–14; *see also* skill
tempering 6, 49
temporality 19; *see also* time
therapeutic horticulture 148–50
timber, *see* wood
time
    measurement of 46–7
    perspectives on 151–2, 160
    reversible and irreversible 7
    *see also* temporality
Tompsett, David Hugh (1910–91) 66–7, 70, 72–83
tools 120, 137, 154, 185, 188, 200
    becoming dextrous with 209–10
    bodies as 46–7
    for glass-working 206
    for working with corrosion casts 67, 73, 81–2
transformation 4, 19, 52, 58–9, 107
    of materials 45

ontological 122
transmission, versus emergence 214
trees
    body parts as 73–4, 80, 83, 85
    bark of 101
    as containers 101–2
    of life 74, 80
Trenoweth Quarry, Cornwall 221, 224, 226–7
Turner, Terence 115

Verner, James, furniture maker 191–4, 197
Viveiros de Castro, Eduardo 91–2, 107, 116

waste 8–9, 20, 225, 234–5
watching 209–12, 216

weeds 156
wellbeing 159–60
willow 1–2, 163, 166, 168, 171–2
    as plant and material 168–9
    sculpture 169–72
witchcraft, as making 10–11
wood 2, 185, 188, 195–7
woodwork 1–2, 8, 183, 185–6, 194, 198–9
working groups 215–16
workshops 12, 168, 184
    in early modern Europe 45, 46–9, 58–9
    versus working groups 215
*Wunderkammern* 9–10, 45